LLEWELLYN'S

2008

Magical Almanac

Featuring

AarTiana, A.C. Fisher Aldag, Elizabeth Barrette,
Nancy Bennett, Boudica, Kaaren Christ, Dallas Jennifer Cobb,
Sorita D'Este, Raven Digitalis, Nuala Drago, Ellen Dugan,
Denise Dumars, Bryony Dwale, Ember, Emely Flak, Sybil Fogg,
Lily Gardner, Karen Glasgow-Follett, Magenta Griffith,
Laura Gyre, Elizabeth Hazel, Christine Jette, James Kambos,
Sally McSweeney, Mickie Mueller, Muse, Paniteowl,
Diana Rajchel, Roslyn Reid, Janina Renée, Steven Repko,
Cerridwen Iris Shea, Michelle Skye, K. D. Spitzer,
Mark Stavish, Kari Tauring, Ladyhawk Whispers,
Gail Wood, and Zaeda Yin

Llewellyn's 2008 Magical Almanac

ISBN 978-0-7387-0553-8. Copyright © 2007 by Llewellyn. All rights reserved. Printed in the United States. Llewellyn is a registered trademark of Llewellyn Worldwide, Ltd.

Editor/Designer: Ed Day

Cover Illustration: © Grizelda Holderness/Illustration LTD.

Calendar Pages Design: Andrea Neff and Michael Fallon

Calendar Pages Illustrations: © Fiona King

Interior Illustrations © Melissa Gay, pages 15, 27, 56, 95, 108, 127, 146, 168, 235, 252, 255, 282, 298, 303, 315, 339, 362, 381, 383; © Carol Coogan, pages 19, 45, 91, 99, 123, 139, 164, 239, 263, 290, 319, 328, 357, 377; © Mickie Mueller, page 268; © David Wallace, pages 17, 22, 25, 37, 81, 97, 103, 119, 133, 154, 236, 242, 260, 275, 310, 313, 317, 352, 371

Special thanks to Amber Wolfe for the use of daily color and incense correspondences. For more detailed information, please see *Personal Alchemy* by Amber Wolfe.

You can order Llewellyn annuals and books from *New Worlds*, Llewellyn's catalog. To request a free copy of the catalog, call toll-free 1-877-NEWWRLD, or visit our website at www.llewellyn.com.

Astrological calculations are performed by the Kepler 6 astrology software program, specially created for Llewellyn Publications and used with the kind permission of Cosmic Patterns Software, Inc., www.AstroSoftware.com.

Llewellyn Worldwide
Dept. 978-0-7387-0553-8
2143 Wooddale Drive
Woodbury, MN 55125

About the Authors

AARTIANA has practiced many forms of natural spirituality since the early 1990s. She lives in Western Montana with her husband, her two teenage children, and an old black tomcat with white whiskers named Chuckles. She is a professional astrologer, tarot card reader, dowser, and has become a certified Master Herbalist in 2007. She has an organic garden, crochets professionally and is co-creating Tië eldaliéva, meaning the Elven Spiritual Path. Find out more by visiting www.myspace.com/aartiana.

A. C. FISHER ALDAG is one of the founders of Caer na Donia y Llew, a legal Pagan church in southwestern Michigan. She helps to sponsor Paganstock, Kalamazoo Pagan Pride, and the Midwest Pagan Council's Pan Pagan Festival every year. A. C., her husband Dave, daughter Rhiannon, and son Brandyn, live on a small farm near beautiful Lake Michigan. They're owned by two large and obnoxious magical mutts.

ELIZABETH BARRETTE serves as the managing editor of *PanGaia*. She has been involved with the Pagan community for more than seventeen years, and has done much networking with Pagans in her area, including coffeehouse meetings and open sabbats. Her other writing fields include speculative fiction and gender studies. She lives in central Illinois and enjoys herbal landscaping and gardening for wildlife.

NANCY BENNETT has had her work published in various places including Llewellyn's annuals, *We'moon*, Circle network as well as many mainstream publications. Her pet projects include reading and writing about history and creating ethnic dinners to test on her family. She lives near a protected salmon stream where the deer and the bears often play.

BOUDICA is reviews editor and co-owner of the *Wiccan/Pagan Times* and owner of the *Zodiac Bistro*, two online publications. She is a teacher with CroneSpeak, teaching both on and off the Internet, and a guest speaker at many festivals and gatherings. A former New Yorker, she now resides with her husband in Ohio.

KAAREN CHRIST is a social work consultant and freelance writer living in Prince Edward County, Ontario. She shares her world with two beautiful children and a dog named Lukki. When not performing domestic goddess duties, you will find her in the garden crafting children's stories.

DALLAS JENNIFER COBB lives in an enchanted waterfront village. She's freed up resources for what she loves: family, gardens, fitness, and fabulous food. She's forever scheming novel ways to pay the bills when she's not running country roads or wandering the beach. Her essays are in the recent Seal Press anthologies *Three Ring Circus* and *Far From Home*. Her video documentary *Disparate Places* appeared on TV Ontario's *Planet Parent*. She is a regular contributor to Llewellyn's almanacs.

SORITA D'ESTE is an author, Witch, and priestess. She is the co-author of *Circle of Fire* and *The Guises of the Morrígan* and is a regular contributor to many MBS publications. She lives and works in London.

RAVEN DIGITALIS lives in Missoula, Montana, is a student of anthropology, and is the author of *GothCraft* (Llewellyn Publications). He is a neo-Pagan priest as well as a Gothic-Industrial radio- and club deejay and an animal rights activist. He lives with his Priestess Estha McNevin, both of whom hold community rituals, tarot readings, and co-operate the metaphysical supply business Twigs & Brews.

NUALA DRAGO is an author, musician, and solitary Wiccan. She is an avid reader and a life-long student of extinct languages, folk

magic, and ancient herbal lore. Nuala enjoys country life, riding and training horses, and rehabilitating abused animals.

ELLEN DUGAN, the "Garden Witch," is a psychic-clairvoyant and has been a practicing Witch for twenty years. Ellen is a master gardener and teaches classes on flower folklore and gardening at a community college. She is the author of several Llewellyn books, including *Garden Witchery, Elements of Witchcraft, 7 Days of Magic, Cottage Witchery, Autumn Equinox, The Enchanted Cat, Herb Magic for Beginners,* and *Natural Witchery.* Ellen wholeheartedly encourages folks to personalize their spellcraft and to go outside and get their hands dirty, so they can discover the wonder and magic of the natural world. Ellen and her family live in Missouri.

REV. DENISE "DION-ISIS" DUMARS, M.A., is co-founder of the Iseum of Isis Paedusis, an Isian study group chartered by the Fellowship of Isis and is an Isian minister. Her book: *Be Blesséd: Daily Devotions for Busy Wiccans and Pagans,* was published in May, 2006. She teaches college English and is, appropriately enough, a volunteer for the American Cinematheque at the Egyptian Theater on Hollywood Boulevard.

BRYONY DWALE has lived in Southeastern Ohio her entire life and has been practicing paganism for three years. She is an Eclectic Pagan with an interest in Fairies and herbs.

EMBER is a freelance writer, poet, and regular contributor to Llewellyn annuals. Her interests include collecting rocks and minerals, gardening, and nature photography. She lives in Missouri with her husband and two feline companions.

EMELY FLAK is a practicing solitary Witch from Daylesford, Australia. When she is not writing, she is at her "day job" as a learning and development professional. Recently, this busy mother of two and partner of one completed training to be a civil celebrant.

Much of her work is dedicated to embracing the ancient wisdom of Wicca for personal empowerment, particularly in the competitive work environment.

SYBIL FOGG has been a Wiccan practitioner for eighteen years, first as a solitary and later with her four children and partner, a group she considers her coven. She is a fiction writer, freelancer, bellydancer, and adjunct faculty member at area colleges. She holds a BA in English and an MFA in Creative Writing and is currently working on a novel of autobiographical fiction.

LILY GARDNER continues to pursue and write about her lifelong passion of folklore and mythology. She has been a practicing Witch for thirteen years. In addition to her work in folklore, she writes short stories and is working on her first mystery novel. Lily lives with her husband, her son's cat, and two spoiled Corgis in the rainy but magnificent city of Portland, Oregon.

KAREN GLASGOW-FOLLETT has been practicing Witchcraft since 1972. Karen lives in the Midwest with her husband (and in close proximity of her two adult sons). Karen's résumé includes: Reiki healer, psychic medium, craft designer, writer, psychic development educator, magical energy educator, and obstetrical nurse and educator. Karen does spend some of her "spare" time trying to figure out what she wants to be when she grows up.

MAGENTA GRIFFITH has been a Witch for nearly thirty years, and is a founding member of the coven Prodea, which has been celebrating rituals since 1980. She has been a member of the Covenant of the Goddess, the Covenant of Unitarian Universalist Pagans, Church of All Worlds, and several other organizations. She presents workshops and classes at a variety of festivals and gatherings around the Midwest. She spends her spare time reading, cooking, and petting her cat.

LAURA GYRE, a Pennsylvania-based freelance writer, was recently shocked to realize she has been practicing eclectic witchcraft for fifteen years. She and her partner James live in a collective house in Pittsburgh, where they devote their time to exploring the intersections between spirituality, radical politics, holistic health, and the arts. They are also eagerly anticipating the birth of their first child. Visit www.gyreworks.org for more.

ELIZABETH HAZEL is an astrologer-tarotist who follows the pagan path. She is the author of *Tarot Decoded,* and writes the syndicated newspaper horoscope "Third Rock Almanac" and new-Witch's feature column "Astro-Spell." Liz lives in Toledo with beloved kitties Bart, Pixie, and Selkit. Reader comments are welcome at vala@bex.net.

CHRISTINE JETTE (pronounced Jetty) is a registered nurse and holds a bachelor's degree in psychology. She is the author of *Tarot Shadow Work, Tarot for the Healing Heart, Tarot for All Seasons,* and *Professional Tarot.* Visit her on the Web at: www.findingthemuse.com.

JAMES KAMBOS is a folk artist and writer who has had a lifelong interest in folk magic traditions. He holds a degree in history and is a regular contributor to Llewellyn annuals. He lives in the beautiful hill country of southern Ohio.

SALLY MCSWEENEY is the owner of Triple Aspect Herbs, a metaphysical herbal apothecary. As a Pagan hedge Witch with leanings toward Celtic and Norse traditions, she is working on a book about healing with the energies of the Moon throughout the wheel of the year. Also a master herbalist specializing in aromatherapy, she lives in Oregon with her husband and two cats.

MICKIE MUELLER is a Pagan artist and writer. She is also a Reiki teacher and Pagan minister. Her art has appeared in publications worldwide as well as in *The Well Worn Path* and *The Hidden Path,*

both by Raven Grimassi and Stephanie Taylor. Visit her website at www.mickiemuellerart.com

MUSE has been studying alternative religions, spirituality, and magic since an early age, and has always had a fascination with the unseen world. Among many other things, she is an avid traveler, writer, yoga practitioner, and a perpetual student. She holds a degree in European History, and hopes to see every bit of the world her professors taught her about. She currently lives in Colorado Springs, Colorado, where the great weather, amazing hiking, and fantastic people are a constant inspiration.

PANITEOWL lives in the foothills of the Appalachians in northeast Pennsylvania, where she and her husband are in the process of developing a private retreat for spiritual awareness. She is co-coordinator of two annual events in Virginia known as the Gathering of the Tribes. She is founder and elder high priestess of the Mystic Wicca tradition.

DIANA RAJCHEL is a third-degree Wiccan priestess with a bent for intelligent cartoons and good food. She lives in Minneapolis, surrounded by her friends and Pagan family. Someday she hopes to learn the name of the local city spirit.

ROSLYN REID, Discordian Druid, is a member of the Richard P. Feynman Memorial Cabal in Princeton, NJ. She teaches yoga and tarot, which she has studied for over twenty-five years. She is currently in training to become a dreamworker. A longtime contributor of art and articles to Llewellyn and other Pagan publications such as *Sagewoman* and *Dalriada* (a Scottish magazine promoting Celtic heritage), her work has appeared in consumer magazines such as *Tightwad Living* and *Thrifty Times*. She has also contributed to Susun Weed's book, *Breast Cancer? Breast Health!* Her ongoing

project is rejuvenating the former fruit farm where she lives in New Jersey with her husband and two Corgis, Bonny and Molly.

JANINA RENÉE is a scholar of folklore, psychology, medical anthropology, the material culture of magic, ritual studies, history, and literature. She has written five books for Llewellyn: *Tarot Spells, Playful Magic, Tarot Your Everyday Guide* (winner of 2001 COVR [Coalition of Visionary Retailers] award for best Self Help book), *Tarot for a New Generation* (2002 COVR winner, best General Interest Title), and *By Candlelight: Rites for Celebration, Blessing and Prayer* (2005 COVR runner-up, Spirituality). Janina continues to work on multiple books, including *Loved by a Dragon*, an ongoing research project about the representation and treatment of Asperger's Syndrome in folklore and healing traditions.

STEVEN ERIC REPKO is an elder and founding member of the Coven of NatureWise. Channeling the "Natural Tradition" since childhood, he has studied within the craft for more than three decades. An astrologer, medium, musician, and poet, he and his wife Bonnie are Pagan parents of three children, and owners of Gem N Aries, in Mays Landing, NJ. They provide free online horoscopes and online shopping at www.gemnaries.com.

CERRIDWEN IRIS SHEA is a writer, teacher, and tarot reader who loves ice hockey and horse racing. Visit her redesigned website at: www.cerridwenscottage.com; visit her blog Kemmryk, which discusses working with tarot and oracles at: tarotkemmryk.blogspot. com. She also wrote the magical realism serial *Angel Hunt*.

MICHELLE SKYE has been a practicing witch for over ten years and has been working with the fey since she was a child. Although solitary, Michelle presents various workshops and classes in Southeastern Massachusetts, as well as at Womongathering, a Goddess

festival in Pennsylvania. She is an ordained minister through the Universal Life Church and performs legal handfastings, weddings, and other spiritual rites of passage. She recently published her first book, *Goddess Alive!* (Llewellyn, 2007). She shares her home with elfy husband Michael and little Witch-in-training Neisa.

K. D. SPITZER is a Witchy writer living in coastal New Hampshire. She walks a labyrinth every chance she gets, taking problems to its center and walking out with a peaceful heart. Sometimes she casts a spell in the heart of the labyrinth.

MARK STAVISH is a practicing alchemist and one of the leading authorities in Hermeticism. His work has been widely published in academic, specialty, and mass-market publications. His new book, *The Path of Alchemy*, is a useful, comprehensive guide for students of alchemy, Kabbalah, elemental witchcraft, and herbalism. Mark is Director of Studies for the Institute for Hermetic Studies in Wyoming, PA.

LADYHAWK WHISPERS lives in Northern Michigan, where she practices witchcraft and natural Shamanism, and is a healer and tarot reader. She is an Outer Court member of the Correllian Nativist Tradition, a mix of Scottish and Native American flavor, plus an online school for witchcraft. She is also a solitary who works with the beautiful nature that surrounds her and the native energy that abounds in the area.

KARI TAURING is an interdisciplinary performance artist and educator. She has been studying, teaching and publishing about runes and other Nordic Roots material since 1989. She also conducts workshops on storytelling and dream work; teaches voice, guitar, and piano lessons; and operates a children's environmental learning program in the summer. Her newest music combines Norse Shamanic women's chants with traditional huldre stille.

GAIL WOOD has been a Witch and Wiccan priestess for more than twenty years, practicing a shamanic path celebrating the Dark Moon. She is a clergywoman, teacher, ritual leader, tarot reader, and Reiki Master. She teaches workshops and classes on alternative spiritualities, Wicca, tarot, ritual, shamanic journeywork, and Reiki. She is the author of *Rituals of the Dark Moon: 13 Lunar Rites for a Magical Path* (Llewellyn, 2001); articles in a variety of Pagan publications; and *The Wild God: Meditations and Rituals on the Sacred Masculine* (Spilled Candy, 2006). She is a member of the Coven of the Redtail Hawk, and is high priestess of the Coven of the Heron, both of the RavenMyst Circle. To learn more, read her blog at www.rowdygoddess.blogspot.com or visit the website, www.witchesinprint.com.

ZAEDA YIN contributes to varied publications under various pseudonyms, of which one was S. Y. Zenith. She is three-quarters Chinese, one tad Irish and a lifelong solitary eclectic Pagan. Zaeda has lived, studied, and traveled extensively in India, Nepal, Japan, Hong Kong, Taiwan, Singapore, Malaysia, Thailand, and Borneo over two decades. Now based in Australia, her time is divided between writing and teaching the use of gems, crystals, holy beads, and sacred objects from India and the Himalayas. She is also a member of the Australian Society of Authors.

Table of Contents

Almanac Section.................................

Fire Magic ....

Earth Magic

Winter: The Realm of Earth

by Sorita D'Este

Earth is the most solid and physical of the elements. Earth gives us form, and we walk and live on the earth beneath us. It gives us the strength and endurance of physicality, the ability to touch. Through the physicality of earth we eat, we work, we make love, and we give birth. Earth is the nurturer, the womb, and the tomb, patiently and steadfastly supporting us, whatever we do.

The silence of earth reflects its nonjudgmental nature, but its very selflessness encourages us to be the same, to be responsible in our actions, to try and make our world something of beauty, and leave it better than we found it. The silence of a winter's day when the world is blanketed with snow, when even water has been given the solidity of earth as ice and snow, emphasizes the elemental tide of earth at its peak.

Earth is both nature and nurture, and all we do affects the people we are and the environment in which we live. Earth is the element that is most often taken for granted, yet it is our home, supplying all our needs.

The beings of Earth make up a huge range of creatures. The gnomes (or pygmies) appear in a variety of forms: animal, plant, and mineral. The Ruler of Earth usually appears as a very beautiful and well-built woman with long brown hair and green eyes. She wears a simple green robe and has a wreath of corn on her head. In human form, the gnomes usually appear as short and stocky figures that almost seem to have been hewn from the very rocks of the earth.

Meditation

This meditation is best done on the earth itself, whether in a garden or woodland. Make sure that you are comfortable, take a few deep breaths, and close your eyes.

Focus your mind on the solidity of earth beneath you and in your mind's eye visualize a huge green pentagram on

a black background. See the pentagon in the center of the pentagram shimmer and disappear, opening a doorway to the elemental realm of earth. Through the doorway you can see a mountain range rising up with a dense forest, lit by the morning Sun, covering the lower slopes.

Send your awareness through the doorway in the center of the pentagram and into the elemental world of earth. As you do so, you feel the cool, rich soil beneath your feet and find yourself standing in a forest clearing with trees rising up toward the heavens. Look around; take note of the different types of trees in the forest as well as the many different wildflowers, herbs, and other small plants.

You notice the stillness that surrounds you, a sense of peace permeating every particle of your being. Listening carefully to the sounds in the forest, you hear movement nearby and see a stag bounding through the undergrowth. This seems to be a signal for other animals that start appearing in the forest around you. You see a bear lumbering by and a fox hurrying through the glade. There are other forest creatures lurking in the undergrowth.

A sharp breeze catches your breath and you feel flakes of snow on your face. Soon the snow is blanketing the ground and you are struck by the transformation, as everything is covered with a layer of crisp ice. The verdant greenery is now a white tableau. You reflect on how life retreats into the earth during winter, and activity is reduced. At this time, although you feel no inclination to move, you realize this is not a time for stillness, so you walk through the trees toward the mountains.

Soon you find yourself at a cliff face, and see a cave opening in the rocks. You decide to enter the cave. Caves are entryways into the earth and this one will provide you with shelter as the snow turns into a blizzard. Crossing the threshold of the cave, you feel yourself changing. Your skin turns into fur, your body grows larger, and you become a bear. Warm in your protective fur, you curl up in a corner of the cave and consider hibernating. Your thoughts are interrupted by other animals entering the cave in search of shelter from the blizzard. A fox, a badger, and a deer all enter, their desire for finding shelter stronger than their desire to fight with each other. They all approach you, settling down against your warm fur. The sensation of the animals against your skin makes you focus on the pleasure you get from nurturing others, sharing your warmth to help them survive.

Time passes and the blizzard lets up, and the animals all get up and leave. You realize that it is time for you to leave as well. With your ursine sense of smell, you easily retrace your tracks back toward the pentagram in the forest clearing through which you entered this realm of earth. As you stand before the pentagram you take a last look around. Then, walking through the doorway, you feel yourself transform back into your human form. Awareness returns to your body, you take a few deep breaths, and open your eyes.

Earthing Yourself: Getting in Touch With the Earth–Really!

by Denise Dumars

Hey! You there, air sign, with your mind on your computer instead of your head in the clouds. And you, water sign. Swimming in your emotions instead of the ocean. And you, fire sign, burning your way up the corporate ladder when you should be sitting around a campfire. Last but not least, earth sign. Take off those Birkenstocks and feel the real earth for a change.

Let's all get grounded. This means, yes, we actually have to get our hands dirty. What a concept!

Sitting in front of the computer is not the way to get in touch with your Pagan roots. If you do indeed profess what is called the earth-based religion, then you need to be in touch with some of the Earth.

So to make an earth-based altar, let's take a cue from Count Dracula and find some soil from your native Earth. Yes, this means taking some soil from your own yard or from an area near where you grew up. (Using commercial potting soil for this exercise is OK only if you do not live in or near the place where you grew up or lived for many years, or if you live in a building with no opportunity to touch the soil.)

And if you're one of those people who insist on bringing your own paper cup to a ritual where everyone else is going to drink from the same chalice, never fear. Putting a cookie sheet of earth in the oven at 450 degrees F for a few minutes will sterilize it. Now that you've got your earth, about three handfuls, place it in an oblong open container, something that looks like a small trough.

Now we're going to decorate our altar. You will need some tree bark. Please do not strip bark from a living tree! Find some fallen bark or wood shavings. If you live in an area that does not have trees that have bark, you may substitute something such as part of a fallen bract from a palm tree. Continue to decorate your altar with fallen leaves, flower petals (as from a rose whose petals have fallen), pine needles, or other plant matter. Now add another essential element: something made of metal. Most of us might not have some naturally occurring metal just lying around the house, such as a piece of what we call fool's gold, or galena, or hematite, although hematite can be found easily in most rock shots. A small brass bell such as those sold in Indian stores will be fine. And now you'll need a stone. The stone must be in its natural form. It may NOT be a crystal from a New Age or

metaphysical store! You must find it in nature and it must be in its natural state.

Now you have your earth altar. Place it on a table with a ceramic, glass, or earthenware cup or bowl of spring water to which you have added some sea salt; a candle in a similar holder; make sure the candle is made of a natural substance like soy or beeswax—not petroleum. You'll need a large shell for an incense burner with some sand and a wand of sage, sweet grass, or cedar. If you wish to place an image or statue of an earth deity such as Hecate, Baba Yaga, or Bragi on the altar you may do so, but this is not necessary.

Now we are ready to unite with nature. Light the candle and the incense. Plunge your hands into the altar of earth, and close your eyes. Feel the dirt between your fingers. Do not concentrate on any visual images; simply concentrate on the tactile feel of the soil, stone, and other objects in your earth altar. Now open your eyes and gaze upon everything in the earth altar trough. Then touch and look at each item individually. Feel your connection with the earth becoming stronger. Do so until you feel truly grounded. Work with your earth altar as long as you wish.

And perhaps you do want to take a cue once again from Count Dracula: place some of the earth from your earth altar into a small sealed box or container and place it under your bed so that you are indeed sleeping on your native Earth. Why not give it a try to feel more in touch with your "roots." Our society has suffered greatly from our disconnection with the Earth. We as Pagans need to try to rectify some of these problems, but we cannot do so until we ourselves become more connected to the Earth.

Hellhound on My Trail

by Cerridwen Iris Shea

*Moonlight glinted on Jasper's knife. "No one will ever find you," he said.
"Or, if they do, they'll assume you're some 6,000-year-old bog person."
"Forensics are better than that," I said. The night was damp and cold. I
tried not to shiver. I didn't want to give him even that small satisfaction.
"Bog people were sacrifices," he smiled, "and that's a fitting end for you."
A single howl cut through the air as Jasper honed the knife to cut my body.
Perhaps Gareth had called someone. Perhaps they were looking for us now.
If I could only keep Jasper talking . . .
The howl came again, closer, and the hair stood up on the back of my neck.
Where there'd been no wind a moment ago, suddenly it was strong enough
to almost knock me off my feet. More howls joined the first, building to a
cacophony. I looked over Jasper's shoulder—glowing specks of white bore
down on us from the distance.
Impossible! And yet . . . not.
"Who's dumb enough to let their dogs roam out here?" Jasper snapped.
"These aren't just any dogs," I said. "Look. Their paws aren't touching the
ground."
He turned, and his eyes widened in disbelief. "But . . . they're a myth!"
"That myth has your scent," I said.
"Could just as easily be you they're after."
"I'm not the one running around killing people."*
—from *Murders on Litha Moor,* by Cerridwen Iris Shea

Celtic and European legends are filled with the sounds of the Wild Hunt, the hounds traveling across the night sky: Arawn, Celtic god of the underworld, has a pack of white hounds with blood-red ears; Lugh has a magical hound, as does the family of Harlequin, the Oskerei, Gandreidh, and Herne and his brutal band of wild men. Sometimes it's called the "Furious Host." An Orkneys version of the tale calls it "The Raging Host." Some of the German and Scandinavian tales have a headless rider on a black, white, and gray horse with his pack of baying hounds. Could those tales have been in the back of Washington Irving's mind for the tale of the Headless Horseman in my own home of the Hudson Valley?

Pagan-based tales of the Wild Hunt focus on the energy, the noise, and the joy of the Hunt. Non-Pagan based tales use it as a fear tactic—they're coming to get the souls of sinners! Some of the northern European versions of the tale have the hunters tracking down a woman and then killing her. Of course, the versions I've come across thus far give no reason why they would Hunt and kill a woman—it seems merely being a woman justifies being hunted and killed. Still other versions detail a woman as the leader of the Hunt, sometimes referred to as Hulda, Befana, Diana, or Satia.

The Wild Hunt is depicted as happening around Yule. Inspired by Karl Masaus's tale, Washington Irving's "The Legend of Sleepy Hollow" kept the headless horseman, lost the hounds, and moved the events back to autumn.

The Underground Connection

Many of the books loosely tie Cerridwen and hounds—the hounds seem to be in the background, resting before their next adventure. To explore Cerridwen's connection to hounds, to connect the dots, we have to look at myths and connotations of Cerridwen, the meaning of hounds in the pantheon, and then find where they intersect.

Cerridwen is a dark goddess, a goddess of prophecy, inspiration, transformation, and rebirth. She's in the underworld, and she keeps the cauldron of knowledge there. She is connected with the dark half of the year, which covers both the autumn and the Yuletide season. The most famous legend associated with her is the birth of Taliesin, the bard. An encapsulation of the myth is that Gwion, Cerridwen's helper, splattered himself with a few drops of the cauldron's contents while stirring it. Unthinking, he sucked the finger and gained the knowledge (some versions have him deliberately stealing a few drops of the potion). Cerridwen, who'd planned the contents to be imbibed only by her son, was furious when Gwion ran away. They began a chase, with each of them shape-shifting until finally Gwion became a grain of corn and Cerridwen (also a corn goddess) shifted into a hen to eat him. Once ingested, he became the fetus born as Taliesin, the bard. Bards called themselves the Sons of Cerridwen (Cerddorion). Her cauldron holds the secrets of transformation—of course, anyone who drank of it could shape-shift. Personally, I always felt if Gwion had taken responsibility and faced Cerridwen, they could have spared themselves a lot of drama—but then we wouldn't have the legend to teach us about transformation.

Although most often associated with either the hen or the white sow, Cerridwen had also transformed into a greyhound in order to chase Gwion in his form as a hare. Greyhounds are one of the swiftest animals on earth. A cheetah's speed can reach 60 MPH, a thoroughbred racehorse's speed 47 MPH, a greyhound's 43 MPH. An amazing human might reach 27 MPH. Some versions of the legend specify a black greyhound (black symbolizing the underworld); others indicate a white (the Hounds of Hell are white dogs with red ears). Ancient murals show that the ancient greyhounds of 4,000 years ago resembled those of the present day. Argus, Odysseus's dog, was a greyhound. The Brythonic fighting dogs shown in the *Book of Kells* are thought to be ancestors of the Irish wolfhound (a sight hound in the same general family as the greyhound). The greyhound was in Britain as early as 1014, when King Canute created the Forest Laws, which stated that only noblemen could own and hunt with greyhounds.

Anubis, Egyptian god of the underworld, may be called the "jackal-headed god," but his features remarkably resemble that of the greyhound. Again, there is a connection with the underworld, Cerridwen's realm. White dogs are also believed to be corn spirits—and Cerridwen is a corn goddess. Myriad legends speak of "harvesting souls" as often as harvesting crops.

Dogs are known for carrying messages between worlds, for hunting down souls (on several planes), for loyalty, and for reminding a person of his or her geis (oath, vow, promise). Loyal people keep their promises—it makes sense for a dog to symbolize keeping an oath. Cerridwen, as the dark goddess of transformation, inspiration, and rebirth, feels strongly about keeping promises (perhaps why Gwion was so afraid when he disobeyed her). It makes sense that Cerridwen would send a dog to remind someone of a geis.

From mythological and anthropological references, we move to the experiential. Although in real life, and often in my spiritual work, I tend to be surrounded by cats (and jaguars and tigers, etc.), when I pathwork with Cerridwen, there are always hounds involved. While I am happy not to have made acquaintance with Cerebus (yet), in my time spent at Cerridwen's cauldron, a variety of dogs have shared the space. Some look like the traditional Hell Hounds, white with red ears; some are greyhounds, animals with whom I feel a strong sympathy and affiliation in life; and some are the big, black, shaggy hounds that are rumored to roam the dark nights and snatch up souls. I've never felt threatened by them, although they've always been interested in the new arrival. As an urban dweller, I've gotten out of potentially dangerous situations on late night streets only to have someone say to me, "Damn, girl, that's one big white dog you got there. Think his ear's bleeding." Neither anecdote is textbook proof that Cerridwen keeps hounds, much less sends them to help (she is one of my patrons), but there's an ever-growing experiential understanding on my part.

Working Like a Dog

How does one work with Cerridwen and her Hounds? Working with underworld energy requires training and caution. You're dealing with subconscious energies—energies and motivations that are often hidden. You're peeling away layers, digging well below the surface, to reveal what's been hidden from yourself for a lifetime and beyond. When I work with Cerridwen (I'm still in the early stages of learning), the work is often challenging, and having a dog or dogs nearby is comforting. I don't feel I am in any position to "send" them out—but I'm receptive when they bring messages to me. I'm not someone who's going to stand on the platform chanting and calling up the hounds of the underworld when the subway's late. And, while Jaguar (who's been with me since I was a small child and before I even knew I was a Witch) has walked with me down many a dark street when I felt the chill on the back of my neck, I've still had the experience of the hounds inserting themselves between me and those who wish me harm. I don't fear them because I've done nothing that would set them upon me. (In other words, if the sounds of the Wild Hunt are blaring past, I'm not afraid nor do I feel guilt about something that makes me think they're looking for me.)

A fellow traveler I know as Rowena always finds hounds in the vicinity when she works with Cerridwen. "A sow is well and good as a symbol," she says, "but a sow is not going to carry a message. A dog will. It's up to you to learn how to interpret it." Arnica Bee, another acquaintance whose patron is Cerridwen, agrees. "On those dark and stormy nights, the hounds can find the way home. They guide my car through storms." Paganjack, who prefers to work with birds, only experiences the hounds when something bad is about to happen. He doesn't seek them out, and he'd prefer they return the favor. Yet even he admits their warnings have helped him avoid tragedy on more than one occasion. The strange black shapes in the movie *Ghost* that take away the bad guy at the end always make me think of Hell Hounds (even though they're black, conforming to modern connotation, instead of white as in most of the myths).

I've worked with Cerridwen for over a dozen years now, and every experience is a rebirth and a transformation. The hounds only recently made themselves known to me, although I'd grown up with the legends. I feel about them the way I feel about dogs in general—as friends, protectors, and companions. They live closer to their instincts than I do—when their instincts kick in, I'm going to listen.

Overcoming a Fear of Driving

by Sybil Fogg

For years, I was afraid of driving. As a teenager, I dropped out of my driver's education class because I was convinced I would run someone over. As I matured, I lived in the Boston area, where it was easier to not own a car than to pay for parking and drive in endless circles. When I married my husband, he didn't have a license either. He grew up in Ireland, where it was rather difficult to obtain a license, so the idea of getting one in the United States never occurred to him. Eventually, we moved to Maine and had to depend on friends and family to cart us around. By the time our second child was born, I realized we desperately needed a vehicle of our own. But I was still scared to get behind the wheel. I tried to convince my husband to get a license, but he had too many other obligations.

Finally, I decided I had to take the plunge. I took lessons and got my license by the time I was twenty-six, but my fear was so immobilizing I only drove my car for short, absolutely necessary trips. I still depended on people to drive me longer distances. Soon I was involved in a car accident because my

fear affected my judgment. After that, I gave it up altogether, convincing my husband to take over the duty of designated driver.

When my third daughter was three years old, my husband and I divorced—he took the car, so I resorted to using unreliable public transportation and taxicabs for such mundane chores as grocery shopping. Each day, I had to leave home two hours before work to walk my daughters to school and daycare. At the time, I was finishing up my master's of fine arts and had to rely on classmates and friends to get me to and from school. Within two years, I obtained a teaching post at a college forty-five minutes away from my home. Now I was going to have to drive.

I decided to take control of my fear and turned to the goddess and god for strength. This spell is simple and straight to the point. Just be sure to follow the correspondences.

Moon: New Moon in Taurus to govern self-esteem and protection

Time: Sunrise to govern travel

Tools: A white candle

Bright blue altar cloth

Frankincense incense

Cardamom (or any other protection) oil

A working knife to carve candle

Preparation: Sometime before you cast the spell, wash the candle and rub it with blessed earth and water. Charge it under a Full Moon. June's Mead Moon is a good time for this particular spell, but any Full Moon will do. Use the knife to carve the following symbols into the candle:

A pentacle for protection

A symbol of the goddess to call upon her aid

The god's symbol to call upon his assistance

A mark to symbolize travel (The Internet is a handy tool for this if you don't have one in mind.)

A deosil (clockwise) spiral to bring courage

A widdershin (counterclockwise) spiral to banish fears.

Make sure you are alone when you do this spell because it is important to convene with only yourself while focusing your intention.

1) Anoint the candle with the oil.

2) Drape the blue cloth over the altar. Light the incense and candle.

3) Meditate on your fear. Visualize it. Allow it to well up inside you until you feel as though you are actually driving. Breathe in the fear, inhaling deeply. As you exhale, visualize releasing your fears. Say:

O Princess of the waxing light
Beautiful lady of the night
Maiden, who doth burn bright
Silvery glowing, glistening sprite

I'm asking for your gentle tears
To wash away this binding fear
Release me, make my vision clear
I must drive to work from here

O Great Maiden, lovingly
Hear my call and set me free
I ask to drive courageously
I ask for confidence, so mote it be

Repeat as many times as you deem necessary. Focus your energy on the candle's flame. Then simply let the candle burn down.

Rituals that Reach Out

by Magenta Griffith

Like everyone else, Pagans and Witches have a variety of abilities and disabilities, strengths and weaknesses, assets and liabilities. These can affect everything we do, especially rituals. Abilities such as a good singing voice can contribute to rituals, but not everyone can carry a tune. Similarly, not everyone can fully take part in every ritual. How can ritual planners design a meaningful experience that is open to as many people as possible?

Coven and other small group rituals can usually accommodate the special needs of their members, be it a partial hearing loss or ongoing time constraint. When planning a larger-than-coven ritual or other activity, potential difficulties need to be taken into account.

Perceptual disabilities are often the hardest to accommodate. A ritual that has few or no spoken words may be meaningless to someone with a severe visual impairment. Colorful banners to distinguish the directions could confuse someone with color-blindness. A crowded ritual may obscure the sightlines of a short person or a child. On the other hand, a ritual that is mostly words would not mean much to a deaf person unless there is an ASL interpreter. Poor acoustics or ritual cast members with soft voices may make it hard for everyone to hear clearly. This means an effective ritual that reaches as many people as possible needs both words and some visual components. Besides, people have different ways of relating to the world. A visual person wants things to see, a kinetic person wants to move, an auditory person reacts best to sounds and music.

Moving Along

Mobility problems can take many forms. Being in a wheelchair presents one set of problems, but walking with a cane is an entirely different situation. For a person in a motorized wheelchair, a ramp may be the perfect solution. However, the extra distance of a ramp could be an obstacle for people who wheel themselves or use a cane. Even a few steps up or down can be a problem for certain people. Many mobility impairments will make rituals involving much movement or dance tricky. Someone who is missing an arm may not be able to hold hands with the next person or easily pass a chalice. The space used for an open ritual needs to be handicap accessible, should have chairs available, and the ritual needs to be designed so that people sitting down can fully participate as much as possible.

A different kind of mobility problem is getting to the site of ritual. If the site is not on or near public transit, can rides and carpooling be arranged? Email lists are excellent for this if the ritual is mostly people in a particular organization. On the other hand, free parking nearby is also a plus because some people cannot afford expensive parking in a downtown area. "On public transit" and "free parking" is a nice combination, but is difficult to find in some cities. But some people who don't have a car may not want to have to ask for a lift. However, if you have a family of six or seven, including small children, the logistics of busing anywhere may be a nightmare, and so parking for their vehicle nearby is necessary.

Allergies

Allergies present a range of problems at open rituals. First, asthma is on the rise, and many asthmatics are allergic to incense and smoke in general. With proper ventilation, censing the space may be safe, but this is an issue to keep in mind when planning.

If you are going to pass around cakes and wine, will it be something everyone can consume safely? Having two chalices, one with wine or another alcoholic drink, and one with fruit juice or water is a solution. At the very least, announce before the ritual starts what will be passed around, so people who need to abstain may do so.

Many rituals end with a potluck feast. Because of food allergies, and differences in chosen diet, dishes that are not completely obvious should be labeled. A roast chicken is a roast chicken, but a salad that has cubed ham in it is an unpleasant surprise to a vegetarian. Food allergies and sensitivities vary so widely that the only good solution is identifying the ingredients in home-made dishes; organizers can provide 3 × 5 cards and a pen for this purpose. Also, have the list of the ingredients on packaged items available, which might mean leaving the lid to a container or wrappings from a box handy.

Language Barriers

Languages can be another set of obstacles. If you speak one language, and the ritual is in a different language, you may have no idea what is going on. If you speak English and the ritual is in Gaelic or Greek, the ritual may be meaningless for you. This means all the advance information about the ritual should make it clear what language or languages will be used. It's OK to have a short passage in another language, especially if you also use the translation. Having long sections in a different language make it hard for people to follow and appreciate the ritual.

Even when everyone can understand the words, comprehension can present another difficulty. Some open rituals need to be understandable to children and beginners, people who may not have any landmarks in Pagan country. As a rule, rituals can include mythology that most people have learned. But it is unwise to assume everyone has read a particular book, fiction or nonfiction. Referencing a TV show or a movie when planning a ritual has pitfalls, too. Unless it's meant as a humorous ritual, it may seem juvenile to anyone who isn't a big fan of the show. Not everyone is a fan of *Star Trek*.

Safety First

Safety is important for everyone. Is there a basic first-aid kit at your ritual site? If there isn't, one of the organizers can buy or assemble one with supplies from the drugstore. Will the ritual be reasonably free of interruptions? Open rituals often have a doorkeeper (or two), who can handle intrusions from the mundane world. Even if it isn't an open ritual, it's a good idea to designate someone to handle the unexpected.

Our children are our future, but this doesn't mean every ritual is suitable. A crying baby can interrupt a quiet meditative ritual, and an active three-year-old could create a hazard for all involved in a ritual with lots of movement. We need to think about if and how children will fit into a given ritual. Whenever possible, arrange child-care on site or elsewhere. Some rituals might be OK for older children, but not for toddlers. Other rituals would be boring to a ten-year-old, who might prefer to sit and read or play nearby.

These are just some situations ritual planners might want to consider. Because each group or community has specific circumstances to account for, the best thing to do as an organizer is put yourself into as many people's shoes as possible. Think of the mother of a young baby, an older person with arthritis, the asthmatic as well as the handicapped person in a wheelchair.

Yuletide! Seasonal Meditations

by Michelle Skye

Meditation is not the first thing we think about during the hectic holiday season. Meditation? Who has time? We're too busy driving from store to store, jostling for a parking space, crafting Yuletide cakes and cookies, and wrapping the ever-growing mound of presents. Yet, the holiday season is one of the best times to indulge in meditation. Not only will it help you to relax, center, and feel refreshed, the holiday season is full of unique and celebratory sights and sounds that will guide you in honing your meditation skills. What better time for meditation!

Unfortunately, Yuletide lapses in many regimens are common, and often the result of our own lofty goals. So before setting up an elaborate meditation routine, be sure to take a look at your life truthfully and honestly. Don't plan to meditate every day for twenty minutes if your schedule simply won't permit it. Creating an unrealistic plan sets you up for failure, leaving you feeling frustrated with yourself and less likely to meditate in the future. Instead, promise to meditate once a week for ten minutes or twice a week for five and then do it! Allowing yourself to "slide" only creates an internal negativity that, if continued, can begin to permeate your subconscious mind, setting up false obstacles on your life path.

Once you've decided on a reasonable schedule, take some time to figure out your meditation style. When you meditate, do you see things when you close your eyes, either as snapshots or a movie? If so, then you would be most attuned to receiving information through clairvoyance. Visual interpretation is the most commonly accepted and understood form of receiving information during meditation. We live in a very visual society that inundates us with images. We are culturally programmed to accept them and create them ourselves. However, we need to remember that we have five senses, not one.

Many people will not experience meditation visually, but rather through sound, scent, touch, or an inner knowing. These people will not see a campfire flickering, but will hear it crackling, smell its rich scent, feel the warmth of the flames, or simply know the truth of the fire. Inner knowing is perhaps the most difficult interpretative style to accept and believe. It's easy to get caught in the trap of self-doubt, thinking you imagined the whole thing. In my opinion, if a certain thought, idea, or speculation pops into your mind during meditation, it is a good idea to pay attention. Once you have been meditating for a while, you will know which thoughts are inspirational and which are simply lists of chores. Knowing your most comfortable meditation style is important, so you can build on your intuitive ability and (eventually) expand your meditation skills.

The following is a list of meditation activities that are simple, quick, and especially designed for the Yuletide season. They are divided up into the five meditative categories: sight, sound, scent, touch, and inner knowing. If you are not sure of your meditative interpretation style, try all the exercises and see which one is easiest for you. Focus on the exercise from your innate interpretative category first. Once you feel you have mastered it, try another interpretative category. Continue in this way until you feel confident with a majority of the meditation styles. Don't be afraid to completely stop an exercise if you are feeling frustrated and aggravated. Not everyone can perform every interpretative style. See the annoying experience as a chance to learn more about yourself, as one more step in your path to reaching your goal of meditative confidence and competence. Above all, enjoy your time away from the pressures of the holiday season! After all, you're doing this for yourself.

Sight Exercise ~ Light Displays

Take the time to really look at the holiday displays in your town. Are they tasteful or gaudy? Are they comprised of multiple colors or one color? Are they religious or secular? After you've scoped out all the beautiful (and unsightly) decorations, choose one that resonates with you. Study it intently, then close your eyes and try to re-create it in your mind's eye. You might want to do this a couple of times in front of the display so you can see how accurately you remember. Throughout the season, when you meditate, focus on the holiday display, its vivid colors, and bright lights. Work on re-creating the display in its entirety in your mind.

Sound Exercise ~ Christmas Carols

Christmas carols are a part of our culture whether we agree with their sentiments or not. Without thought, allow a carol to pop into your mind. Write it down and then search through all your old cassettes and CDs for different versions of that particular carol. (The Internet is also a great source of songs.) Pick a version you particularly like and listen to it. During meditation, close your eyes and work on "hearing" the carol. Not just the words, but also the actual voice of the singer. Hear the intonations and inflections, the emotion and power. Once you can successfully reproduce that exact version of the carol, pick another version and notice the differences. Do this exercise until you can hear the differences between the versions of the song without having to turn on a CD player.

Scent Exercise ~ Pine Greenery

Even if you live in a tiny apartment, you can still enjoy the greenery of the season with a small door wreath or simple window swags. Decide on how you'd like to bring greenery into your living space. Purchase the pieces and hang them, paying special attention to their scent throughout the process. When you are done, meditate away from your decorations and work on re-creating the scent, actually smelling it. If you have difficulty, go to your decorations and take a big sniff. Keep practicing until you can recall the pine scent without difficulty.

Touch Exercise ~ Soft Feathers

Find a feather boa, a cashmere scarf or sweater, or a fluffy tree ornament. Close your eyes and explore the object with your fingers. As long as you own it, don't be shy about rubbing it on your

cheeks or across the back of your knees. Feel the softness. Note if you feel ticklish or irritated by the object. When you are done, place the object aside and try to feel it moving on your skin. Does it feel different behind your knees than on the palms of your hands? How about across your cheeks or lips? Compare the sensations while focusing on truly experiencing the touch, not just remembering it. Once you have mastered the touch of something soft, move on to an object that is cold or hard or prickly.

Inner Knowing Exercise ~ Card Images

Most of us receive a holiday card or two during Yuletide. Before you rip into the envelope to discover a smiling angel or quirky reindeer, take some time to meditate on the card. What colors are most prominent? What images decorate the front flap? Will this card be funny or religious, beautiful or plain? Write down any impressions and thoughts you have about the card. Don't overthink your answers—just allow them to flow out of you. When you think you have an idea of the design of the card, open it up and see if you were right. Don't judge yourself if you are completely wrong. Remember, not everyone is going to have this type of meditative interpretation style. See this exercise as a fun way to truly connect to your holiday cards. After all, someone went to all the trouble to buy the card and send it to you. The least you can do is spend five minutes thinking about it!

Ayurveda

by Laura Gyre

If you have an interest in world religions, yoga, alternative health, or the occult, you've likely encountered the concept of Ayurveda in one form or another—perhaps an Ayurvedic diet, Ayurvedic doctor, or maybe even Ayurvedic toothpaste! But what exactly is Ayurveda? Simply put, it's a body of ancient Indian teachings on the subject of personal health and interpersonal healing.

The Ayurvedic philosophy is based on the Vedas, the primary holy texts of Hinduism. However, it is a living tradition that has been growing and changing ever since. For thousands of years it has contained insight into aspects of medicine, such as surgery and antibiotics, that have only been rediscovered by mainstream medicine during the past few hundred years. Amazing as these types of knowledge are, however, they are not the primary focus of modern Ayurvedic practice.

According to Ayurveda, the body is composed of a careful balance of the elements: earth, air, fire, water, and space. Every person has a tendency toward a certain combination of these elements, but this balance also fluctuates over time and is affected by such forces as the position of the stars and the activities of the individual. The Ayurvedic therapies aim to balance the individual through a combination of cleansing therapies (such as fasting and purging) to remove any surplus elements, and supportive therapies (such as herbal medicines and massage with oils) to nourish the depleted elements. Therapies also vary in intensity, from the monthlong pancha karma cleansing therapy administered by Ayurvedic doctors, to simple teas and other preparations that can be made at home.

The Three Constitutional Types

The three common constitutional types are Vata, which is dominated by the elements air and space; Pitta, which is dominated by fire and water; and Kapha, which is dominated by water and earth. A person of the Vata type is likely to be thin, often cold, with dry skin and hair, and probably spiritually inclined—but also somewhat absent-minded or nervous. The Pitta type, on the other hand, is more often characterized by an athletic or moderate build, a lot of internal warmth and energy, and a "fiery" personality with passionate feelings and perhaps a quick temper. Finally, the Kapha type tends to have a heavier body with oily skin, thick hair, and a slow, but steady, pace of life. While many people actually exhibit a combination of these types, which can fluctuate due to lifestyle changes, in most cases one type will consistently be more apparent.

Many aspects of Ayurvedic therapy are tailored to the patient's constitutional type. For example, there are yearly cleansing therapies and a certain season to practice them suggested for each type. Many therapies for specific conditions are also recommended only for one or two of the constitutional types. In fact, Ayurvedic prescription is incredibly complicated—taking into account such things as the time of year, day of the week, and time of day as well as the person's constitutional type and their particular complaint and symptoms—so it needs to be practiced by a thoroughly trained expert for best results. Luckily for the person with a casual interest, there are certain simple recommendations for each constitutional type that are easy enough to try at home.

The Ayurvedic Diet

Diet is a very important part of the Ayurvedic philosophy. The fundamental diet principles are the same for all constitutional types. Eating a primarily vegetarian diet with lots of organic produce and few highly processed ingredients is considered beneficial. Also, it is important to eat and drink in moderation—the classic suggestion is to fill half the stomach with food and one-quarter with water, leaving the last quarter empty to facilitate digestion. Another way to explain this is that no one should eat more food than they can fit in their two hands cupped together (about one to two cups for most adults). Afterwards, it is best to relax a while or walk around a little to promote digestion, and wait at least three hours before eating again.

In addition to these general principles, there are dietary recommendations for each constitutional type. Kapha types should eat more bitter and spicy foods because these are energizing, and less oily or heavy foods. Pittas should increase their intake of cooling sweet and bitter foods, and consume less animal products, alcohol, and caffeine to keep their energy from getting out of control. Vatas should have more naturally sweet, sour, and salty foods because these are considered grounding, and decrease their consumption of caffeine, sugar, and any hard-to-digest foods.

Although the guidelines can be complicated and somewhat rigorous, great emphasis is also placed on the taste and enjoyment of food. Ayurvedic practitioners often prescribe foods and medicines according to their taste—appreciation of life through the senses (including taste) is considered to play a vital role in well-being. Also, much like the elements should be balanced within the body, the tastes should be balanced within food. Although each individual requires more or less of certain tastes, a variety of food is important to good nutrition for everyone.

Ayurvedical Medical Treatments

One of the most powerful and common Ayurvedic medical treatment is pancha karma. *Pancha* means "five," and describes the five main portions of the monthlong treatment. Actually, only four of the five components are generally practiced today, because the fifth, bloodletting, has come under scientific scrutiny. Still, pancha karma is believed to be a powerful cleansing and restorative therapy. It is also fairly strenuous, so people with serious health conditions are generally given gentler restorative therapies first to build up their strength. Everyone preparing for pancha karma is started on a special light diet and a daily regimen of oil massages and sweating. These preliminary therapies are intended to dislodge the unbalanced elements from the body and prepare them to be removed. Next, the four main cleansing treatments, which include induced vomiting, purgatives, enemas, and inhaling medicated powders, are administered over a period of several weeks. Finally, a normal healthy diet gradually replaces the special cleansing foods.

While pancha karma is probably the most dramatic, many other Ayurvedic medical treatments have powerful healing effects. These include some of the practices described above administered separately, and also herbal medicines, anointing oils applied to different parts of the body, acupressure, fasting, special diets, prayers, and exercise routines as well as many different types of sauna and steam therapies. The range of conditions that can be treated with Ayurvedic techniques is vast, and in some cases includes problems of which mainstream medicine has little knowledge.

Do-It-Yourself Ayurvedic Therapies

Many types of healing therapies with Ayurvedic roots are gentle enough to use at home. It's outside the scope of this article to describe these practices in much detail, but most can be investigated easily enough by reading a book or two and purchasing a few readily available supplies.

Ayurvedic massage: This massage uses herbal oils and vigorous rubbing to cleanse the skin and stimulate certain energy lines and points throughout the body.

Aromatherapy: This increasingly popular art uses scents to bring about desired physical and mental states, from energized to relaxed.

Flower essences: Every flower is believed to have its own energy and properties, which can be accessed by using these preparations.

Gemstone therapy: Certain gems and semiprecious stones are also believed to have healing properties.

Herbalism: Many Ayurvedic herbs and herbal products are readily available, ranging from teas to toiletries to supplement pills.

Homeopathy: This science is based on the idea that problems should be treated with a substance that resembles the problem in some way. For example, warts are treated with a warty looking plant, or fever is treated with a plant that causes warming of the body. This principle goes against a lot of scientific thinking, but has produced some interesting results. It is also safe enough to experiment with at commonly available doses, which are so diluted that they are unlikely to contain even a single molecule of the root substance (the theory being that the energy of the material is maintained even though it is physically not present).

Yoga: A much more complex system of action and philosophy than many people are aware, but even physical yoga poses alone are considered to be good exercise that tones and strengthens the body, enhances flexibility, and promotes a healthy balance of energy and relaxation.

The Ayurvedic Life

Besides prescribing therapies for specific problems, Ayurveda suggests a daily routine that is conducive to maintaining health and balance. According to this philosophy, you should wake up early, around sunrise if possible, and drink a glass of water with a little lemon squeezed into it. Next comes a sequence of cleansing activities. Brush your teeth, clean your tongue with a tongue scraper or the edge of a spoon, and gargle with saltwater or herbal tea. Clean your eyes with an eyecup, and exercise them by looking from side to side and then up and down several times. Rub the insides of your ears and nose with a few drops of sesame oil, or use a neti pot (which can be purchased at many health food stores and comes with instructions) to clean your sinuses. If you like, brush your skin gently with a natural-fiber brush to exfoliate it. Following these practices, take a bath, then moisturize your skin with natural oils or creams, and dress in clean clothes made of natural fibers. Ayurveda places great value on maintaining cleanliness, and on using natural materials as much as possible in every aspect of life.

After completing the cleansing activities, observe a short period of religious devotion. You could say prayers, chant, maintain your altar, and so on. After this, have a healthy, moderate breakfast, and start your work for the day. The main guidelines related to work are that it should be enjoyable and meaningful, but not overly exhausting. Also considered beneficial is working with the hands as much as possible, rather than relying unnecessarily on laborsaving devices. This is because you benefit from the sensory experience of touching things, and also because using your hands allows your energy to directly infuse the things you are working with.

During the workday you will probably take a break for lunch. Because it occurs while you are wide awake and generally engaged in active pursuits, lunch should be the most substantial meal of the day, and should be followed by a short rest. In the afternoon, try to get in some gentle exercise, especially if your job is not very physically demanding. Holistic forms of exercise that work with the energy field as well as the body, such as yoga or tai chi, are especially beneficial.

Relax during a light dinner and spend the early evening having fun with friends and family, enjoying nature, or doing creative activities. Later in the evening, have a period of meditation, which will help you prepare for restful sleep. Trading massages with someone or massaging your own feet and hands at this time is also considered helpful for relaxation and general health. Make sure to go to bed in plenty of time to get up with the Sun again tomorrow, feeling refreshed and full of energy.

Magical Mutts
Working Magic with Man's Best Friend
by A.C. Fisher Aldag

When you imagine a Witch's familiar, you often think of a black cat riding pillion on a flying broomstick, not a Pomeranian or a poodle. Well, witchy dog owners will be pleased to learn that man's best friend is just as enchanting as any mere feline. In fact, mystical mutts have a long history of magical talent, including helping their humans to raise energy, celebrating seasonal rituals, and guarding shamanic journeys into the otherworld. Dogs are depicted as familiar spirits in ancient woodcuts and as brave companions of gallant knights in medieval tapestries. Fairy tale Fidos have been featured in literature from Greek ritual dramas to the King Arthur sagas, not to mention the modern Fluffy of the popular Harry Potter series.

These charmed canine legends are based on genuine magical practice. Many pet dogs truly enjoy being included in a spiritual working. Dogs can be trained to behave during rituals and

may actually help channel the flow of energy. Some even join in the ceremony, barking cheerfully as the human participants call "Blessed be." A dog may take pleasure in dancing around a bonfire or lounging beneath the drummer's chair, tail thumping to the beat. A wet canine nose might help to sniff out the most auspicious card in a tarot reading. When your dog presses close to you, bares its teeth, and raises its hackles at something only a canine can see, it may be time to grab the salt and perform a banishing rite. If your dog rolls on its back and sighs with contentment, you can be assured that all is well in your magical world. And of course, a pooch always appreciates sharing the abundance of a holiday feast. When you pass around the cakes and ale, remember to give your pet a special treat, too.

Fortunately, more and more Wiccan sabbats and Pagan gatherings welcome animal companions. The literature provided by festival organizers should have information and rules for pet owners. Check with the ritual leader to make sure it's OK before bringing any animal into a circle. It's best to try including your dog in solitary rites at home, or a small coven celebration, before hauling him along to a huge Pagan Pride Day gathering. Make sure your pooch is comfortable around large numbers of people and can get along with other animals at the rite. Having a dog-fight right in the middle of your healing meditation is no fun. Please be kind to your canine friend and fellow coveners, and keep your dog on a leash.

Most dogs fit right in during a ceremony, keeping pace as you circle deosil around the altar, licking your hand as you invoke the quarters. However, a magical ritual is not the place for every pet. If Rover is whining in fear, clamping its tail between its back legs, or is barking or growling uncontrollably, it might be time to ask the priestess to cut you out of the circle. The energies of the rite could be too much for a dog's psyche, the drumming and chanting may hurt the delicate canine ears, or the incense might overwhelm his keen sense of smell. Even a "good dog" might not behave during every magical gathering—especially if there is something tasty on the altar! Don't be upset with your pal, who, after all, is only doing what comes naturally. Just like people, dogs may be "solitaries" or very attuned to one single individual. A dog can dislike a big Pagan campout, but still feel a profound connection with the ancestor spirits at a Samhain ritual.

If you're planning to include your buddy in your magical workings, it might be a good idea to first protect him with a talisman or spell. You can create a simple charm of wood or clay, inscribed with magical symbols such as runes, ogham, planetary sigils, or Theban writing, charge it with energy, and hang it from your dog's collar. Or use a permanent marker and draw your words of power directly on the collar. Bill Whitcomb's *The Magician's Companion* contains many symbols useful for this purpose. You may wish to perform a rite to name your familiar, and ask the gods and/or elements to guard and protect your dog from any harmful energies and also from mundane, worldly dangers. Diana, Odin, Arawn, Kwan Yin, and Cernunnos are a few deities associated with the dog. Anoint him with a few drops of plain oil, remembering that some scented potions might be harmful to canine skin. Of course, you'll want to "act in accord" with your magic by confining your puppy in a safe yard, keeping candles away from wagging tails, and putting poisonous herbs out of reach.

Although the dog has been somewhat maligned in Western society, canines have a better reputation in other cultures. "Fido," a common name for dogs in the movies, comes from the Latin word "fidelity," a term for loyalty and devotion. Dogs were honored by the Romans and Greeks for their allegiance to mankind. Diana, the Greco-Roman goddess of the hunt, was accompanied by sacred hounds that protected her maidenhood from satyrs and a marauder disguised as a stag. The qualities of faith, honesty, and dependability are found in those born during the Year of the Dog in the Chinese zodiac system. Repeating the cycle every twelve years, the next Dog Year is 2018. (Count backward by twelve to see if your birth year falls under the sign of the Dog.) Foo Dogs, intricate carvings of canines that resemble the chow breed, are placed on either side of a doorway as guardians of the home. "Foo" means fortune, bringing good luck to all who dwell within. Chows are known for their protective instinct, and were sacred companions of ancient Chinese emperors.

The dog was revered by other rulers as well. Egyptian tombs are frequently protected by a pair of solemn-looking stone hounds, ornamented by gold and precious gemstones. Many hieroglyphs depict a priest, queen, or deified royalty with a dog at their feet. King Arthur had several pet dogs that slept beneath the Round Table and accompanied the knights on their quests. The historian Nennius claimed that Arthur's dog Cafal (pronounced "CAH-vall") left his paw prints embedded in a solid stone monument.

Mab, Queen of the Fairies (a.k.a. Mabh, Maub, or Medbh), was said to use Welsh Corgis to pull her tiny chariot. These small, sturdy herding dogs also served as the hunting steeds for the Wee Folk. According to legend, a fairy prince fell from his mount into an iron trap, and was in dire peril, as iron is poisonous to the Fair People. A young human lad heard the barking dogs and came along just in time to rescue the prince. In gratitude, Queen Mab gave the boy a breeding pair of Corgis to herd his tribe's cattle.

The dogs of the Celtic nations were held in high regard, and the Druidic Brehon Law governed their well-being. When the Irish hero Setanta mistakenly killed a craftsman's valued wolf-hound, he was obliged to take the dog's place for a year, guarding the land and protecting the family herd animals. He even took on the name Cu Cullhain, which means "Cullhain's Hound," until another dog could be properly trained to replace him. In Welsh legend, the leader Gellert left his trusted hunting hound to guard his baby son. When Gellert returned, the cradle was on the floor and the dog was covered in blood. Believing that the animal had eaten his son, the enraged nobleman killed his own dog with a sword. Then he heard a whimpering sound, and found the baby, alive, lying on the floor surrounded by dead wolves. The brave dog had actually protected the child. Gellert was so contrite over killing his hound that he raised a stone tomb, drove his sword into the rocks, and named the cairn "Bedd Gellert" (Beth Gellert, or Gellert's Grave) in honor of the faithful dog. This site still exists in Wales today.

Some mystical canines have a much darker aspect. Anubis, the dog-headed Egyptian god of the underworld, is considered a fearsome deity, although he also has the role of comforter and guardian of the mysteries. If a seeker makes a polite request, Anubis can help to guide him on a spiritual journey. An offering of meat or golden jewelry may be required. Cerberus, the vicious three-headed monster dog of Greek mythology, guarded the gates of Hades, ensuring that the living could not enter and the dead could not leave. Cerberus was responsible for the demise of many a hero until Hercules won his obedience by treating him kindly. The Wild Hunt of Germany was accompanied by ferocious hounds, who sought dead men's souls to drag off to the underworld. A similar legend exists in the Celtic lands, attributed to the hunt of Arawn, Herne, or Cernunnos. The otherworldly dogs are either pale white with cropped ears and blood-red eyes, or coal black and indistinguishable from the night. There are hundreds of black dog legends in Great Britain and continental Europe, most associated with the spirit world. Encountering a black dog on Samhain is said to predict certain death within a year. However, a ghostly hound can also retrieve a seeker from a journey into the fairy realms. The Cwn Annwn (pronounced "coon AH-noon," the dogs of the Celtic Summerland) were sometimes considered to be helpful and benevolent, driving negative influences out of a forest, snarling to warn of danger, and herding deer toward starving hunters.

There are several other dog-related sabbat traditions. Because sheep were so important to the Irish economy, herding hounds were honored at Imbolc with a bowl of milk. In the Hebrides, the islands of northern Scotland, a Lammas "bickle" dog constructed of straw was presented to the farmer who was late harvesting his grain. Although the straw dog was given in jest, it was also considered a talisman to protect the village from starvation. And at Beltane, young maidens would sometimes adorn their pet pups with ribbons and flowery wreaths. Of course dogs are remembered at esbats (Moon ceremonies) too, when hounds and their wolf or coyote cousins sing praises to the Full Moon. Some believe the figures outlined on the Moon are a dog chasing a rabbit.

If you're planning on being owned by a mystical, magical mutt, please consider rescuing your new best friend from an animal shelter. Because of superstitions related to large black dogs, they are often considered to be undesirable, and many are destroyed every month. Yet I've found that black Labradors and rottweilers can be wonderful companions. I've also discovered that magical qualities are not breed-specific; a beagle or a Bouvier can be sensitive to energy, a dachshund or a Dalmatian can be a fine spiritual helper. Do some research into the best type of dog for you and your family. And don't forget your own spiritual talents . . . do a reading, perform a rite of divination, ask your guides to help you find the perfect pooch. Honor and bless your pet by having your dog neutered or spayed. Make certain your pal has all the necessary shots, and if you live in an area where heartworms are a problem, have your veterinarian conduct the test and provide preventive medicine. Your dog will reward you with years of magical energy, wet doggy kisses, and boundless love.

Midsummer's Clearing

by Ladyhawk Whispers

Sometimes things happen that you have no control over. Sometimes you just have to wait, walk slowly, and hold on through the shadows. This is just life; this is where the lessons are, where we learn.

I have been practicing witchcraft all my life—even before I knew what it was. I too have ridden the wave of my life's lessons, all the while my soul knowing what to do to better my life or make me happier. My mundane self (the self I show to the world) hurt, got depressed, sick, or just plain miserable. Although my higher self knew just what I needed to do, the doing eluded me as I waded through the shadows dragging my life along wondering how a Witch who knew so much (I thought) couldn't raise enough energy to even work a spell.

That small voice kept calling to me, "you know it's always dark in the shadows, but light will prevail." And the good news is it does! Being Wiccan means that your life is a cycle, influenced by Mother Nature herself. You cannot force nature any more than you can force the seasons of your life. Hold on, a break will come and the Sun will shine again. It always does!

The following came to me on Midsummer's Eve. All the pondering and praying finally brought to fruition just what I needed to clear the debris from the shadows of my life's lessons, to get back to the soul's planting of new ideas, new direction to a more fulfilled self. Spring is also a good time to do this, but sometimes you need to do a late planting so that you might harvest the goodness through the rest of the wheel of the year.

Midsummer is a time of bonfires, flower rings, and thanking the Goddess and praying for a bountiful harvest to come. Some colors associated with this time of the wheel are red, gold, and yellow, symbolizing the Sun and its warmth, energy, and love. The light has returned and is shining on us, some of our hard lessons have been learned and we are ready to reap the benefits.

Do this spell the day before Midsummer (June 21) in the noon hour when the Sun is at its highest.

Materials

3 herbs—I chose chamomile, marigold, and rosemary seeds because they are herbs whose correspondence is the Sun.

3 terra cotta pots

3 candles—red, yellow, and gold

Water-based acrylic paint (or stickers if you don't feel artistic, but energy runs in you when you try to create and it pleases the Mother, so try to paint)

Potting soil

A lighter or matches—I prefer matches because I love the smell of the sulfur and it kind of relates to this spell.

Plan enough time to complete the ritual (mine took about three hours). You don't want to be interrupted right when you have a good energy flow going. Gather all your necessary items before you start, like a newspaper and a spoon or trowel. You can do this spell inside, but outside is nice too. I also used some music that reminded me of happy summers as a child.

Erect a circle of light by visualizing it all around you and your workspace. Set your candles out one at a time. Start with the red one, placing it in the direction of the south. Do not light it yet. As you are facing the southern candle, place the gold candle to the left and the yellow candle to your right, making a triangle. Place one pot in front of each candle. If you are playing music, make sure it is low so you won't be distracted or turn it off at this point. Stand in front of the triangle with the flat side nearest you and the top point farthest away from you. The bottom of the triangle would then be at the north.

Light the candles in a widdershins pattern, counterclockwise, starting with the red one. Ground and center yourself, then begin your plea to the Goddess.

Your words will hold more power for you if you do them in rhyme, chant, or a singsong manner. Be very sincere and let your emotions show—she knows what's up, but you need to get it out of your system— let your heart pour out to her. Mine went something like this; you can use my words or make up your own.

Mother, Mother I plead to you,
Give me strength to not be blue.
Send my healing right away,
For I fear I might have lost my way.
I need you now so desperately,
Please oh please I beckon you now,
Come to me Mother as I sow.
Hear me hear me this Midsummer's Eve,
My will has been weak,
My spells haven't been working,

My energy level has been low,
Weakness is not something a Witch wants to own.

Take this from me I plead,
Take it from me with each planted seed.
With your warm love and the energy from the Sun,
I now walk out of the shadows and into the light of my life.

As you make your plea to her, plant your seeds in a clockwise manner. Again, start at the red candle, plant the rosemary. At the yellow candle, plant the chamomile, and plant the marigold at the gold candle.

Now that you have your seeds sown, you will now affix a symbol to each pot. Start with the pot in front of the red candle. Paint a heart on it while thinking of how the goddess is in your heart and really bringing that love out for yourself to own, love of yourself, because you are the goddess.

Next move to the yellow candle. Paint a big Sun on it and think of how you can bring more fun into your life. Feel what it was like to play in the Sun as a child, remember, and embrace that feeling again.

Finally, move to the gold candle and paint a dove on it thinking of the peace you will manifest in your life through the Goddess. Then give her a heartfelt thank you and eat something or put some salt on your tongue to ground your energy you have just raised.

Watch your herbs grow and grow, and your life shine in the future remembering that although you had to go through some difficult times to get to where you are in life, it was all worth it because you have come out in the Sun to play with just a little more wisdom to share and enough love in your heart to sustain you.

Happy planting and planning!

Appalachian Folk Magic

by James Kambos

The magical traditions of Appalachia are complex and varied. The folk magic practiced in this region is a blend of old magical customs from around the world. Over the centuries many different ethnic groups have lived in Appalachia, with each bringing their own magical beliefs.

To fully understand why these magical traditions are so deeply rooted here, you must first learn what makes this beautiful rugged region of the eastern United States so unique.

The Appalachian Mountains are the most ancient mountain chain in America. More than two hundred million years ago, after North America rose from the oceans, a tremendous upthrust of energy created a massive line of majestic mountains and valleys stretching from present-day Quebec south to northern Alabama. These mountains became known as the Appalachians, and the region became known as Appalachia.

The rich magical history has carried on the most in central and southern Appalachia. This area extends from southern Ohio and continues through the Virginias, portions of Kentucky, Tennessee, the Carolinas, Georgia, and northern Alabama.

The first people to leave the imprint of these myths and magic in Appalachia were Native American tribes, such as the Cherokee and Shawnee. Next, the descendants of freed African slaves settled primarily in the lowlands just east of the Appalachians. Due to their close proximity to the Appalachian highlands, much of their magical lore eventually assimilated into the folk-magic melting pot of Appalachia. Soon after, cheap land, the rich soil of the bottomlands, and the great forests attracted a wave of European immigrants, bringing with them their rich magical traditions.

They came from many countries, including Germany, Great Britain, France, Hungary, Iceland, Poland, Italy, and Greece. These nationalities had one thing in common—a closeness to the earth. Working together in this new environment, they cleared forests, farmed the land, and mined for coal. It was only natural that their magical lore and legends were shared, passed on, and changed to suit their individual needs. This blending of old magical beliefs formed the basis of Appalachian folk magic, much of which is still practiced today.

Appalachian folk magic has endured mainly due to geography (and not the offensive, inaccurate stereotype casting Appalachians as ignorant, superstitious hillbillies). The region is made up of mountains, hollows, valleys, and foothills. Flat stretches of land are rare. The rugged topography of Appalachia has kept the region isolated well into the twentieth century. The majority of the population are devout Christians who have blended the old ways of their European and African ancestors into their belief systems. Luckily for those of us interested in studying magical traditions, the hardy people of Appalachia have been able to preserve the mystical folklore of the old world.

The Magic of the Hills

Born and raised in the Appalachian foothills of southern Ohio, I have witnessed spells being cast and charms bringing a wish to fulfillment. I have known conjure women who read cards sitting by a potbelly stove, while taking a "chew" of tobacco. What follows is a potpourri of folk-magic practices common to Appalachia. This is my home, and this is my magic.

Quilt Magic

Combining artistic craftsmanship with magical intent is common in Appalachia. This is especially true in quilting. The quilts of Appalachia are known for their quality and command high

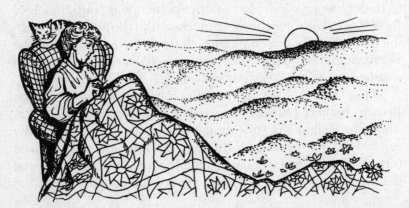

prices. What many people don't realize is that quilts are more than art; they can also contain powerful magic.

Quilts were usually made to mark life's milestones—births, weddings, and so on. To charge a quilt with a positive aura, the quilter may weave special blessings into it for things such as a long life or happiness. The designs also have mystical meanings. A ring shape would represent eternity. Flowers could stand for abundance and beauty. A cabin design would symbolize hearth and home. And a star would represent divinity.

The quilter could also tuck a bit of dried herbs, a lock of hair, or a feather into the lining of a quilt to bind the spell to the recipient. This is powerful magic because the act of stitching makes you concentrate on the magical outcome.

To perform your own quilt magic, select a pattern and colors appropriate to your goal. Bless the needle, thread, and fabric. When your quilt is done you'll have a beautiful heirloom blessed with positive energy.

Magical Apple Dolls

In Appalachia there is a charming folk-art custom of making apple dolls. These rustic-looking dolls can sometimes be found for sale at craft fairs. Although they certainly can be displayed in the home as folk art, their original use was magical. They are similar to poppets and were used for spells, protection, or love charms. The ones that you make yourself are the most powerful. Here's what you do.

In the autumn, when apples are in season, preferably during a waxing Moon, select an apple you are drawn to. Peel and carve a face into it while concentrating on your magical goal. Hang the carved apple by wire to dry in a dark, airy space for about three weeks. Don't disturb it or the enchantment will be lost. As the apple dries, it will take on its own characteristics and "speak" to you. After drying, attach the apple to a stick and dress with scraps of fabric to create a folk-art doll. No one needs to know about its magical purpose. You may keep your apple doll on display, or burn in a fire after it has done its work. If the doll was used for fertility or prosperity magic, you may also bury the apple doll wherever you feel is appropriate.

Appalachian Scrying Techniques

The ancient art of gazing at a smooth or shiny surface to predict the future or to seek answers to questions is very popular in Appalachia. However, instead of using mirrors or a shiny stone, Appalachian scryers are more apt to use water. The methods most typically used in Appalachia are an ordinary water glass or a well.

To "read" the water glass, fill a clear glass with water. Gaze into the water intently. As with most scrying techniques, the water will look misty at first, then clear. Now is when the images will come. Watch for symbols, faces, or actual events. Many people see images in color; there are also times when you might see movement. To prevent eyestrain keep your water glass sessions short, perhaps no longer than ten minutes at first. Write down what you see in a journal, and then see if it comes to pass.

Gazing into a water well is one of the oldest magical traditions to be found in Appalachia. This type of scrying was even depicted in the major motion picture *Cold Mountain*, when the character Ada wanted to see her future.

Since water wells are deep and dark, it is easy to see why they would make an excellent focal point for scrying. Magical lore surrounding this type of gazing is interesting and may vary from different regions of Appalachia. In some areas it's believed the best time of year to scry into a well is spring, especially during the month of May. A friend of mine from Kentucky claims her family has used well-gazing to see the face of a future mate. The steps for gazing into a well are the same as looking into the water glass.

The Diviners

Some people call them fortunetellers or seers. As a child growing up in Appalachia I heard many stories about certain people who had the "second sight"; that is, the gift of prophesy. These diviners normally lived in isolated areas deep in the back hills. Most were loners whose reputations spread by word of mouth. In general, their favorite divining tools were ordinary playing cards.

On a spring afternoon many years ago I met such a person.

The locals knew her simply as Ma. She lived in a weatherbeaten farmhouse framed by waist-high weeds on a rutted dirt road. Just for the heck of it I went to her for a "card reading." I had heard she was the best. I was not disappointed. Her thin bony hands shuffled the cards and I cut the deck. She quickly turned seven cards face-up and began predicting future events—many of which didn't make sense at the time. That is until a week passed, and I realized her predictions were dramatically on target.

Like most Appalachian card readers, Ma used a deck of playing cards, not tarot cards. The technique of reading playing cards can take some time to master, but is well worth your time. The best thing to do is take no more than five cards at a time and meditate on what they mean to you. Don't rely on how-to books too heavily. Let the cards "speak" to you. Then begin by doing simple readings for yourself. It may take more than a year, but you'll find your way.

Some Appalachian Spells and Magical Beliefs

Spells and charms have been used in Appalachia for generations for protection, health, love, and many other reasons. Here is a sampling of spells you may find interesting.

Wood and ashes are popular materials used in Appalachian protection magic. To bind a curse and return it to its sender, a person would frequently take a small flexible twig or sapling, split it, and twist it. The name of the suspected evildoer would be muttered and the twig would be left on the ground. To complete the spell, the practitioner would walk away without looking back.

To break a spell, try this. Upon a sheet of white paper with soot from a candle or fireplace, write the problem or the name of the person you think cast the spell. Do this with your finger. Then burn the paper until it is consumed with fire and has turned to ashes. The spell will be destroyed.

Magic to destroy pain was popular in this remote region because doctors were scarce; however, the following spells should never be used in place of medical treatment.

When a person was suffering from pain and regular treatment didn't seem to help, an ax would be driven into the floorboards near the patient. Or, a knife would be placed beneath the bed; the purpose was to symbolically "cut" the pain. For a more modern version, take a length of gray yarn, and while concentrating on the painful condition, cut the yarn with scissors. Lastly, throw the yarn away.

I've also seen the ancient art of knot magic used in Appalachia to locate lost objects. To do this, take a handkerchief and tie it in one knot. Picture the lost object in your mind's eye as you tie the knot. Insert the knotted handkerchief into the earth, or the soil of a potted plant: and whisper, "come back to me." This charm was practiced in my family and is very effective.

For prosperity, here is an Appalachian charm given to me by a ninety-year-old man who swore by it. At night during a waxing Moon, hide a dollar bill outside your front door. The next morning place the dollar in your pocket, and spend no money for the next twenty-four hours. To ensure wealth for the coming year, you may also perform this spell beginning on New Year's Eve.

Conclusion

Life for many Appalachians has been difficult. Poverty is common and the people have been the victim of prejudice. But, through the years their faith combined with a belief in ancient magical practices have helped many Appalachians survive hardship.

For the most part, the folk magic of Appalachia has remained unchanged. It is magic that is literally as old as the hills.

For Further Study

Gainer, Patrick W. *Witches, Ghosts, and Signs: Folklore of the Southern Appalachians.* Morgantown, WV.: Seneca Books, 1975.

Plants, Planets, and How to Make a Better Potion

by Mark Stavish

Working with plants offers experienced and neophyte practitioners of various esoteric paths the opportunity to connect not only with the energies of the material world and the elements, but also to their astral and cosmological counterparts.

In esoteric cosmology, the universe is described as going from the very abstract to the very concrete with many stages or levels of transition in between. In alchemy and kabbalah, these levels are referred to by their relationship to the seven ancient planets, and in some instances the zodiacal signs, and are known as the Doctrine of Correspondences. The Doctrine of Correspondences is the key to all magic, as it allows for a linking of ideas, images, emotions, forms, and energies across the spectrum of existence from the very subtle, to the very dense; within ourselves and external to our mind and body. A proper understanding of the correspondences involved in an herbal or alchemical operation is essential for success.

Once the level of matter, or earth, is reached, energy-matter is seen less in terms of the unique expressions of the planets and more so in terms of the elements. These elements are expressed as follows: fire, energy; air, gas; water, liquid; and earth, solids. They also have a subtle expression as well: fire, self-consciousness; air, mind, or organizing capacity; water, emotions; and earth, physical expression, or density.

At the dense material realm of physical life, energy rests until acted upon to reverse its polarity, or move from matter back into energy. It is important to recognize that primordial energy—chaos, nothingness, or alchemical First Matter (*Prima Materia*)—is indestructible, yet, when it combines with and moves through the phases of creation, it is altered until matter is formed, leaving little energy to spare. This is done through alterations to its essential vibratory nature, which is similar to how a musical note can be the same, but simply of a different octave. Matter is simply dense energy, whereas energy is potential matter, and can be understood as being at the lower end of the musical scale, whereas energy is at the higher end. Only when acted upon by consciousness do they accelerate their evolution or transition between states. This action of consciousness upon matter is often slow and laborious, taking eons of casual and haphazard causes and their effects, unless it is done with an understanding of natural laws, such as expressed in the techniques of prayer, meditation, ritual, or alchemy.

When energy combines with existing matter, or transitions into it, the energy begins to go through the alchemical stages of decay, which separates pure energy from impure matter. Purity is a perfect expression of an ideal; impurity is an imperfect expression, or form, of an ideal.

The purified energy then seeks a new materialization until the ideal of energy is perfectly expressed in the form of matter, "as above, so below." In essence, energy is constantly reincarnating to express itself.

Cornelius Agrippa states in Chapter LXVIII of *The Three Books of Occult Philosophy*, "That which is above binds that which is below and assimilates it; that which is below is then changed to be like that which is above or is otherwise operated on."

The increasing of vibratory rates causes a temporary relaxation or even total release of the bonds between consciousness (the control mechanism) and matter, thereby allowing more energy to enter the relationship. All magical operations are aimed at simultaneously alternating polarities while raising the mental, emotional, and, as with alchemy, even the physical vibrations to a specific level to tune one's consciousness to a specific frequency—similar to turning the dial on a radio to a specific station.

When this temporary relaxation or release occurs in the plant or mineral realm, it is similar to the human out-of-body experience. When the consciousness (or soul) experiences expansions in awareness—and the body experiences deeper rest and release from tensions that obstruct the mind-body interface, there is an alternating of the polarity of the body. When the physical world is passive, it attracts energy and consciousness into it. When consciousness becomes passive, it attracts the psychic and the spiritual phenomena.

Everything is in a constant state of flux and alternating of polarity. Magic and alchemy actively participate in this polarization and direct it to specific ends, aimed at creating a balance or whole whereby polarity is transcended and primordial unity re-experienced. Humans, animals, plants, and minerals all go through the same experiences, but with varying degrees of awareness. When alchemists or magicians use a plant or mineral in their work, and assist in raising its vibrations, they are, in effect, raising their own.

With each stage of decay or death, matter also benefits or is made more exalted. From the experiences of mineral life arise plant life, and from plant life the experiences of animal life, and from animal life, our human self-awareness. Herein we see the progression from earth (mineral), water (plant), air (animal), to fire (self-awareness).

Fire (energy/self-consciousness) exalts and purifies earth (matter/physical expression), which is why slow heat through infusion, a low boil, exposure to the Sun, distillation, or alchemical digestion are used to extract the energetic qualities of a plant from its physical matrix and transfer it to the liquid it is steeped in. From this newly charged liquid, the plant energy becomes accessible to us and can be used in magical, alchemical, or healing practices.

What makes our earthly, material existence unique is that it encompasses the elements in their most concrete form, as well as the concrete expression of the planetary energies, or all of the subtle planes that preceded it. Whereas any experiences we might have of say, a solar plane, would be unique and distinct to it. Here on Earth we have the challenge and the task to fully express all of the planes of experience that preceded it, or to literally create within and through ourselves, "Heaven on Earth."

In working with plants, we have an opportunity to increase our awareness of the expression of cosmic energies in our material life and the emotional energies most closely connected with the psychic and astral experiences that are critical to linking our inner aspirations with our "outer" life.

Elemental Aspects of a Plant

Whereas the planetary nature of a plant will vary from plant to plant, the elemental nature of each plant will be more or less the same. While some plants will emphasize one or more attributes, and thereby a primary elemental nature, all plants will have all four elements in common.

Fire – Seed: The source of everything. As it grows, the essence takes form and expresses its full nature, passing it on to future generations in the form of seeds.

Air – Leaf: Absorbs sunlight, energy, and stimulates the process of photosynthesis, the creation of chlorophyll in plants.

Water – Trunk and branches: Transfers nutrition throughout the plant, principally through water.

Earth – Roots (also bark for trees): Provides a connection to the mineral world.

If you want to create a tincture that would keep you grounded so as to not fly off into fantasyland, using the roots either exclusively or predominantly would do the trick. (However, caution is needed here, as the roots of a plant can be toxic even if the stems, leaves, or seeds are not.) If you needed more energy and vitality in your interior experiences, use of the seeds would be preferred. To add more emotional qualities, as well as aid in the transfer of energy between levels, use the stalk and stems for their watery predisposition. To increase a mental awareness and clarity, the leaves would be emphasized.

Planetary Aspects of a Plant

The planetary aspect of plants is based upon the traditional use of the Doctrine of Signatures. Here, plants are assigned according to planetary influences, as well as zodiacal signs. Plants usually have only one planet that rules them, although some can share aspects of more than one planet and therefore these particular aspects should be identified.

For example, horsetail is ruled by Saturn; lemon balm by Jupiter; basil by Mars; eyebright by the Sun; lady's mantle by Venus caraway by Mercury; and mugwort by the Moon.

If you want to make a tincture that would improve intuition, a tincture of eyebright could be made. In addition, other tinctures made from herbs corresponding to planetary qualities also apply. To increase psychic or physical strength, try a Mars-related herb; to harmonize relationships, Venus; to enhance intellectual and mental speed and acuity, Mercury; for general health, happiness, and well-being, Jupiter; and for concreteness, firmness, and an understanding of causes and their effects, a tincture, infusion, or other magical extracting using a plant corresponding to Saturn would suffice.

A tincture of mugwort could be added to strengthen the two aspects of insight (i.e. "knowing") and psychic perception (i.e. actually seeing, hearing, smelling, etc., the phenomena on a visceral psychic level). They could be combined in equal doses or in ratios of 1:2 to accentuate one aspect over the other.

Planets and the Days

Along with having a correspondence to plants and to various psycho-spiritual qualities, each planet also has pronounced influence on a day of the week. This cyclic rotation of planetary energies across the week (and the day) allows us to maximize meditation, ritual, or herbal work to obtain the most harmonious environment. The period of rulership begins at sunrise and ends at sunrise the following morning. Thus, on sunrise Saturday morning the influence of Saturn is strongest, and lasts until sunrise on Sunday, when the psychic energies of the Sun are dominant. This continues until sunrise on

Monday when the energies of the Moon take its place. This continues across the week with the cycle repeating itself on an even smaller scale within each day. For our concerns however, the planet of the day is all we need to know, because its energies are strongest at sunrise and about the first thirty minutes thereafter.

Corresponding Influences

Day	Planet	Herb	Quality
Sat	Saturn	Horsetail	Groundedness
Sun	Sun	Eyebright	Intuition
Mon	Moon	Mugwort	Psychic Perception
Tues	Mars	Basil	Strength
Wed	Mercury	Fennel	Mental Sharpness
Thurs	Jupiter	Lemon balm	General Well-being
Fri	Venus	Lady's mantle	Harmony

The only additional consideration is lunar phases. Simple work with plants is best done during a waxing or Full Moon. Try to avoid starting work on the waning and dark phases of the Moon.

A Simple Alchemical Process

While not everyone may feel up to distilling alcohol to make a spagyric tincture, it is still possible to derive some benefit from alchemical theory. The simplest way is through digestion. In alchemy, or any of the occult arts that brings benefit into the material world, we learn that we can either work with time or technique. Working with time requires less equipment and skill, whereas working with technique produces results more quickly, but requires greater skill. The following method uses time as our friend and is open to anyone. Simply arrange to have the materials on hand for the start of the operation.

It is important to start any spagyric or alchemical operation with a sincere prayer or invocation of divine assistance prior to starting the actual physical work. This prayer should be simple, direct, and devoid of any ritualistic actions. If you like, you may visualize the desired end of the operation as you pray, but avoid any complex images, symbols, or extended techniques of any kind. Keep it simple and to the point. Ritual is not to be used in any form, be it as a means of "setting the tone" of the operation, or as a means of directing them once it is underway. We are to be open to the natural energies of the hour and to use them, and that is it.

1. On a Friday morning with the Moon waxing or full, place an ounce of dried, crushed, and ground herb (such as lady's mantle) in a canning jar.

2. Pour 180-proof grain alcohol over the herb, using enough to allow for about one finger's width (half an inch) above the herb.

3. Cover the jar top with plastic food wrap. Seal tightly with lid.

4. Wrap in aluminum foil and place in a warm, dark location where it will not be disturbed.

5. After no fewer than forty days, and preferably three to six months, open the jar and pour out the tincture, filtering it. Place it in a sealed jar or vial for future use.

6. Burn the plant residue to a fine gray-white, or white ash, and add back into the tincture. After the initial burning, outside as it produces some smoke, grind the ash to a fine powder and place it in an oven at 400-450 degrees F for several hours. Grind it regularly as smaller particles work faster.

In this method, unlike traditional herbal products, you have the entire plant in your potion or medicine. The "body" (salt) of the plant is not thrown away, but is "resurrected" and added back to the plant's essential energies—or in alchemy, called the sulphur (essential oils) and Mercury (life force). If you have used a whole plant in your work, it will also contain all the elements of fire, air, water, and earth.

The herbs listed above use standard attributions and are generally considered safe for ingestion in small doses of 10 to 20 drops. Clearly, any plant should be cross-indexed for toxicity before ingesting. If you are not sure, check with a certified herbologist or naturopathic physician.

The tincture could then be ingested in small quantities of 10 to 20 drops in distilled water or wine. After it has been created and the laboratory work is completed, the tincture could also be used in ritualistic feasts such as the magical Eucharist, also called the Mass of the Holy Ghost, by adding it to the bread or host as well as the wine. If you didn't want to ingest the tincture, then it could be used to anoint a candle for use in meditation or ritual work aimed at the same goal of increasing your intuition.

Alchemically prepared tinctures are considerably stronger in their effects than infusions and simple extractions. Known as spagyrics, plant alchemy is a simple process of utilizing plant energies that can provide the aspiring alchemist with a series of important initiatic experiences in a short period of time.

While these operations fall under the domain of what was called—and increasingly being referred to again by its proper name—Natural Magic, one should not fall into the error common to both those words.

There is hardly a person who has not been misinformed about the effect of an herbal product by either a well-meaning friend, stranger, or sales person who says, "It is natural, it can't hurt you." Lead, mercury, arsenic all are formed and exist in nature. Each one, along with a laundry list of additional plants and minerals, will give you a one-way trip to the Invisible. Nature is both life and death, and always remember that fact.

The second misunderstanding is magic. In the last decade or so there has been an increasing emphasis on the idea that one can simply make it up as they go. While this is possible, it is also a sign of considerable disrespect for both the forces of nature, of which magic is a part, and oneself as a reflection and mediator of those forces. To quote Israel Regardie's introduction to *The Golden Dawn*, "Power without wisdom is the name of Death . . . Know thou that this is not to be done lightly for thine amusement or experiment, seeing that the forces of Nature were not created to be thy plaything or toy. Unless thou doest they practical magical works with solemnity, ceremony, and reverence, thou shall be like an infant playing with fire, and thou shalt bring destruction upon thyself."

Magic is the key to understanding nature. Nature has laws, so does magic. Know the laws, and in the words of the old (and new) alchemists, "Know the theory before the practice." The only danger in any of this work is in ignoring this simple preliminary.

Author's note: A special thanks to Paul Bowersox and Dr. Joseph Lisiewski for their kind assistance with this article.

Jade Magic and Healing
A Smattering of History and Lore
by Zaeda Yin

Jade is a gemstone of auspiciousness, peace, beauty, love, virtue, purity, healing, and protection. For centuries, it has been of invaluable importance to peoples of the Far East, especially the Chinese and Southeast Asians. The name jade was derived from the Spanish term "piedra de hijada," which literally means "stone of the flank." This originally came from the ancient Indian use of jade as a curative for kidney diseases. The virtues of jade are mentioned in the legends and folklore of Chinese, Indo-Chinese, Japanese, and other Asian cultures.

In olden-day China, emperors, imperial families, nobles, high officials, and affluent merchants coveted and collected the finest jade objects d'art, sculptures, and jewelry during different eras. Religious leaders and Buddhists also wore jade for spiritual purposes and some temples installed jade Buddhas and Bodhisattvas for worship. Today, jade continues to be obtained and used in large quantities by the Chinese throughout the world and has become rather synonymous with Chinese and Asian cultures. Throughout the reign of every Chinese dynasty, specialized sculptors and craftsmen were commissioned to make intricate imperial seals, adornments, jewelry, accessories, ornaments, and signature stamps to be used with ink, pendants, bangles, incense burners, vessels, vases, goblets, figurines, statues of Chinese gods, fairies, altars/tablets, dragons, phoenixes, flowers, lions, horses, ships, birds, and many more.

Styles, shapes, textures, and forms used by sculptors were reminiscent of specific ruling dynasties of the time. Common folk were also able to obtain smaller and lesser-quality jade or nephrite with their more spartan financial means. Many pieces, mainly pendants, were used as amulets and talismans or exchanged between lovers as tokens of devotion. Before a person embarked on a long journey, they were usually given a piece of jade with wishes and prayers for protection and safe return. Children wore jade pendant amulets for protection against diseases and malignant spirits. Jade items were given during special occasions such as weddings, birthdays, inaugurations, New Year's, and other important celebrations or festivities.

Jade was also presented as a token of gratitude to helpful persons of high rank for assistance gained, but was also widely used as bribes. Eminent scholars, poets, artists, and calligraphers used jade signature seals etched with their names to stamp rice-paper scrolls with ink upon completion of their works as marks of authenticity. Between strangers in circumstances when lives were saved or loyal brotherhoods formed, jade pendants were exchanged to cement sworn alliances. Most Chinese families pass jade heirlooms down the generations to ensure that descendants continue to reap good fortunes and maintain health, protection, and longevity.

Two Types of Jade

There are two types of jade. First is the highly revered jadeite. The second is nephrite, which is quite similar to jadeite in healing qualities despite the color of nephrite being creamier, lighter, and less translucent. Nephrite costs less than jadeite as it is more commonly found. The crème de la crème of jade that is jadeite is actually "Jadeite Burmese Jade." The most treasured is known as "Imperial Jade," an emerald-green, transparent jadeite from Burma, today known as Myanmar. Before the eighteenth century, only creamy white nephrite was available in China. By the mid-eighteenth century, the finest jadeite was imported from Burma and quickly accorded high status as the most powerful gemstone with mystical properties that can generate prosperity and posterity. Jadeite was also believed to deflect evil and preserve wealth, name, fame, glory, and existing good fortune. To avoid confusion in this article, the term "jade" is used for "jadeite."

Where Jade Is Found

Contrary to common belief, jade of the best quality does not originate in China but from Burma (Myanmar), the only country in modern times to produce top-grade jade. The most valuable deposits are located in upper Myanmar, intermixed with layers of serpentine or in secondary deposits of conglomerates and in river gravels. However, some nephrite jade is found in China, but very little in Tibet and Guatemala. It is also discovered in small crystals in the Swiss Alps. In Japan and the former Soviet Union, there are also some high-quality deposits. Other countries where jade deposits exist are Central America, South America, Canada, Mexico, and the United States (Alaska and California). In Wyoming, there is also nephrite jade. The metallic elements in the respective mines of these locations geologically determine the quality of jade formations, colors, textures, and market value.

Jade Magic

Jade is long believed to dispel negativity, confer protection, repel malevolent spirits, and prevent evil thought-forms and hexes from afflicting a household or person. Amulets and talismans can be worn or hung in the home. For better immunization, jade objects should be placed in strategic parts of the house by following intuition or instinct. Jade's mystical properties are versatile and varied with the ability to also draw good luck, abundance, harmony, peace, and serenity; maintain good health; rid ill fortunes; and ease suffering. Statues of deities carved from jade when installed on home altars can generate sacred vibrations that are conducive to meditation, prayer, spellcasting, mystical pursuits, and solving difficult problems. Once installed, it is necessary to make offerings such as fruits, nuts, flowers, water, milk, sweets, mead, and anything else you wish out of sincere devotion. Edibles are then blessed and can later be partaken for good luck. Be sure to keep houseflies out in the meantime!

A pair of jade or nephrite lions placed near the entrance of a home, shop, office, or business premises will ward off undesirable entities and preserve existing positive vibrations. Sleeping with a piece of jade under the pillow can help prevent recurring nightmares and in some cases, sleepwalking. The wearing of jade pendants is also beneficial for children, the frail, and the elderly who are vulnerable to unseen baneful forces. Lifelong wearers of jade bangles and pendants reportedly mentioned that whenever personal health or fortunes were about to undergo shifts, the hues of their jade items would noticeably change color—the more serious the circumstances, the more intense the shift in shade.

Colors and Healing Qualities

Jade colors include white-cream, lavender, blue, brown, reddish-orange, yellow-orange, and green. Most jade pieces are spotted or fused with different hues. Although all jade and nephrite possess healing influences, each color relates to certain conditions. Worn for health reasons, jade strengthens the body's filtration and cleansing systems, thereby facilitating removal of toxins. The Chinese consider jade and nephrite to be suitable for all signs of the zodiac. Colors and healing properties are described as follows:

White/Cream (Off-White or Grayish-White)

Hues of white, milky or cream, in jade and nephrite assist in directing energy to positive outlets. They filter out distractions and stimulate focus on the best possible outcomes for difficult situations. They also motivate realistic decision-making and enhance the clarity of thought. Some gem healers suggest that white/cream nephrite is beneficial for soothing tired, inflamed, or diseased eyes when worn or placed upon closed eyelids while resting or napping.

Lavender (Lilac or Purple)

Lavender attunes with spiritual and emotional states. Recommended for those who find it hard to let go of partings or are experiencing bereavement. It also brings about the understanding of restraint and subtlety in affairs of the heart. Lavender jade paves the way to steadfast confidence and self-acceptance for those with low self-esteem and self-loathing issues. Spiritual practitioners will find it useful for meditative purposes and achieving higher levels of consciousness and awareness.

Blue

Blue jade is symbolic of peace, heaven, inner reflection, calm, serenity, and relaxation. Recommended for relieving tension from an overwhelmed nervous system or one that is on the verge of emotional or physical burnout before things get out of hand. For volatile temperaments, blue jade soothes and mellows the soul.

Brown

Believed to connect to earthy and Mother Nature's energies, jade with brown hues is grounding. It gives a sense of balance, well-being, comfort, practicality, and reliability. Where domestic friction is rife, use brown jade to settle frayed nerves, dispel anger, and find appropriate solutions to problems. When moving to another location, brown jade facilitates smooth transitions, adaptation, and acclimatization.

Red (Reddish-Orange)

Usually associated with love, passion, action, anger, and delusion, caution is required when pondering whether to use red jade. This especially applies to persons whose negative emotions have been mostly suppressed, repressed, or oppressed over many years. In such cases, depending on individual childhood conditioning or traumas, red jade may or may not stimulate agitation, resentment, and anger. While it may help release buried anger, remember that venting anger must be done without harm to oneself and others. If personal intuition persists that red jade is "right" for you at any given time, be sure to make positive affirmations that you intend to release unpleasant emotions using healthy methods. After that, the past no longer has any hold over you. Red jade extracts negative feelings hidden in the subconscious and at the same time helps the forming of closures to sad situations. It also steers the soul away from delusion and opens channels to relevant recovery. When used with mindfulness, it is great for untangling the soul's cobwebs and clearing stagnant "inner clutter."

Yellow/Orange

Jade with hints of yellow, orange, and some green is regarded as being one color grade. Associated with the Sun's energy, the warmth of this variety is energizing, motivating, and stimulating. This variety of jade teaches the interconnectedness of all beings. The Chinese believe in its auspicious powers and capability to bestow joy, happiness, and longevity. Gem healers also use the yellow/orange variety to unclog sluggish organs so that food, nutrients, and waste can be processed without hindrance within the physical body.

Green

Green jade contains all the properties and healing qualities of the other colors mentioned above. For thousands of years, it has been long revered for its potency in maintaining abundance, prosperity, growth, love, virtue, spirituality, good health, body strength, and longevity. Green jade of reasonable quality is more commonly used due to affordability. The elusive top range "Fei Tsui" jade requires a deep wallet to obtain. "Fei Tsui" is a term in the Cantonese dialect that refers to the phenomenally best quality that is usually a translucent emerald green. It was favored by imperial dynasties, but today it is largely found in museums and in private collections of wealthy collectors. "Fei Tsui" is also called "Imperial Jade." Nevertheless, small pieces of "Fei Tsui" jewelry set in gold or platinum are available at jewelry stores. If you want a piece, be sure to source a specialized jeweler who provides an authentification certificate.

Types of So-called Jade

Reputable dealers will never use misleading terms, but be aware that there are some ignorant or even blatantly unscrupulous sellers who showcase serpentine as jade. Other examples of so-called jade are:

a) "Amazon Jade" and "Colorado Jade" are actually amazonite (crystal-grade green feldspar).

b) "American Jade" is the Californian green variety of idocrase.

c) "Indian Jade" is actually aventurine.

d) "Korea Jade" and "New Jade" are serpentine.

e) "Imperial Mexican Jade" or "Mexican Jade" is in fact green-dyed calcite.

Note: In Alaska and Wyoming, jade is the U.S. State Gemstone. It is also the Canadian State Gemstone of British Columbia. The characteristics of genuine jade and nephrite continue to ensure that their uses will always remain timeless. For ideas on creating magical rituals and spells using jade or nephrite, the book *Cunningham's Encyclopedia of Crystal, Gem & Metal Magic* by Scott Cunningham is invaluable. The book contains a wealth of further information, provides profoundly useful guidance, and many spells that can be adapted by novices as well as advanced magical practitioners.

Labyrinth
by Emely Flak

Imagine taking a walk to the core, where your journey on foot features paths that take you forward and back in a circular pattern. Finally, you reach the center, but this is not the end of your journey. Instead, it's only just beginning as you reflect, contemplate, meditate, pray, or simply relax. When you are ready, you walk again, retracing in reverse, the same steps that brought you to the center to return to your starting point. You have taken the walk that represents birth, death, and rebirth. You have walked the sacred labyrinth. Carl Jung once referred to the labyrinth symbol as an archetype of transformation.

Throughout history, across various locations around the globe, the labyrinth pattern has been found on cave walls, coins, pottery, cathedral floors, fabric and basket weaves, and in outdoor structures, suggesting that this sacred design has been a potent symbol in many cultures. The labyrinth is recognized as a magical geometric form, on par with structures such as the ancient pyramids and Stonehenge. Because they have been constructed by many cultures over thousands of years, some claim the labyrinth represents a universal pattern in human consciousness.

Characteristics

The labyrinth pattern is usually in the form of a circle, with circular, meandering pathways to its core. A labyrinth is typically described as unicursal, meaning one path. The pathway that takes you to the core is the same one that returns you back out. As the labyrinth is often confused with a maze, it's important to make the distinction. A maze is designed to confuse. With its twists and dead ends, the maze is a puzzle that tests memory and persistence, making it a left-brain task demanding analysis and logical thought. Contrast this with the labyrinth that features only one path and no trickery. Whilst a maze can stimulate and confuse you, the labyrinth soothes and balances without the distraction or stress associated with decision-making. When walking the labyrinth, you make turns of 180 degrees, which not only shift your direction, but also shift your awareness from left to right brain. Through these mind shifts engaging both sides of the brain, you are transported to a state of relaxed alertness, making you more receptive to a meditative state. It is also believed that this open state of consciousness helps balance the chakras.

Although each labyrinth is designed differently, most feature one of the two main patterns. The main ones are the seven-circuit classical labyrinth (the ancient form) and the more recent eleven-circuit design that appeared during medieval times. Interestingly, in some literature, the seven-circuit form has been linked with the seven chakras of the body. The circuit describes the path or ring that leads to the center. In history, the more famous ones appear in mythology in the story of King Minos at the Palace of Knossos in Crete, along with actual representations of the labyrinth pattern that are believed to exist in buildings in Ancient Egypt. In the Middle Ages, the labyrinth enjoyed a revival, appearing in gothic cathedrals in the more complex pattern of eleven circuits.

Symbolism

As the spiral circle in the labyrinth pattern is an ancient symbol for the divine mother, the symbol is believed to represent the sacred feminine. The labyrinth walk can represent both Mother Earth and the Triple Goddess. As you walk to the core, you symbolically enter another world. As you return, you are reborn to experience the end of one state and the beginning of another, making it a symbol for life, death, and rebirth. In the Hopi Indian culture, the labyrinth was symbolized for Mother Earth and the underground world out of which their people emerged. The knowledge to walk the labyrinth, to its core and back, was regarded as an ability to travel to the other world. In this cultural context, the center was believed to be the mother's belly—a place for birth.

As a design that is typically circular and combined with spiral patterns, the labyrinth expresses a visual image of wholeness and natural cycles. Interestingly, the labyrinth pattern has been likened in design to the Buddhist mandalas. In Buddhism, a mandala, circular in design with a focus on its center, is a visual meditation aid as it depicts a physical representation of the spiritual realm.

History

In Roman history, mosaics portrayed labyrinths as fortified cities, making the pattern a symbol of protection appearing above door-ways. In this culture, the design was often adapted in a square shape, also appearing as patterns on floors. In mythology, the labyrinth features in the story of King Minos of Crete. The laby-rinth design, created as a structure with walls, was built to hold the Minotaur—a fearful creature that was half man and half bull. Eventually, the hero, Thesus, takes the brave journey into the lab-yrinth to kill the monster. The Minotaur at the center of the laby-rinth appears on ancient coins and gems dating from this period. In this context, the successful return journey to the core repre-sents courage and victory.

Religion

In Gothic cathedrals during medieval times, the labyrinth emerged as the more intricate eleven-circuit design divided into four quad-rants. The most famous of these, built around 1200, can be vis-ited today at Chartres Cathedral, near Paris. It is believed that this floor labyrinth, in a Christian setting, was walked to represent a

quest to connect with the divine, and to replace an actual pilgrimage to Jerusalem as it was named *Chemin de Jerusalem*, which means "Road to Jerusalem." By taking this simulated pilgrimage, you would be transformed, leaving the old you behind and emerging ready for new beginnings in your life's journey. As additional penance, some pilgrims walked the labyrinth on their knees. This exercise would take about an hour, or the time needed to walk three miles.

During the same medieval period, about 500 labyrinths as stone structures, emerged in Scandinavia, most found near the coast. As secular constructions, they were believed to be built by fishing communities to trap evil-spirited trolls and winds in the spirals, for protection of the fishermen at sea. In recent times, the labyrinth has appeared in contemporary churches, such as Grace Cathedral in San Francisco and in the King Lutheran Church in Torrance, California. Today, you will come across labyrinths in gardens, parks, and meditation retreats and in respite facilities or hospitals as a healing tool.

The Labyrinth Walk

Each time you take a walk through a labyrinth you will experience it differently. You can take as long as you wish. Some journeys will be shorter than others depending on your purpose, intent, and response to your journey. If you can, take the journey barefoot to connect with the earth's energies as you walk. Quintessentially, the walk represents a form of pilgrimage to the symbolic center to recovery or enlightenment. The return passage back to the entrance symbolizes rebirth, recovery, or liberation.

Each time you walk the labyrinth it may be for a different reason. You may be seeking:

- Balancing or centering
- Healing
- Connection to higher self
- Contemplation
- Focus
- Meditation
- Prayer
- Help with a decision
- Opening awareness

Once you reach the center of the labyrinth, or at the conclusion of your journey, you can experience:

- Relaxation
- Answers, solutions, or insight
- Sense of peace and present being
- Warmth
- Liberation
- Energy
- Empowerment
- Healing or recovery

If you cannot find a labyrinth near you to walk, you can simulate a walk on various websites or trace one with your finger. Alternatively, get together with some friends and draw one in the sand or create one on the ground with twigs, sticks, or chalk markings. Take the journey and see where it takes you!

The labyrinth is both secular and spiritual. With no alignment with a specific religious path, the symbol is a powerful one across all cultures and beliefs. As an exercise, the labyrinth walk provides numerous experiences that meet varied needs. Overall, the sacredness of the pattern and the walk helps us experience a greater sense of oneness and being, making it a metaphor for the movement of spirit in our life.

Sacred Rituals, Public Spaces

by Dallas Jennifer Cobb

So much of our lives are lived in the public sphere, and while many Pagan rituals and gatherings take place in private spaces, there are times when a public space is the most fitting place for a sacred ritual.

While living in Toronto's downtown west end, I took part in many sabbat gatherings held in Dufferin Grove Park. As the name intones, the space was a public park and natural spot that lent itself to festive gatherings. With tall stands of maple and oak trees, a community garden area, adventure playground, and community bake oven, the energy of the park was magical.

We found the space one autumn at equinox. My circle mates, a relaxed and eclectic bunch, were eager to have a large fire as part of the ritual and our gathering. Because most of us were apartment dwellers who lacked direct access to an outdoor space, Dufferin Grove was an ideal setting: lush, green, and accessible.

We went through the proper channels to get permission to use Dufferin Grove's fire pit. We went to the park authorities, applied for a fire permit, reserved the fire pit for the times and date we required, and described our gathering as a "festive celebration" on our application. Our request was approved, and a permit issued—free of charge!

We had only to identify two responsible people from our group who pledged to ensure that the fire was maintained safely and fully extinguished when we were finished. The park authorities even supplied the pre-cut firewood for us, and stacked it neatly beside the fire pit.

After our initial sabbat in Dufferin Grove, the consensus was that we wanted to hold most of our sabbats and celebrations there—around the fire, under the oaks, in the open air, beneath the Moon. Winter and summer, spring and fall, we found our way there in all seasons. Not just the open fire, but also the wide expanse of space, the tall trees, and the feeling of empowerment that came from holding a sacred ritual in a public space thrilled us.

These days I live in a waterfront village of 1,700 people. A small rural community, there are few Pagans here. But that hasn't stopped my practice of magic ritual or public witchery. I have organized a baby-blessing ceremony on the public beach and done sabbat rituals in both the local provincial park and public beach. While my Pagan community here is much smaller, I have modified rituals to include more of my community, friends, and neighbors, but still utilizing public spaces in an effort to be both visible and magical. While my circle has shrunk, my sacred practice hasn't.

If you are thinking of coming out of the broom closet into the public realm, there are many things to consider when planning sacred rituals in public spaces. Part of the magic that we weave is the preparation and planning. We ready ourselves, the space, and our community for the upcoming ritual. But whatever the occasion, and whatever the setting, planning for safety and security are primary requirements for ensuring the sacred.

Finding a Magical Space

The best spot to practice magic is one that feels good to you and the people involved. Choose a physical space that holds good memories, meaning, or generally is associated with good happenings. A place that brings as many of the elements together in one spot is an ideal ritual or celebration space. Whether you live in a city or a small rural village, these spots are there. You just need to look, and let your witchy senses be engaged.

Search for elements that lend themselves to your magic. Groves of trees honor the historic practice of magic that often took place within the security of groves. Water elements like streams and ponds are great, but even a fountain or a bucket of water to put out the fire can represent the element. Because our gatherings usually involved some dancing, my circle liked to have an open space large enough to accommodate us.

And don't forget the effect of ambient light. If you are gathering at night and want to see the Moon, stars, and sky, choose a spot with natural darkness to make viewing the night sky possible.

Finally, think about practical stuff like where can people sit, and what is there to sit on. Grass is nice, but those with physical limitations like to have something up off the ground. The wonderful thing about parks is that there are often benches provided, or at least large logs like those around our fire pit.

Consecrating Public Space

Once you have found a suitable public space, how do you make it a sacred space? Parks and public lands are areas open to everyone and may be affected by divergent energies. It is important to work with the energy of the space before holding a ritual. Take the steps to sanctify the public space.

Like sanctifying yourself, it is important to purify and protect public spaces. Take the time to visit the space prior to the ritual. Walk the earth, intone your intention, and spread your energy throughout the space. Ask permission of the earth to celebrate there. Ask the gods and goddesses to join you, and ask for the protection of the Fates.

Burn sage and sweet grass to clear old, stale energy or sprinkle water to bless and consecrate space. Once, when our usual fire pit had been in use up until our time to use it, members of my circle used branches from the community garden compost pile to symbolically sweep away the energy of the previous people and happenings.

It is also important to clear any dangerous objects from the space, so make sure you pick up any broken glass, sharp objects, or metal that could easily injure someone. And remove any garbage or trash that could draw down the energy.

Sacred Safety and Security

While most public spaces are safe, planning for safety and security is important for the people involved and for the energy of the ritual. Use your common sense. Make plans to arrive in twos or clusters, and depart in the same fashion. Provide clear directions so people don't get lost and end up wandering through some other area of the space. Dress in comfortable, functional clothing in case you need to gather more firewood, stomp out stray embers, or purposefully leave the presence of negative people.

Our circle always had a keeper of protection. That was the person designated to carry a small first-aid kit, a whistle, and a cell phone. These items are only needed in times of emergency and were rarely used, but provided us with a sense of safety and preparation. Our keeper was a part of the ritual, but also had the role of keeping watch over any intruding energy and, where possible, diverting it from the group and the ritual.

Positive Pagan Images

There are a lot of negative images of magic and Pagans out there. I take it upon myself to try to balance out the misinformation not by fighting against the negative images, but by supplanting and spreading my own positive images. The strongest magic is the transformation of thought or misconception, at will.

When planning a sabbat or a ritual, I try to imagine what it would look like from the outside to someone unfamiliar with ritual. I want it to look inviting and interesting, so passersby feel intrigued and inquisitive, not frightened and angry. To give a gathering a lively, festive presence, I incorporate songs, chants, storytelling, and miming into a sabbat ritual.

When a gathering looks interesting, you may find people attracted to your circle, and interested in joining you. If you are holding rituals in public spaces your circle will need to discuss, in advance, whether or not the ritual is open to visitors, and if so, during what parts of the ritual or celebration. Having a clear agreement beforehand ensures that decisions are made for the good of the group and no one feels excluded.

During our sabbats in Toronto, we often had people wandering through the park join us. Attracted to the fire, the brightly garbed people, or perhaps intrigued by the chanting, singing, and storytelling, they drew near to watch. We had all agreed to open our circle at any time to include a wanderer. And this practice paid off. Several people became regularly involved with the circle, and attended other sabbat celebrations.

So even if you live in close quarters and lack access to nature, it is possible to find a gorgeous natural setting for your rituals and gatherings. Spread the magic of the craft, and make plans to hold sacred rituals in public spaces, weaving safety and security into the fabric of the sacred.

Shoe Magic

by Elizabeth Hazel

Put on your dancing shoes . . . or running shoes, working shoes, snow boots, sandals, or clogs. Whether you have an all-out shoe addiction like *Sex and the City*'s Carrie Bradshaw, or just buy what you need to because you have to, shoes are an item of both pleasure and necessity.

The feet are the farthest from the brain, and our means of locomotion. Feet have to work all day, every day. But feet love to be joyful, too, luring us to skip, dance, jump, leap, and even trip—all movements that shake up a stuffy brain. Feet are the body's interface with Mother Earth, a pair of five-toed reminders that we're earth-bound creatures.

Because they're at the end of the line, so to speak, feet are ruled by the watery, final zodiac sign of Pisces, and its mystical ruling planet Neptune. So although feet bind the individual to the earth, in occult terms they're imbued with deep emotions and vast, boundless spirituality.

Shoes are a perfect medium for practical magic because they're a necessary item of apparel in every situation. Shoe spells should be conducted when the Sun or Venus is in Pisces during the spring, or during the Full Moon in Pisces (late August or September). At other times of the year, spellcast when the Moon is in Pisces (once every month).

New Shoe Boon

This is a spell for the magical shopper on the hunt for new shoes. Since there are two feet, work with two candles and two deities. Mercury rules the extremities and commercial transactions, so include Mercury or his equivalents (Hermes, Odhinn, and Thoth) as one of the deities. Choose the second deity to represent the purpose of the shoes. Use a combination of Mercury-Vulcan for tough work boots used for demanding physical labor; for dance, try the muses Charis (grace) or Terpsichore (dance); for attraction, Ishtar/Aphrodite; for rituals, Hecate or Selket; for office work, Vesta; for luck and protection, Zeus-Jupiter.

Set up two candles, yellow for Mercury and a second color appropriate for the second deity. Light the candles and chant this spell three times. Repeat for three days until the candles are burned down. Pair the first verse with a second verse that fits the purpose of the shoes you're trying to find, or write a second verse of your own:

Shoes, shoes, come two by twos—
Shoes, shoes; Mercury and (goddess or god), help me choose.

Second verse (choose one of the following three couplets):

A working pair, sure foot and fair,
Tough as rock, soft as a sock.

A dancing pair, light as air,
Bow and glide, just like a bride.

A sexy pair, like siren's hair;
Magnetic charm, but safe from harm.

After casting the spell, go shoe shopping. You should find your shoes quickly and easily, and, if you've done a good job with your spell, on sale.

Sacred Shoes

Arrange new shoes on the altar for consecration. Charge a magical circle, light a purple candle, and start by consecrating them with the four elements:

By the Lord and Lady,
I consecrate you with fire (pass shoes over a lit candle)
I consecrate you with water (pass shoes over a bowl of water, or
sprinkle a little)
I consecrate you with air (pass over burning incense)
I consecrate you with earth (sprinkle with sand or salt)

Return the shoes to their place on the altar and chant:

Shoes – take me where I am going,
Shoes – secure on Earth are knowing,
Shoes – Hermes, bless this pairing,
With these shoes I'll be wearing.
Keep my balance sure and true,
Keep me on my pathway through,
Guard me well through every day,
(God/Goddess's name) (quality) leads the way.
So mote it be.

In the final line of the chant, fill in with the name of a deity and energy that emphasizes the purpose of the shoes: "Zeus's protection leads the way." (Hephaestus' crafting, Selket's magic, Ishtar's beauty, Athena's cunning, Vesta's dedication, etc.)

Shoe Charms

After shoes are consecrated, you may choose to add a general-purpose charm. Other occasions might call for a special charm for a specific purpose. Experiment and invent, listen to your feet, and pay attention to results.

Take advantage of the way a shoe is built: The tongue of a shoe "tells" the shoe what to do. Use a piece of chalk, a pen, a permanent marker or fabric paint to inscribe a meaningful symbol on the tongue of the shoe. The sole of the shoe is its spiritual interface with earth, and can also be inscribed with symbols, both inside and on the bottom of the sole.

Harmonize charms with the directions and orientations of shoes: the toe is where things are initiated by taking a first step, or where one can put their best foot forward; heels are at the back, where things are banished, crushed, completed, or resolved in a satisfactory manner. The right shoe is for gain, acquisition, or attraction. The left shoe is for releasing and banishing.

A simple charm involves placing a kamea (magical square), a sigil or bind rune, a picture or symbol of a god/goddess, or a totem image inside of a shoe. For attracting good luck, draw the symbol for Jupiter, the Inguz rune, or a picture of Ganesha on a tiny piece of parchment and stuff it into the toe of the right shoe. For maintaining good health, draw a Tyr rune for protection on the soles; or place an image of a caduceus in the heel of the left shoe to banish or crush any germs.

Shoes are perfect for binding charms. Use colored thread or lightweight string: red for luck/protection, gold for wealth, pink for love, green for abundance, yellow for speed and communications, etc. Tie three knots around a strap or on a shoestring, or tie three threads with three knots (totaling nine knots) for a little more magical oomph. Trim off excess thread when finished. Say a simple binding spell like:

> As I tie these knots, three by three:
> Luck and wealth are drawn to me,
> So mote it be.

Or
> Fresh new love will come to me, so mote it be.

Or
> No foul or harm will bother me, so mote it be.

Power Rubs

A sympathetic technique that turns shoes into magical magnets is a power rub. To perform a power rub, take a physical symbol of what you want to attract and rub it all over both shoes while announcing aloud what you want to acquire. If you're trying to win money or get a raise, rub your shoes with a dollar bill on a Thursday (Jupiter). For romance, rub shoes with a rose or with rose petals on a Friday in the hour of Venus. To charge lucky shopping shoes, rub with coupons and say something like, "Every time I wear these shoes, I'll find great bargains, clearance items, unadvertised discounts, discounted floor models, and other terrific deals." Keep talking while you're rubbing the shoes inside and out. For a superlative pair of dancing shoes, rub with a feather: your feet may grow wings.

Green Toes

Herbs and flowers are perfect complements for shoe magic. Place a pinch of a dried herb inside the right shoe to attract, left shoe to repel, and in both for gathering power.

- Winning a lawsuit – bay leaf (right shoe)
- Protection from harm – dogwood leaf or flower (left)
- Love – rose or vervain (right)
- Quick thinking on feet – lavender or yarrow (both)
- Repel harm or negativity – cayenne pepper (left)
- Accomplishment/potency – basil (both)
- Heal from sorrows – willow (left)
- Heal from lost love – bleeding heart (left)
- Dancing – Johnny-Jump-Up petals (both shoes)
- Good luck – four-leaf clover or red clover petals (right)
- Triumph over opposition – High John (right) and cayenne (left)
- Magical power – mandrake or dragon's blood (both)
- Attract new friends – zinnia petals (right)

Shoes can also be carefully anointed with magically charged oils, but exercise caution with uncut essential oils as they may damage the finish or leave spots.

Accessorize Your Spells

Shoes can be a substitute or secondary talisman or amulet, acting as day-to-day emissaries of a bigger, ongoing spell. Include a shoe charm as a part of a larger ritual.

For example, as part of a new employment spell, charm a pair of job-hunting shoes. Do a discreet binding knot, and tuck a cloverleaf into the right toe for luck. As part of a protection spell, place a banishing pentagram in the heel of the left shoe. As part of an initiation ceremony, consecrate a pair of shoes dedicated to magical working, and inscribe personal sigil, wizard mark, or other symbol on the soles of the shoes. Sprinkle dragon's blood or mandrake into both toes. Wear this pair only for magical rituals or on rare occasions where extra power will be needed.

With a pair of spell-charged shoes, your magic goes with you everywhere!

Air Magic

Spring: The Realm of Air

by Sorita D'Este

Air is the most subtle of the elements, the invisible essence of life that surrounds us throughout our lives as we continually breathe in its power to vitalize ourselves. The gentle breeze, the refreshing wind, the raging tornado—all are expressions of the changeable power of air, which can be transformed from one to the other in a moment. Air brings beginnings, like the tide of air that starts the year each spring.

Air embodies the hope of a spring day, the clarity of a sharp intake of breath, the joy of a cooling breeze, the freedom of a bird gliding on the winds. It brings inspiration (literally and physically) and is associated with the powers of the mind such as intellect, the quality of discrimination, logic, and the ability to analyze, to see the whole picture with a "birds-eye view," along with the wisdom of experience.

The qualities of air are reflected in the beings of air. The sylphs (or sylvestres) of air appear as winged creatures such as birds, insects, and butterflies, or as tall beautiful ethereal humans. The Ruler of Air usually appears as a tall, slender, and beautiful man with fine features, piercing blue eyes, and blond hair. He wears a gossamer yellow robe that blows around his body and is crowned with a wreath of white lilies. He exemplifies the way sylphs look when they take human form.

The winds themselves all have qualities associated with the direction they come from. Eurus, the east wind, is cool and crisp; Notus, from the south, is warm and can be fierce; Zephyrus, from the west, is humid and changeable; and Boreas in the north brings enduring force.

Meditation

If possible, perform this meditation on a hilltop or a place you can feel the wind blowing and swirling around you. Make yourself comfortable and make sure you will not be disturbed.

Close your eyes and feel the air on your skin as you relax. In your mind's eye, visualize a huge yellow pentagram, pointing upwards, on a sky blue background. See the pentagon in the center of the pentagram shimmer and disappear, opening a doorway to the elemental realm of air. Through the doorway, you can see a clear blue spring sky with a few white clouds gently scudding by. The Sun shines brightly and you feel the call of the freedom of air.

You know that you need a different form to explore the air realm, and so you allow the power of air that pours out of the doorway to surround you and transform your energy body. As its power permeates your being, you feel yourself changing. Your body starts to sprout feathers and your arms turn into wings. Your nose elongates into a beak and your eyes move to the side of your head as you change. You feel your legs shortening and your toes becoming claws. A feeling of energy and freedom flows through you as you change into a golden eagle. With a mighty cry, you push off with your strong legs, leaving your physical body behind and launch yourself into the air, straight through the doorway in the center of the pentagram.

You beat your mighty wings, each stroke propelling you through the air as you fly through the sky of the world of air. In your aquiline shape you feel new sensations. You are aware of the invisible currents within the air, and you glide luxuriously on the thermal currents that lift you higher. Your vision is super-sharp,

and you can see for miles, picking out every detail of the other birds and creatures which share the sky with you. In the distance you see a beautiful white Pegasus, and a "V" of geese flying lower in the sky.

Now you glide with the air currents as free as the wind, experiencing the wonder of air as you see the ground far below you. From your vantage point, you can see every detail of the landscape—the woods, the hills, the rivers, and the fields. Everything feels like it is in sharp focus and you unconsciously adjust your position with the occasional flap of your wings as you ride on the wind. Spend some time flying through this realm exploring and learning about it and its inhabitants.

After a while, you start to feel tired and decide to return to your place on the hilltop. As you scan the landscape, you see a tiny figure sitting on a hill below you. As you glide down lower, you realize it looks like you. Lower and lower you fly, getting closer and closer to the figure on the hilltop. You fly toward the figure and realize it is you, and head straight for it. As you get closer you feel yourself becoming more insubstantial and ethereal, like the wind, and as you reach yourself you have become completely airy and pass into your physical body, bringing the experiences and wisdom of air back into your human form.

Pendulum Divination for Imagination & Wisdom

by Denise Dumars

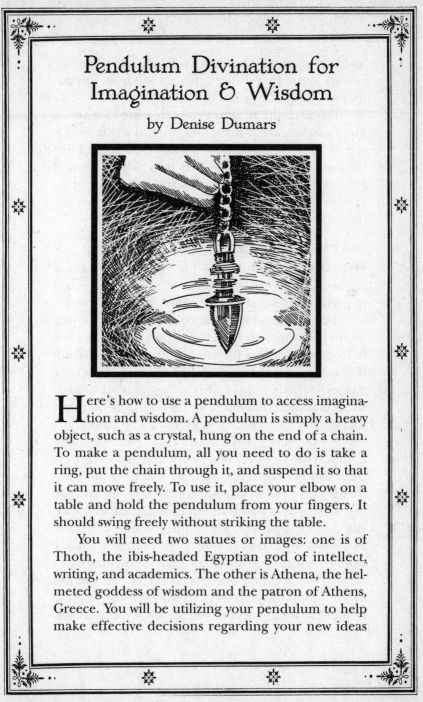

Here's how to use a pendulum to access imagination and wisdom. A pendulum is simply a heavy object, such as a crystal, hung on the end of a chain. To make a pendulum, all you need to do is take a ring, put the chain through it, and suspend it so that it can move freely. To use it, place your elbow on a table and hold the pendulum from your fingers. It should swing freely without striking the table.

You will need two statues or images: one is of Thoth, the ibis-headed Egyptian god of intellect, writing, and academics. The other is Athena, the helmeted goddess of wisdom and the patron of Athens, Greece. You will be utilizing your pendulum to help make effective decisions regarding your new ideas and their applications. Thoth will help you whenever you are creating a project. Athena will help you put that new project to good use.

Although the pendulum is often used for yes or no questions, there are other ways to use it in this context. For example, if you have the question: I feel blocked; should I try to work on my writing or should I try to do something else? Ask the question first as, should I work on my writing? Then ask the pendulum, should I work on something else instead?

How to Interpret the Pendulum

Many times a pendulum will not give you a definite answer. If it swings wildly from side to side it could mean one of several things. Either your question was not clear or the powers that be are not ready or willing to give you a clear answer. Many people use the following guidelines for interpreting the pendulum: if it swings around in a circular motion, deosil (or clockwise), this is a yes. If it swings around widdershins (counterclockwise), the answer is no. If it just hangs there like a lox, then we're all in trouble!

But seriously, working with these two deities will help you in any intellectual work and in any applications of your work. We often see Thoth depicted as though he were writing on a tablet. When you are just writing up a proposal, for example, he would be the one to appeal to. He is also the one to appeal to the when you need answers while doing academic work or creative, business, or academic writing.

On the contrary, Athena, as the Greek goddess of wisdom, is more concerned with the wise application of knowledge. For example, she was considered the patron of shipbuilders in ancient Greece, and of other builders, engineers, and others who created large projects. Also, when you are ready to apply your new idea, you want to work with Athena.

If you're wondering if you are on the right track to begin with, then you may wish to work with both Thoth and Athena. Place your statues or pictures of Thoth and Athena on a table or altar about twelve inches apart. First, ask Thoth if the project you are thinking of is a wise one to start. If the answer is a clear yes, then ask Athena if your idea for the application of it is a good one. If she also says yes, then continue on with your project. If you find that you have good luck with this procedure, then you may repeat it for each new project.

In addition, do not be afraid to ask Thoth for inspiration for any new creative project. Burn some incense and simply speak your prayer aloud to him along with offering a lit candle to him. Or you may write down your petition and place it before or beneath his statue. Similarly, you may appeal to Athena for guidance. As with Thoth, you may simply speak your prayer or write it down. Traditionally, use kyphi for Thoth and Greek Orthodox Church incense for Athena. You may also use a scent related to the intellect, such as rosemary, orange, clary sage, geranium, or lemon. Or you can choose to simply use frankincense and myrrh.

As you learn to use the pendulum, it will become more accurate and useful to you. Feel free to use the pendulum for guidance, but remember, as the creator of your idea, you are the one who decides the right course of action!

The Spiritual Battle of Sarah Winchester

by Muse

There is a fine line, sometimes, between madness and inge-
nuity—and between fear and passion. Sarah Winchester's
house, now called the Winchester Mystery House, in San Jose,
California, is a testament to those fine lines. The maze of twisting
passageways, false doors, and stairways to nowhere was thought to
have been designed by a madwoman who claimed to be guided
by spirits. But was she truly mad? Or was she fighting a spiritual
battle with occult tactics?

Sarah Pardee married into the Winchester Repeating Arms
Company fortune. The company manufactured and sold the
famous Winchester rifle—"the gun that won the West." She
married William Wirt Winchester in 1862 in New Haven, Con-
necticut. A few years later, in 1866, she gave birth to a daughter, Annie Pardee Winchester. Although Sarah's life started out
charmed, the enchantment did not last. In a terrible twist of fate,
baby Annie died less than a month after she was born. Sarah was
devastated. Shattered and on the edge of madness, it took her
years to recover. She never did have another child. To make matters worse, too quickly after her recovery from her first loss, her
husband, dear William, contracted tuberculosis and died. Sarah
inherited more than $20 million and received 48.9 percent of
Winchester Repeating Arms. She was left a wealthy widow—but
completely alone and distraught.

Grieving deeply, Sarah consulted a spiritualist medium who
confirmed her belief that there was a curse on her family. The
medium informed her that the spirits of those killed by the Winchester rifle were after her family—and she was next. The only
way to avoid this curse was to move west and build a house. As
long as the construction continued, Sarah would survive the curse
and the spirits would be kept at bay.

Sarah promptly took her fortune and moved to California,
where she purchased an eight-room farmhouse in the Santa Clara
Valley. Construction began in 1884 and continued for the next 38

years of her life. Hundreds of workers labored on the house, 24 hours a day, 365 days a year.

Sarah herself designed what the workers built, drawing "blueprints" on pieces of paper (a master set of blueprints for the house was never drawn up). She gave the workers detailed instructions each day. Often they were asked to stop one project to move onto another, thus many of the rooms and architectural details to this day are half-finished.

The house is a labyrinth of oddities. It includes stairways that lead to ceilings, chimneys that stop short of the ceiling, closets that open into walls, trap doors, windows in the floors, stained glass in hallways that never see the light, and a door that leads to a multistory drop to the lawn below. Almost every post in the house was placed upside down. Rooms were constantly added and removed. The house spread upward and outward, like a tumor.

During the building of these chaotic architectural designs, Sarah continued monitoring the spirits with a medium. A séance room had been built early on for nightly meetings with the spirits. The route through the house to this room was a maze of hallways, and the room itself was built with one entrance and three exits. So if any servants happened to figure their way into the room, once they exited the other side they could not turn around and go back in. Also, a bell in a tower that only three people knew the entrance to was installed and rung every night at midnight to welcome the spirits, and then again at 2 am to tell them to depart. During these nightly meetings, it is said that Sarah received instructions from the spirits.

The house reached seven stories before the 1906 earthquake. During that earthquake, the top three floors collapsed and Sarah was trapped inside one of the many rooms. Given the massive damage this earthquake caused in the San Francisco area, the destruction was relatively minimal. But, in order to confuse the spirits, the eccentric woman had never slept in the same room on consecutive nights, so it took her staff more than an hour after the earthquake hit to find her. When Sarah was found and dug out of the room she was trapped in, she took it as a sign from the spirits that she had spent too much time on the front of the house. So she had the front thirty rooms boarded up—including the ornate front door that only she and the worker who created it had ever stepped through.

Sarah died in her sleep in 1922, at the ripe old age of 85. Construction stopped for the first time in 38 years at the very moment her death was discovered. To this day, you can see nails driven only halfway into the wall, a mark of the sudden end to the madcap building project. At the time of Sarah's death, almost $6 million had been spent on building the house. There were 4 floors, an estimated 160 rooms, 2,000 doors, 10,000 windows, 47 stairways, 47 fireplaces, 13 bathrooms, and 6 kitchens. The true numbers may never be known because the layout of the house is so confusing that every time a count is taken, the result is different!

Crazy by Design?

To this day, many people think Sarah was crazy. They say she lost her mind with the death of her family, and blame the macabre architecture of the Winchester house on this insanity. But if you look at occult history throughout the world, her actions aren't that abstract, given her beliefs. Sarah strongly believed that the ghosts of people killed by the Winchester rifle were after her. Labyrinths, mazes, intricate stained-glass designs, even the prevalence of the number thirteen throughout the house are all indicative of efforts to confuse, deter, and even trap ghosts.

The labyrinthine design of the Winchester house is the first thing you will notice when touring the property. Sarah herself gave her workers orders every morning, thus controlling the crafting of every aspect of her home. While her spiritual guide told her to continuously build onto the house to appease the ghosts, Sarah could very well have been designing the house to confuse or discourage the ghosts at the same time. Not only are ghosts thought to be naturally confused by such mazes, but also the constant changes and additions to the house would make it even more difficult for them to navigate and come after Sarah.

One historic method of getting rid of ghosts involves either remodeling the current house or moving to another home completely. Perhaps ghosts are easily confused by such changes in environment, or maybe the disruption in their home drives them away. Many occult books and ghost-hunting guides also recommend loud noises such as shouting or slamming doors. Thus, the constant hammering and shaping of the Winchester house may have served as yet another deterrent for the ghosts.

The Winchester house features dozens of stained-glass windows. Some feature geometric designs, others flowers, and quite a few incorporate spider web designs. One of the most famous Tiffany glass windows features two large spider webs with thirteen small colored orbs. Spider webs can be incorporated into a house or a room in order to "trap" negativity—in this case, maybe the ghosts were what Sarah was trying to trap. One very beautiful and incredibly expensive stained-glass window was even built in an interior hallway that never saw the Sun. Perhaps Sarah thought that if sunlight could not pass through, neither could the ghosts that were hunting her.

In addition to the spider web designs, the spiritually potent number thirteen is also prevalent in the stained glass windows, and throughout the house. Nearly all the windows contain thirteen panes of glass, the walls have thirteen panels, many rooms have thirteen windows, the greenhouse has thirteen cupolas, thirteen lights on the chandeliers, thirteen palms line the driveway, and most of the staircases have thirteen steps. Even Sarah's will had thirteen parts and was signed thirteen times.

Mankind's belief in the power of this number can be attested to throughout history. Floor numbers in high-rises and skyscrapers often skip the number thirteen. Friday the 13th is considered an unlucky day. Maybe this is because there are thirteen Full Moons in a year, and the Moon is a very powerful influence upon spiritual energy. Or in Christian terms, maybe the number became powerful because there were thirteen people at the Last Supper. Given the heavy energy of this number, it is no wonder that Sarah chose to surround herself by it. Not only to represent the spiritual struggle she was undergoing, but perhaps also to defend herself against the spirits she believed were after her. Many books on the subject note that Sarah thought the number thirteen was lucky for her.

The Mysteries Continue to Evolve

As you get to the end of the Winchester Mystery House tour, you visit the Grand Ballroom. A beautiful, expansive piano graces one ornate wooden wall. Rumor has it that Sarah hosted her ghostly guests in this room and played piano to entertain the spirits. But the oddest thing about this room is a set of two stained-glass windows, one on either side of the fireplace. To this day, no one has been able to figure out what Sarah meant by the words so elegantly placed in the glass. The window on the left reads, "Wide unclasp the tables of their thoughts." The window on the right reads, "These same thoughts people this little world." Is this the poetry of a madwoman? Or verses given to Sarah from the beyond?

Today the Winchester house is a tourist attraction during the day . . . but some say a haunted place at night. Sarah Winchester, although a recluse in regard to society, always had dozens of craftsmen, construction workers, and servants at the house. People literally lived their lives in the service of the Winchester building project. Sarah was admired by her employees as being a strong, firm woman, but also generous and kind. She was rewarded by the loyalty and dedication of her employees and servants. With such energy put into the house, it is no wonder people still see and hear ghosts at the mysterious mansion.

The mystery of Sarah Winchester and her odd mansion will probably never be solved. But the energy and draw of the house will continue on as long as the structure stands and the mystery remains. Visitors to the house have different reactions. Some get a scared feeling. Some see spirits or hear ghostly hammers echoing through the walls. Some visitors see flashing lights, experience cold spots, or see spectral "orbs" in the photographs they take inside the Winchester house. Some just shake their heads at the "insanity" of the late Mrs. Winchester. But I felt sadness in that house. And desperation. Sarah Winchester spent her life fighting unknown pursuers and lamenting the death of her family. But she survived, and she left an amazing legacy for us to behold.

The Winchester Mystery House is located at 525 South Winchester Boulevard in San Jose, CA. Daily guided tours are offered most days of the year, and special events are hosted around Halloween and Friday the 13th. Get the details and times of the tours at www.winchestermysteryhouse.com or call for information at 408-247-2101.

Technomagic, Classic Concepts

by Diana Rajchel

Arguably, all magic classifies as technology, just as technology can be perceived as magic. Complex operations (or mystifyingly simple ones) happen unseen that allow us the unspoken luxuries in our daily lives: the flick of a switch for light, the speed of microwave heating, and even the pictures and stories contained inside the television box. While magic as an esoteric practice doesn't always produce the immediate results that technology provides, technological tools lend themselves well to magical application.

The principles of technomagic don't differ from any other magical practice. As determined by James Frazer, author of *The Golden Bough*, all magic operates on the following concepts:

1. The Law of Sympathy
2. The Law of Similarity
3. The Law of Contact

The first law, the **Law of Sympathy**, is the principle that arches over the other two. Sympathy indicates that any object connects intrinsically to the greater whole of reality. Two things utterly unrelated are, somehow, related and an action upon one will have an effect upon all else connected to it.

Magic is the process by which a practitioner can target an objection or person through forming a sympathetic connection. Technological tools, such as cell phones, computers, and palm pilots particularly lend themselves to this use because they are designed to reach through space and connect seemingly disparate objects.

The **Law of Similarity** indicates that an act upon one object or being will have a similar effect upon an object or being like it. For instance, if you use your cell phone to transmit a sigil via text messaging, the effect the sigil has upon your phone will also have the same effect upon the phone or other messaging medium that receives it. Links can be formed between objects in an electronic medium through use of runes or sigils.

The **Law of Contact**, on the other hand, supports viral and meme concepts such as those never-ending quizzes posted on Internet journals. As a repetitive concept with symbolic arrangement and empowerment, it can become a method of magic by contagion, spreading the magical/psychological contact to each person who encounters or views the sigil. Similarly, a talisman deliberately left on a public bus can spread magic by contagion, affecting dozens upon dozens of disparate passengers getting on and off the bus as it travels around the city.

Technomagic in particular lends itself to contact magic. Use of sigils connects well with technomagic of this model. Sigil magic consists of condensing a specific desire or purpose down to a single symbol. You can designate emoticons, a single line, or even graphics to post a drawn sigil online in order to emit the intended energy continuously until the purpose has been achieved. Memes in particular can be used to spread a magical concept through the Internet. Encode a blog quiz to show specific empowered symbols and you can continue to feed an energy concept in near perpetuity.

Also as a form of contact magic, email can be used to delivery energy. Simply attach energy to a symbol in an email before hitting "send." Attach the symbol, meditate on it, and visualize it glowing, or visualize energy flowing from a chosen source into the symbol you've attached to the email. This can be used either to send to a person you previously agreed to share an energetic bond with, or to send to yourself when you need to tap into a specific emotion or inspiration in order to perform a task.

Tools and Tasks

By combining an understanding of the three laws of magic with the development of skills necessary for magical practice, you can use nearly any tech toy as a tool for magic. Necessary skills include inducing a trance and deep meditation. The ability to use tools to alter consciousness—whether using a program on the computer to deepen trance or playing an MP3 that stimulates deep neural responses—can enhance the development of these skills. The more you meditate, the better you get at it, and the more you can do with meditation . . . and by extension, the more you can do with your electronic tools.

Once you have a strong ability to visualize what you want and point energy from one space into another space, you will have the ability to make nearly any object function as a magical tool. Under the Law of Similarity you should be able to imagine two unrelated objects as somehow the same, and under the Law of Contact you should understand that even without touching something you can connect it to a different object or energy by perceiving it so.

It's only a matter of creativity to use gadgets besides computers as magical tools. Palm Pilots can be used to carry essential notes or sigils on hand. You can upload a series of prayers and meditations into the notes fields of Palm Pilots to review if taking the bus or train on a morning commute. Some intrepid magicians have gone so far as to write small program scripts, such as prayer wheels, that can work near-continuously; just program in a prayer, and the wheel continues as long as the Palm Pilot has power. For people who use "words of power" (where specific trance triggers are applied), the calendar function can be particularly invaluable. At specific points during the day when the trigger is needed, the Palm Pilot can go off and invoke the necessary response.

Under the Law of Similarity, you can use your Palm Pilot as a method of "healing" a faulty computer. It is, after all, a smaller computer. So, for instance, if you encounter one of the many mysterious hardware faults that happen with computers, you can take even a nonfunctioning Palm Pilot and treat it as a poppet for your computer. All you need to do to link it is etch on the serial number of your CPU to create a magical link. You can begin the healing magic to get past whatever strange fault caused the crash.

However, there are certain steps in magical practice that must be repeated no matter how long you practice magic. While no tech-toy in the world can replace all the elbow grease involved in magical working, some aspects of magical life can be automated, making it easier for you to concentrate on the "meat" of developing magical consciousness. The standard inventions of your home can become magical tools that enhance purity, health, safety, and calm.

Basics Still Apply

Purification is a repetitive and necessary task of any magician. This applies not just to cleanliness of body and spirit, but also to cleanliness of space. Keeping any home constantly clean takes work—and sometimes in the choice between going to work on time or vacuuming, work wins by default. While there is no complete shortcut to purification, the implements used in the home to control dust and clutter can also work on the psychic level. Drawing a sigil or spraying a solution of lemongrass and saltwater onto the outside of air filters can promote purifying vibrations throughout the home. It keeps anything overly negative from "sticking" so when you do get around to doing that house cleansing and purification, everything lets up nicely. The vacuum can be charged to "suck up" any negativity or stagnancy in the air as well.

You may also be able to channel the lights in your home to give you energy when you're feeling low, or empower the stove as an altar that transmits safety and peace throughout your home. Dropping essential oils on light bulbs can subtly change your moods and give you a healthier outlook, or a calm view best oriented to magical study. You can empower your furniture to give you a relaxing or energizing vibration. You can empower your car to feed energy toward a specific purpose beyond getting where you're going, whenever you drive it. Technology affects all aspects of human existence, and by extension, manifests in each corner of the elemental division. Technology manifests in all parts of our lives, and magic can be added to the most banal of our daily routines.

Technological magic takes the new tools and applies them to old concepts. We use magic for prosperity, health, and happiness no matter what tools we apply. Technomagic is subject to the same laws; we use our cell phones, computers, cars, and other gadgets to send out magical energy the same way we use wands and candles. While very modern in its application, technomagic is in its own way a primitive concept that addresses ever-primal needs. Perhaps this is why technoshamanism was one of the first identifications for those who use technology in their magic—it brought technological magicians back to the foundation skills of altered consciousness and rethought perception. Unless living an extreme lifestyle, technology is difficult to avoid in Western culture. By making it a magical as well as practical tool, you enhance your own power on multiple levels.

The Blessing of the Truck

by Roslyn Reid

One night not such a long time ago, in a galaxy right here, my best friend decided that her boyfriend's new truck needed to be blessed. Living on the East Coast of the United States, I have always considered this activity to be a necessity. So we got busy. The blessing we constructed that night can be used on any form of transportation—truck, car, bicycle . . . even a skateboard.

The optimum time to conduct this ritual is under a first quarter Moon in a prosperous sign. (It's not necessary to wait until night—you can do it just as well during the day.) Sagittarius is a particularly good sign for transportation, although Cancer may be a better sign for commercial vehicles. We did this spell with the Moon in Libra because I felt that the truck was quite beautiful, and I thought it should stay that way!

Here are the materials we chose for our blessing:

Candles:	2 white ones of any kind
Herb:	Periwinkle (myrtle or vinca)
Incense:	Sage
Oil:	Angel's breath
Goddess:	Rhiannon
Rune:	Pentacle or Sun wheel

Periwinkle can be found in many yards, and sometimes growing wild; it is one of the love flowers, symbolizing happy memories. Sage is the most popular plant used for protection; and sage incense is easy to obtain—you can even grow your own sage and dry it. As for the oil, if there is another type of oil you routinely use for blessings, by all means use it. Rhiannon is the Welsh goddess of the wind; but if your tradition is not Celtic, invoke a similar deity from your practice. Pentacles are usually agreeable to everyone. For the modern Pagan, a well-designed spell needs to be flexible above all!

We parked the truck in her backyard to avoid curious eyes. After inscribing the appropriate rune on the candles and anointing them with the oil, we placed them into some blue and red star-shaped candleholders we happened to have. (The shape, color, or inscriptions on the holders can be anything. The important part is to be sure they are designed to prevent you from being burned—nothing can disrupt a ritual faster than screams of pain!) We invoked Rhiannon, lit the candles, and slowly carried them around the truck three times in a deosil direction while chanting the following:

> Salt and sea
> Of ill, stay free
> Fire and air
> Draw all that is fair
> Around and around
> The circle is bound.

Because we were working at night, we used flashlights to help us see where we were going. The lens of the flashlights can be inscribed with a pentacle or rune of your choice with magic marker.

After finishing your threefold walk, place the candles on the ground. (If it is very dry in your region or if you are doing this ritual in an enclosed

114

space such as a garage, you should extinguish them first.) Light the sage and smudge the truck with the smoke, inside and out. Finally, sprinkle periwinkle inside the truck and in the bed. For a bicycle or skateboard, you can sprinkle some periwinkle with oil, place it into a mojo bag, and attach it to your vehicle with tape.

The instant results of this blessing were quite interesting—immediately after we invoked Rhiannon, the wind rose! And five years later, that truck has never had an accident or any kind of major mishap. Thank goddess.

Finding Your Familiar

by Kaaren Christ

If you desire a spiritual connection with the animal world, but think the experience is available only to the spiritually evolved or gifted—don't despair. A "familiar" is simply a living creature having personal and spiritual meaning to you, and the experience is available to anyone who seeks it. No need for otherworldly experiences or altered states of consciousness. Personal awareness and desire are key, not revelation. A gradual opening of your mind and spirit to the animal world goes a long way toward enriching your life and adding another level to your spiritual practice.

Many people describe enjoying a spiritual relationship with a particular animal, but the nature of that connection differs greatly from person to person. Some describe their familiar as a "spiritual teacher," others choose words like "companion" or "messenger." A common misconception is that familiars appear only in the form of animals commonly associated with magic such as the cat, wolf, toad, or eagle. True, these animals seem to enjoy some measure of popularity, but there is no "rule." Such a belief creates a narrow perception of familiars and leaves some spiritual folks feeling left by the wayside. Just as we are all different, there is no "one" way to discover your animal familiar and no "right" way to honor or experience them.

We Are Family

If the idea of having a spiritual connection with an animal feels foreign or strange, try thinking of animals as members of your family. As human beings, we are mammals and already part of a wondrous, intricate web of living creatures that roam the earth, fill the oceans, and speckle the skies. It's easy to lose sight of the similarities between ourselves and other members of the animal kingdom, especially for those of us who live and work in large cities, separated from most animals. However, thinking about our similarities is a great way to raise our consciousness and feel more in touch with them.

Like different animals, individual human beings have unique natures that guide life choices, such as the number of people we live with or our preference for city or country living. Just as animals are instinctively driven to live in certain environments, we also choose "habitats" that meet our spiritual needs and desires. These choices include the type of home we prefer as well as what we surround ourselves with—such as art, music, and furnishings.

Moreover, like any species, we depend on one another, but the amount we socialize differs between individuals. Some people prefer life in highly structured social communities while others prefer more solitary wandering. Our dietary habits also vary widely. Some of us are carnivorous hunters, some vegetarian foragers, and yet others a combination of both. We also show a penchant for particular climates; some people longing for the heat and solitude of the desert while others seek the ebb and flow of the ocean.

Think about your lifestyle choices: your home, diet, and social connections. These things offer hints about the animals with which you share common traits. When you start to think about familiars this way, it becomes easier to find meaningful connections. Which animals seem to be in your "family?"

Search the Ordinary

Most of us know someone who has an extraordinary connection to a particular animal. Perhaps we have an aunt who collects feathers from every bird imaginable or know a photographer with an uncanny ability for capturing images of butterflies in flight. Although these strong connections do occur, many people experience more subtle connections.

Take a few minutes to think about animals you generally feel "kin" to. Think about pets you have kept as companions and what they brought to your life. Which did you feel particularly close to? How did they come to you? Were they orphaned? A gift from a special person? Did you have an instant love affair with them? Did they arrive unannounced at your home and refuse to leave?

You can also take a walk through the rooms of your home or flip through your photo albums. Does one particular animal reappear often? You might also look at your favorite movies and books. Do any of them feature a particular animal character? Many connections between humans and animals are subconscious until effort is made to bring them out.

117

Think in Groups

If you are still struggling to find an animal you relate to, try to find a category of animal that makes "psychic sense" to you. Consider the various groupings of animals and their most fundamental characteristics, and think about them in relation to spiritual principles of air, fire, water, and earth.

Mammals

This is the warm-blooded group of animals humans belong to. We give birth to live young and nourish them with our own milk. Most mammals live in groups and demonstrate quite elaborate social organization—much like us! **Spiritual Dimensions:** Mammals are typically associated with earth qualities, but, depending on their habitat and individual characteristics, may also embody other aspects.

Reptiles

The cold-blooded group of lung-breathing animals has protective, scaled skin and are often very colorful. Many reptiles shed their skin, or re-grow body parts lost to injury or assault. Cold-bloodedness, normally given a "bad rap," embodies the nature of the adaptive, and suggests responsiveness to environmental changes. Reptiles lay eggs and are not particularly doting parents. **Examples:** Lizards, turtles, snakes, crocodiles, and alligators. **Spiritual Dimensions:** Depending on the individual animal, reptiles may represent earth or fire. Their changing and adaptive natures reflect spiritual growth and healing.

Birds

These egg layers feature feathers and lightweight, hollow bones. They have no teeth and high metabolisms—eating a tremendous amount of food and producing much heat. They are known for having beautiful voices and their unique ability to "speak." Complex behavior is found in migration patterns, courtship, and incubation behavior. Birds are often associated with oracles and predicting the future.

Examples: Songbirds, seabirds, carrion eaters, birds of prey, woodpeckers. **Spiritual Dimensions:** Birds belong in the realm of air; the intellectual and realm of the spirit.

Amphibians

The word itself means "double life." Amphibians have cool skin that is usually slippery, making them hard to catch! They have four limbs and no scales. They have toxins in their skins, and are often brightly colored. **Examples:** Salamanders, newts, toads, frogs and caecilians. **Spiritual Dimensions:** Creatures of both earth and water, these animals are highly adaptive, and embody many of both characteristics.

Fish

These egg-laying residents of water do not breathe air. They may inhabit either fresh or salt water. Some make their homes close to the surface while others exist in the darkness of the ocean's floor. **Spiritual Dimensions:** Water. Realm of the emotional, the subconscious, and the instinctive.

Insects

The collective mass of insects on our planet outweighs the mass of all other species combined. These creatures have no backbone, and many—such as the bee and the ant—demonstrate elaborate social organization. They are also known for their ability to undergo incredibly dramatic metamorphosis. **Spiritual Dimensions:** Because insects are found in almost every corner of the

119

planet, they may be associated with any of the elements. A careful look at their individual characteristics will offer hints about their spiritual natures.

Animal Aversion

Are you someone who hates to get animal hair on your clothes? Never had a pet or enjoyed bird watching? Do you feel nervous around dogs and cats? Don't assume this means you are unlikely to have a familiar! Quite the opposite, in fact. Often we fear or avoid those things we repress in ourselves or those things we most desire, but are unable to accept. Examine your fears, aversions and dislikes of animals; you may be surprised what you find there and how much you can learn about yourself!

Honoring Your Familiar at the Altar

There are many ways to increase your connection with the animal world and one of them is to include them on your altar, as part of your everyday spiritual practices. Again, there is no right or wrong way to do this. It is simply a way to turn your mind and spirit to the ways of the natural world and become more attune to the animal kingdom. If after thinking about animal familiars, you feel an attraction to a particular animal, you might find some pictures or representations of them to add to your altar or your home. Such items might include statues, artwork, sheep's wool, feathers, turtle shells, birds' nests, or snakeskins. You might also find poems or songs about the animal, and commit them to memory. If possible, find recordings of the animals' sounds and listen to them, noting the emotions that their noises evoke.

Being connected to the animal kingdom happens through conscious intent, meditation, and desire. There are so many things animals can teach us when we have eyes to see and ears to listen to them. An early step to exploring spiritual relationships with animals is simply raising your awareness about them. Going to the library on a quiet Saturday afternoon and searching for folktales and information about specific animals is a wonderful way to increase sensitivity and enjoy an emerging sense of oneness with creatures of the animal kingdom.

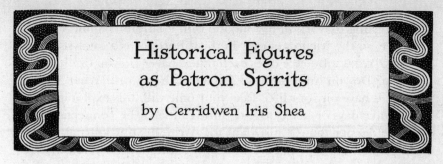

Historical Figures
as Patron Spirits
by Cerridwen Iris Shea

As we wander down the spiritual path trying to connect with each other, the earth, and the numerous entities surrounding us, many of us desire patrons. We want spiritual mentors, both on this plane and on other planes, to guide us, to keep us humble, to lean on, and to honor. Hours are spent in libraries and bookstores reading mythology; days are spent online researching various pantheons.

But what about using an historical figure as your inspiration? Someone who once lived on this Earth and moved on? Is it possible for such a relationship to work?

I think it can. I think it has to be approached carefully and respectfully, but there are ways to allow a respected figure's influence work as a patron spirit to help you on your personal path. But it's much more complicated than saying, "Oh, I admire X and want X to be my patron."

First of all, in order to be a patron spirit, the figure has to be deceased. There's nothing wrong with admiring a living figure, but that's an entirely different relationship. A patron spirit needs to be pursued under different terms, although still with respect for the person's life and privacy. And remember, trying to force someone to be your mentor is interfering with free will. Manipulation is manipulation on any plane of existence.

Just because you admire someone doesn't mean you have the right to force the relationship, dead or alive. It has to be mutually beneficial. All of these relationships are two-way streets. You have to consider what you bring to it as much as what you gain.

Make a list of figures you feel drawn toward. In your journal, write about why each one is important to you. If you're a writer, are you only drawn to other writers? Or to painters? Or to politicians? Why? Are you drawn to figures with similar interests? Or is it more interesting to work with someone with a different frame of reference, so the friction energy in the difference is a catalyst in the work? What influence does each figure have? Do you think about them? Do you hunt down examples of their work? What impact does it have on your life? Take your time with this exploration. It can take days or weeks to sort through it all. The connection has to be deeper than "I just want to." Write in your journal, meditate—don't accept easy answers to the questions. Self-knowledge and your personal goals are important parts of this equation.

Once you've written and meditated through the list, pick the figure to whom you are most strongly drawn. Now, research the person's life as well as the person's work. Is this someone with whom you would have had a positive relationship if you were alive at the same time and moving in the same circles? Don't get caught up in your fantasy of the relationship. Take the evidence of the person's life and honestly evaluate if it is someone with whom you would have gotten along in real life. For instance, just because a woman likes a male singer's music and public persona does not mean it would be a good relationship if, in life, he had a history of abusing women. People don't suddenly nicen up just because they die. Souls can evolve, but probably not over the period of time between its last incarnation and the time you want to connect. A woman who says, "He never met the right girl; I could love him enough to change him"—this is not going to be a healthy relationship. You need to find someone you would respect and get along with in life—who would also respect you.

Again, take your time. Read biographies, autobiographies, everything you can. If there are collections of letters or profiles written by others, research all of that. Although you might feel you want to get this done "right now," taking the time and doing the research will serve you better in the long run.

What if you had an idea that someone would be a great patron spirit, and you research the person and find you don't like him very much any more? Release the energy respectfully and move on. Finding a patron is never a quick fix. It takes time, research, and connection, the same way it does in life. We are people on this plane of existence. We are going to react in specific ways to stimuli. And, since we do exist on this plane, we need to be connected to spirits who support that existence, not try to negate it.

For instance, I am a great admirer of the works of Virginia Woolf and of Eugene O'Neill. However, neither of them is right for me as a patron spirit. Virginia Woolf committed suicide, had frequent breakdowns and a complicated emotional life, and was often nasty to people she felt weren't as smart as she was. I don't want to embody those qualities. Nor are they qualities I seek in a teacher. Likewise, Eugene O'Neill had problems with alcohol and expected the women in his life to fetch and carry for him and protect him from the outside world so he could do his work— at the expense of their own creative lives. Why would I want to invoke that? Not only do I not want to be subservient to an historical figure to carry out a legacy, I don't want to embody those qualities and demand that my lover/husband/partner buffer me from the world at the expense of his creative life. As much as I admire their creative work, I don't want to be like either one of them, nor do I want to encourage that sort of behavior. Therefore, I remain a fan of the work, but am glad I didn't know them in real life, and am not attached to them as patron spirits.

Conversely, this doesn't mean you have to agree with every single facet or event in the person's life. Human beings aren't perfect, and those imperfections are as important as the good qualities. But, overall, pick someone with whom you feel comfortable and challenged.

Multiple Patron Spirits?

What if you're drawn to more than one figure? Again, take your time. Meditate, research, try to figure out why both have an equal pull. Do they represent two completely different aspects of your personality or your desired aim? Do you think they work well in tandem, or would it be a constant source of conflict?

There's plenty of debate within the Pagan community about whether or not you can work with more than one patron spirit/deity, and about mixing and matching pantheons or keeping everything in the same pantheon. Each person has to do the work and figure out which way works best for the individual path. I do think one should not spread oneself too thin. While I feel connected to more than one patron spirit, I also try to spend individual time with each, rather than mixing them all together like a spiritual cocktail party. Time, research, reverence, respect, patience, and humor will see you through the process. Your patron should be a source of joy, inspiration, and occasional tough love. It's not about bowing down to someone who makes you feel insignificant. We're on a path of joy, discovery, and reverence—not subservience.

A Final Screening To Seal the Deal

Once you find an historical figure with whom you feel you connect, spend time meditating with and about the figure within a protected circle. Invite the figure in, have a chat. Perhaps you will find that you are not compatible after all. Perhaps you will find the figure isn't interested in being the patron of someone still on this plane of existence. For all we know, the afterlife could be very busy. We can speculate, but we won't know until we reach it ourselves. I, for one, am in no hurry to get there. And you don't have the right to bind a spirit to the earth who is off on its own soul's quest.

Do a series of meditations, the same way you would with a patron deity, to find out if there is mutual compatibility. The mutual aspect is important. You'll be exchanging energy, not just taking energy or advice. Discuss how the relationship will work.

Once the parameters are sorted out and both parties agree to a form of psychic contract, it's time to perform a ritual to celebrate the partnership. Remember, you don't want to bind, you want to celebrate. There's a difference.

Build a joyful altar decorated with items both of you enjoy. Create a medicine bag. You don't have to worry about filling it at this point, but if there is an item or two that feels like a connecting talisman, totem, etc., have it ready to consecrate. Frame a picture of the figure that you can keep near you to remind you of the connection. Decide which phase of the Moon is most compatible to the shared goals, which season works best, and set aside uninterrupted time to perform the ritual. Don't forget to ground and center after the ritual.

Should you build a permanent altar to the figure? That's a question of personal preference. My instinct is not to do so. A picture and a medicine bag dedicated to our work together is the best answer for me. If you wish to, I would say wait until you've established a working rhythm with the patron. Again, remember, you are dealing with an entity that once walked this plane, not a deity figure. A time may come when that soul has to continue on its path without you. This may only be a temporary relationship. We can be companions on each other's soul journeys, but we do not have the right to deflect or divert someone else's soul journey because it's what we want.

Once the connection is celebrated, how often should you work with your patron? You'll have to find that out by trial and error. How often would you work with a corporeal mentor? Would you set up a weekly schedule? In a normal student/teacher relationship, you would have the holidays off to spend with your family, yet you'd remember the favorite teacher. Is that something you want to do here? Or, in your holiday celebrations, do you wish to include the patron?

Put aside one yearly date just to celebrate the presence of the patron in your life. It can be on the figure's actual birthday, or the anniversary of the date of your initial ritual together. But keep that day sacred. Use it for thanksgiving, for re-evaluating progress made together, and for assessing the relationship moving forward.

Sharing the Connection

But what do you do with a patron spirit? For example, if you're a writer and the spirit was a writer, you can learn from the patron's process, work, and legacy. If you're a writer and your patron is a painter, you can learn to see the world in new ways, with brighter color, and apply those ways of seeing to your work. You can learn from the mistakes the patron made in life and apply the lessons to your own life. Honor and respect are important, but don't forget the joy. Time with the patron shouldn't be tedious or feel like a chore—it should be a way of self-renewal.

The time may come when you and your patron decide to part. You may find that you've outgrown the patron, or you may find that your paths are diverging. If that's the case, do a separation ceremony. This can be as simply as sitting in a circle, thanking your patron for the past work, and saying farewell. You could also do a symbolic cutting of a ribbon with your names on each end, or use a pair of candles (with your name inscribed on one and the name of your patron on the other) connected by a cord, which is then cut.

Historical figures remain in our consciousness because their legacy has a lasting effect on our society. Working with such a figure's energy can enhance your own spiritual growth and awareness, and continues the legacy of your patron.

Scatter Method of Rune Casting

by Laura Gyre

In ancient times, many cultures used symbols carved on bits of wood or bone for divination. The caster would throw them to the ground and interpret the pattern of their fall to gain knowledge from the gods. Modern rune reading is one descendant of this practice, though today we generally place the runes in an orderly pattern rather than scattering them. Both types of readings have their advantages, but a thrown method such as the one described below can be particularly good for a quick overview of a situation.

First, be sure to use a set of runes that is unlikely to be damaged by a drop onto a soft surface. Many types of runes that meet this criteria are available, including sets made of stone, wood, or even plastic (or you can make your own by inscribing the symbols onto small pieces of these materials). However, over time even the sturdiest of runes can become worn—if you use this method frequently you might want to reserve one set for throwing and another for other types of readings.

Spread out a cloth where you are working, on a carpet or other soft surface if it is convenient. The reader or the querent then holds the bag of stones and states (or silently concentrates on) the topic selected for study, adding a prayer to an appropriate deity if desired. They then scatter all the stones on the cloth by hand or by pouring them out of the bag. Any runes that fall off the cloth or completely face down are not part of the reading. (You can remove them now if you like.)

Start by looking for the central rune, or cluster of runes, from the perspective of the person who threw them. This method is a variation on a popular cross-shaped spread, so the central area represents the central theme of the reading. Runes found here can give you clues about the nature of the problem, who or what is involved, and the stage it is in right now. Anything to the left of center refers to past influences, while anything to the right suggests future developments if the present course of action continues. Likewise, runes above the center refer to helpful influences, while those below center warn of potential obstacles.

Combining these interpretations leads to a more in-depth reading as, for example, forces represented in the upper left quadrant may have helped in the past, while those in the lower right may indicate future obstacles. Additionally, the nearer a rune is to the center of the reading, the more important its influence is in the current situation. Runes closer to the edges may represent the distant past or future or certain "long shot" possibilities. Since the runes are scattered, sometimes many of the specific positions will be empty. If that happens, concentrate on the information that is present, and ask specific follow up questions about the other areas if you like.

Finally, examine the spread for any meaningful clusters or positions. Two or more runes grouped very closely are probably related to each other, for example a travel rune combined with a family rune might very well refer to travel to visit relatives. You can expand intuitively on this type of interpretation: what comes to mind if two runes are crossed, if one is obscured by another, or if one is pointing in the direction of another? Also, some runes can be reversed (upside down). The total meaning of reversed runes is too complicated to discuss here, but a reversed rune generally means the opposite of the upright interpretation, or possible problems or complications related to its usual meaning. Something unusual in the scatter method is runes falling on their sides, neither more upright nor reversed. I generally interpret them to mean that what they represent will be a factor in the situation, but that its nature will be somewhat ambiguous.

For example, if the rune on its side is Fehu, representing prosperity, then I would interpret it to mean that there will be significant events related to finances, without speculating as to whether it will be a windfall or a financial crunch (though sometimes surrounding runes can give a clue).

This method may seem somewhat imprecise at first, but like most things it comes more naturally with practice. At the very least, the questions you are left with can form an interesting starting point for further questions you can ask with a more structured method.

Below are a couple of sample readings to show how this all works in practice. In your own readings, it's probably best to interpret the individual runes in the same way you normally would, but for the purposes of this demonstration, here are some very basic correspondences:

fehu	prosperity, material goods
uruz	vitality, true will
thurisaz	difficulty, suffering
ansuz	communication, advice
raitho	travel, a journey
kenaz	creative effort, positive attitude
gifu	a gift from the universe, partnership
wunjo	joy
hagall	intrusion of forces beyond your control
nied	need
isa	a helpful period of waiting
jera	justice, results of past actions
eihwaz	protection, often supernatural
perdhro	magic, surprises, secrets revealed
eolh	protective or helpful influence, often human
sigel	power, health
tir	success in competition, or possibly a man
beorc	family, home, birth
ehwaz	physical movement, change
mannaz	cooperation, interconnection with the world
lagaz	intuition, or possibly a woman
ing	resolution of a situation, move to something new

daeg	growth, improvement
othel	heritage, inheritance
wyrd	fate, forces that cannot be understood, no answer (This rune, which is blank, is not present in some sets.)

Reading 1 (Specific Question Asked)

First, let's look at a reading for someone asking about the state of their current romantic life. Close to the center of the spread is thurisaz, which indicates that the situation is fraught with problems. In the lower left quadrant, representing things that have caused difficulties in the past, is Raidho, "travel." Perhaps one or both partners in a relationship have had to travel a lot, or a long-distance relationship is causing strain. Also, closer to the center but in the same quadrant is Perdhro reversed, partly covered by Tir. More recently, we could say, there have been difficulties relating to certain secrets coming to light, which a man involved has tried to hide. However, in the upper left we see Wunjo, which means things haven't been all bad. This person has also had positive experiences with love. On the far right, in the future, we have Gifu, which suggests that a successful partnership is in store for this person eventually.

And at the top, in the region of things that will help are Ansuz and Uruz. Not surprisingly, this person would benefit from communicating clearly with partners and paying close attention to personal priorities.

Reading 2 (No Subject)

For the second example, we'll look at a reading as though we haven't been told the subject. In the center are Hagall and Fehu reversed, which suggest that this person is concerned about financial problems due to events beyond control. Perhaps they have been laid off from their job or suddenly saddled with unexpected bills. In the upper left corner, clustered together we see Othel and Eolh, "a protective or helpful influence" and "inheritance," which might suggest that in the past this person's financial situation has been assisted by family members or even an actual inheritance. However, in the lower portion of the spread we have

Tir on its side. They are currently having a problem related to competition. If it's true that they are unemployed, this could easily refer to challenges in a competitive job market. However, moving on to the right side of the spread, it looks like things will improve in the future. In the lower right (the future difficulties area), we do encounter Isa, which means that there will be a delay, but due to the nature of Isa this is more likely than not to be a productive type of delay during which certain necessary events take place. To the right of center there is a cluster of runes leading off into the far future. First comes Daeg, which suggests that during the period of delay there will be gradual improvement of some type, possibly of work-related skills. Further to the side, in the eventual future, Eihwaz is grouped with Jera. This suggests that the querent's current efforts, assisted by powerful but unseen forces, will eventually pay off (in this case probably referring to an acceptable new way of making a living). A major area that was not mentioned much in this reading is the top, helpful influences in the present and future, so it might be constructive to ask a more specific question about what this person could do now to improve their own chances.

Your Name in Runes

by Kari Tauring

Developing an intimate understanding of the runic alphabet of the ancient Norse and Germanic people is paramount to using them in divination, talismans, or other magical work. The word rune comes from *ru* meaning "secret." While a strict academic study of available source material and texts by modern authors can help you understand the secrets of runes, ultimately, the meaning of each rune must seep into each individual in a personal and intimate way for deep meaning to be fully revealed.

The runes are a living and organic system that connects each user to her or his environment, life condition, and orlag (fate or karma). One great way to begin integrating the runes is through translating your own name into runes and creating a collage of visual meanings for your name in runes.

The interactive connections runes have to their environment have a long, rich history. Linguistically, one can trace the shapes and sounds backward through the Indo-European migration. They appear in Hungary, ancient Erturia, and Phoenicia. There have been rune poems written through the ages. The importance of runes cannot be understated, as the new Christians began burning texts, and other factors made rune poems a dangerous and extremely valuable way to preserve the culture. The poetry inspired by the complexity of their meanings and the impact they have on the emotional, psychological, and spiritual life of those who study and use the runes continues today. And the runes and rune masters communicate with us through their use of runes in art and architecture.

The ever-evolving nature of runes eluded me when I began studying them in the mid-1980s as part of my college linguistics program. Though I quickly saw the complex puzzle that the runes present and the value of pursuing the mystery in my own life, due to academics and other priorities, it took several years before I thought to translate my name into runes. And though it is an easy and personal introduction to the runic system, it carries its own set of complexities.

A Process of Self-Discovery

We start with first names. What's in a name? You'll find out! Each of us has a birth name, abbreviated versions and nicknames, magical or adopted names. What you are called, or what you call yourself, is the key. Start first by writing down in English the letters that create the way you identify yourself to others in this world. For me it is K, A, R, I.

Now the next question arises. Should you translate letter for letter or by phoneme (letter sounds)? Either way is fine, but I prefer sound for sound. The words we speak, the sounds of the vowels and consonants create a vibration both in this world and interdimensionally. If the A sounds more like "ah," use Ansuz, the mouth of the river or the mouth of god. If the A sounds more like "eh," use Ehwaz, the horse rune of complete change. There are some phonemes that are difficult such as the "sh" sound in the name Cheryl. I have used the s and j runes together to create the sound as well as k/c and h for a letter-by-letter translation. Ultimately, the individual must decide which runes feel most appropriate.

Once you have decided which rune sounds translate best into your name it is time to explore the shapes and meanings of these personal runes. Edred Thoresson in his book, *Northern Magik* points out that the runes are much more than a phoneme, or sound-holding place. They are a shape, a sound, and a word, then the levels of meaning flow out from there. Runes were very commonly used in artwork, especially adornment with magical intention. In the classes I teach, each person uses books and charts to look up the meanings of the individual runes. For example, my name is KARI, Kenaz, Ansuz, Raidho, and Isa. Kenaz is torch, with the further meaning of acquired knowledge. Ansuz is the mouth of the river or the mouth of God. Raidho is the wheel and the journey, and Isa is ice.

The next steps are very fun and active. Several techniques to explore these basic meanings are used in my "Your Name in Runes" class. Participants cull magazines, boxes of art supplies, or create drawings for the imagery of the runes that make up their names. We do word-association exercises. Write the word that represents the shape and circle it. Now make lines of connection around the circle of associated words coming from your stream of consciousness. Constantly refer back to the original word the first time. For example, Kenaz is torch, torch is fire, torch is handy, torch is controlled, torch is dangerous, and torch is flashlight and so on. Next you might do a linear stream from torch as in torch, stick, handle, tool, garden, create, divine, etc.

Another technique is to think of how and when the rune appears in your life and tell or write the stories of these incidents. "I remember when my sister and I were in the caves in Wisconsin and they had lined the walls with torches. The light that was dancing on the walls was so strange to me. It made me feel very small and young."

In a visual exercise, take the shapes of the runes themselves and draw or paint the lines separated from one another. We may layer the runes on top of one another to see how they intersect and what new runes form out of their connections. We may draw images using the shapes in different configurations to come up with a unified image of the shapes of our names.

As the collage of images, words, and stories comes together in the artistic creation before you, the secrets within the relationships of one rune to the next as they appear in your very personal name begin to manifest. While there is meaning in the individual runes, side-by-side they take on further meanings. Kenaz and Ansuz together means to me that the torch of understanding will guide my pursuit to the wisdom provided by the mouth of god rune. I see the image of a match cut from a magazine ad glued next to the image of a stream and realize how quickly divine wisdom can snuff out my human understanding. I see the image of the flashlight and the deep wooded bank of the stream picture and realize that it is sometimes my wit that guides me to the deeper knowledge. I see the picture of the wheel next to the stream (Raidho) and realize that combining the wheel with the stream can grind corn! The journey of my life may take place without moving my location. The waters of the wisdom gained through Ansuz may flow through me, turning fresh ideas and deepening my understanding. But then, next to Isa, the ice rune, the wheel may get too rigid and break in the frozen stream. Or perhaps Isa is telling me that my journey will have rest periods during which I can turn back to the fire of Kenaz and create from my newfound wisdom. And in turn, Kenaz will melt the ice.

All this started with the runes for KARI. The secrets that can unfold for you may be surprising, which is why guiding others toward self-discovery through the process of working their own names in runes is a rewarding experience for me. But it can be just the start of your journey. All the possible translation and interpretation become available to us as we work the runes of our names, our family names, and the names of our cities or states. This way, we can truly learn the alphabet, not just memorize the phoneme and what a book says it means. This is how we learn to carry the runes in our blood, in the core of our beings like the women and men of ancient days.

Fairy Godmothers

by Elizabeth Hazel

Well-dressed and wand-wielding, fairy godmothers have successfully made their way into the twenty-first century by evoking delight, fantasy, and much wishful thinking. Fairy godmothers are important, but rare, participants in the panoply of magical characters in folk legends. Their fine, long history runs parallel to their Faerie kinfolk, but with unique lore and patterns.

So what, exactly, is a fairy godmother? Despite cultural variations, their functions are consistent from story to story. Fairy godmothers are very small female fairies. In their true form, they are beautiful and garbed in elegant raiment, and may be winged or mounted on butterflies. Depending on regional preferences, fairy godmothers may wear blue, green, silver, or white, but their costumes are always magnificent. Fairy godmothers are the fashionistas of the fairy hierarchy.

In some tales, fairy godmothers appear dressed down or in other guises. Sometimes this may be the result of "contamination" of the original story as religious imperatives discouraged talk of fairies and magical beings. An "old woman" or "wise woman" may be a fairy godmother in disguise: for instance, an old woman gives magical tools and advice to the young wife in "The Nixie of the Mill Pond" (Grimm); an old woman guides the sister in "The Wild Swans" (Andersen). A fairy godmother may take the shape of an animal. In the Grimm Brothers' version of "Cinderella," she is a white dove. Alternately, fairy godmothers have also been transformed into the more conformable angels, as in "The Pink" (Grimm).

Origins

Tales that use angels instead of fairy godmothers aren't entirely unreasonable. Celtic legends infused with early Christian mysticism relate that the Little People were fallen angels cast from heaven. Since they weren't as evil as the demons, they landed in forests and mountains, in the air and sea, and became fairies, elves, dwarfs, goblins, pixies, kelpies, etc. They can redeem themselves through kindness to humans. So fairies are beings from the starry skies, perhaps the source of their pointed ears and mildly alien appearance. The earliest fairy sightings were the original UFOs—unidentified fairy operatives.

Fairy godmothers may serve a particular family, an association with a two-fold origin. In Teutonic legends, a fairy godmother-like creature called a "fylgja" acts as a family's tutelary and protective spirit. She appears in dreams to give warnings or advice about future events; but should the individual see her while awake, his/her death is imminent. In other legends, the fairy godmother is the spirit of a dead parent, ancestor, or a person who owes a debt to the protagonist, and acts in a supernatural manner to give assistance. Benevolent fairies, spirits of the dead, and angels are somewhat blurred in form and function in fairy godmother lore.

Fairy godmothers also spring from ancient myths. As Christianity spread throughout Europe, the northern European countries were some of the last to accept conversion, and indeed, sometimes this amounted to cheap laminate over hard oak. Teutonic and Nordic myths went underground and were preserved through oral transmission, although dumbed down sufficiently to provide a deity protection program that disguises goddesses as fairy godmothers. This is evident in the Grimm tale "Mother Hulda," a.k.a. Frau Holda, an Earth goddess in a lesser incarnation.

Timely Assistance

Regardless of their form, fairy godmothers are the most kindly and caring of the Little People, giving genuine assistance at times of dire need. When a hero or heroine is in deep trouble, or at an impasse, the fairy godmother appears out of nowhere. The help given is always specific and can take many forms. Sometimes advice and proper tools are given; other times, as demonstrated in "The True Bride," (Grimm) the fairy godmother performs amazing feats of magic in order to assist the heroine. Enchanted clothing, magic rings or cloaks, or disguises may be given. Her help may be tangible but impermanent, disappearing after it's used. And upon occasion, the directions or advice may be incomplete, leading to further troubles that the heroine must surmount.

But the crowning glory of fairy godmothers is babies. They interact during the conception, christening, or naming ceremonies of children. When a poor couple longs for a child, fairy godmothers are fertility specialists and perform an in utero pixilation. Other stories, notably "Sleeping Beauty," show fairy godmothers attending a naming feast. This is traditionally the time when godparents take their vows to protect a child. Noted psychiatrist Carl Jung wrote that godparents assume this symbolic role to remind the child that their parents aren't gods.

Naming feasts were important celebrations, and in northern Europe, a wise woman would be invited to the feast to forecast a child's destiny. In a similar fashion, fairy godmothers bestow gifts on a child to ensure a fortunate

future. In Grimm's version of "Sleeping Beauty," the kingdom had thirteen fairy godmothers (wise women), but
the king had only twelve golden plates, so one fairy was
excluded. In revenge, the thirteenth fairy interrupts the
gifting ceremony and curses the infant. The twelfth and
final fairy godmother cannot remove the curse, but mod-
ifies it so the princess sleeps for a hundred years.

Fairies are extremely sensitive to slights of any kind,
and must be treated with the greatest respect. Even
though fairy godmothers want to do well, they can behave
with great malice if they feel insulted. Because they are
solitary, there is rarely an explanation about their origins, the source of their powers, their advance knowledge

about the hero or heroine's problems, or even where they go when they've finished their tasks. Fairy godmothers are drenched in magical mystery, which makes them even more compelling.

Post-Industrial Godmothers

Disney's cartoon confections based on eighteenth and nineteenth century fairy tales display a delightful mix of magic, whimsy, and humor. Cinderella's fairy godmother is a kindly, white-haired old woman; Sleeping Beauty's are three bumbling, but well-intentioned, fairies who have more problems with color choices than a room full of Martha Stewarts. Yet one author gives a more contemporary version of a fairy godmother in the twentieth century: P. L. Travers' *Mary Poppins* (1934).

Mary Poppins follows all of the typical patterns of a fairy godmother, although she is cast as a nanny. She arrives and leaves when the wind changes directions, helps the Banks children grow and learn through supernatural events, and refuses to explain anything about herself or what happens around her. Various adventures reveal that Mary Poppins is related to the stars, the seasons, and the planets. She remains an ageless twenty-seven, and carries an empty carpetbag full of wonderful things, including a tape measure that declares her "practically perfect." When she leaves the Banks family, chaos ensues; at her return, order is restored as if by magic.

In true fairy godmother tradition, Mary Poppins brings unexpected good luck and adventures, blends imagination with discipline, and untangles the snarls of the entire household. Travers produced a series of eight books about this character, although the Disney film (1964) features episodes from only the first book.

Attracting a Fairy Godmother

Sometimes one's path can lead to a difficult turning point in life, or into a situation where extraordinary assistance is required. This calls for the help of a fairy godmother. Any fairy-attracting operation should be conducted with enormous respect and loving whimsy. Consider the situations enumerated above, where fairy godmothers excel— it's wise to play to their strengths.

A fairy godmother spell may attract an ancestor who wants to help, or some other variety of spirit, but the intent remains the same—assistance in a critical situation. One does not summon a fairy godmother (or any other supernatural entity for that matter) just for a cheap thrill. A real need or impasse has to exist, because fairy godmothers respond to sincere requests for help. Because it is so personal, the ceremony should be conducted in solitude.

A spell and charming-chant are given below. Preparation is important and practitioners may modify the procedures or chant to suit their tastes, and may select objects or gifts that reflect their specific needs.

Fairies are most easily accessible around Beltane and Imbolc. Both sabbats have a strong magical flair that appeals to fairies. Troubles, however, are not restricted to any particular season or time. While performing this spell near a sabbat is preferable, if the situation is urgent, perform the spell on the three nights of the Full Moon, starting the evening before and completing the spell on the evening after the lunation.

As the Moon goes full, make a small batch of fairy dust with crushed sandalwood powder and flower petals (broom flowers, heather, pink roses, lavender, foxglove, sweet woodruff). If these flowers have been saved and dried from funeral bouquets from a beloved relative, all the better. Saturate the powder with perfume or charged magical oil and allow it to dry before putting in a jar. Fairies prefer musky-floral scents.

Next, construct a landing pad for your fairy god-mother. When complete, it should look like a delight-ful fairy garden. Start with a wide, low-lipped bowl or a round tray with a shallow edge. Cover the bottom with dried moss, available at most craft stores. Sprinkle with fresh or whole dried flowers. Add some pretty stones like rose quartz or fluorite. Find a small sculpture of a fairy, or some representational image of a fairy to put in the bowl. If you don't have a sculpture, make a "standee" with a picture of a fairy glued to cardboard with a prop on the back. Place a tea light in a votive glass next to the fairy image to light the landing pad.

"Fix" a tall, pink taper candle with perfume or magi-cal oil. Carve a half-inch deep hole at the bottom of the candle and "load" it with fairy dust. Drip melted wax from a candle stump to reseal the filled hole. Sprinkle fairy dust on the candle, and place it in a candleholder. Find a sweet-toned bell or a tiny set of wind chimes to use during the charm.

Before starting, cast a circle of protection so trick-sey fairies can't enter and make things worse! Add gifts (candies, cookies, crystal beads, sparkly glitter) to the fairy bowl, and sprinkle a wee pinch of fairy dust over the bowl.

Light the votive and the taper, ring the bell or chimes, and then recite the charming-chant three times:

Oh godmother Fey—your magical gifts
Untangle the mire and soothe all the rifts;
Harken to your goddaughter's (son's) prayer —
Send heart's true desire to earth from air.
Sprinkle me with your fairy dust,
In your benevolent care I trust,
All good things will come, they must.

After chanting, concentrate on the specific assistance needed, or say aloud what is needed to help troubles end or free you from impasse. Ring bells or chimes again when finished. Repeat the procedure three consecutive nights, and allow the candles to burn down completely.

Leave the fairy bowl on your altar and burn the landing-pad votive for an hour every evening after completing the spell. Unmistakable intervention should arrive within a few days—at the latest, a couple of weeks. If she can help, a fairy godmother will work fast. Events will occur with a magical flavor, or with magical ease. When the concern has been resolved, it is very important to remember to thank your fairy godmother with incense or other gifts. When the fairy bowl is disassembled, put the gifts underneath flowers or flowering bushes in your garden.

Dragonfly Wishes, Dragonfly Dreams

by Nuala Drago

When the dragonfly weaves its way into your dreams, it is an omen that something in your life is about to change. The dragonfly is a master of change. They were ancient before the birth of the dinosaurs, thrived throughout the 100 million year Jurassic reign, and have continued to flourish long after. Through transformation and adaptation, the dragonfly has survived on our planet for more than 300 million years.

The dragonfly has seen the fluctuation of coastlines as the continents took form and has witnessed the metamorphosis of soft sediments into rock and coal as its steamy, fern-forested, Carboniferous Era home alternately warmed and cooled, creating new climates and environments. During this era, Meganeurids—predatory insects with wingspans up to thirty inches—were precursors to the modern dragonfly. The species have endured vast upheavals that gave rise to new species and mass extinctions.

What wonders the dragonfly has seen! What life-altering secrets is it privy to!

Archaeological evidence shows that dragonflies have captured our imagination since humankind was in its infancy. Their images appear on such objects as unearthed Cretan seal-stone engravings from the Late Bronze Age, Ming Dynasty porcelains, tapestries and murals from China and Japan, coats of arms, and even sculptures of silver and bronze from such places as the Netherlands and Normandy.

Long ago, in Japan, also known as Dragonfly Island, the samurai adopted dragonflies into their heraldic crests, displayed them on sword guards, helmets, and armor. They believed that katsumushi, the invincible insect, as they called him, would give them strength and bring them victory in battle.

In Norse legend, the love goddess Freya was a beautiful, cunning woman who knew how to wield the ancient magic called seidr, which included trance travel, or astral projection. Freya used her power to manipulate affairs of the heart and the sway of battle. Mating dragonflies are Freya's symbol. After a courtship that can last a week or more, during which time the male dragonfly carries the female locked in his embrace, their two bodies join, arcing into the shape of a heart.

Of course, dragonfly and fairy lore are perpetually entwined, and because of their association with otherworldly creatures, dragonflies are often referred to as fairy steeds. It is a common belief that humans are drawn to dragonflies because they are gifted with the same radiant attraction, also called glamour, which makes fairies irresistible to mortals and allows them to change their shape or remain invisible unless they wish to be seen. Many also believe that the dragonfly actually transforms into a dragon whenever he crosses into the fairy realm.

Human fascination with dragonflies has given rise to a number of popular nicknames for them, such as the Hobgoblin Fly, Mosquito Hawks, Horse Stingers, Old Glassy, Adderbolts, or the Devil's Darning Needle—all monikers that reflect the physical traits and behaviors of the dragonfly. The male dragonfly patrols his territory like a tiny, airborne knight in jewel-toned armor, challenging each intruder. The enormous, close-set eyes of the dragonfly impart an imposing, all-knowing appearance, and their aerial feats as they hawk and dive are beyond belief.

One of the most popular stories about dragonflies is that they will sew up the mouth, eyes, ears, or even nostrils of anyone who tells a lie. This was almost certainly invented to frighten misbehaving children. Although the dragonfly is of the order Odanata, meaning "toothed," and has a voracious appetite for mosquitoes and other pest insects, it will not bite a human.

In past centuries, it was popular for young women to try to catch dragonflies. If they were successful, it meant that they would soon marry. Those young women must have been highly motivated since the dragonfly normally cruises at 20 to 30 MPH and can soar at speeds up to 50 MPH!

Another charming belief is that if a dragonfly lands on you long enough for you to count to three, any wish you make will come true. But be careful what you wish for because dragonflies, like fairies, can be notorious tricksters!

The Two Realms

Magical traditions depend upon strong ties to the natural realm, which are usually provided by bonding with an elemental, guardian, or familiar. Since the dragonfly is believed to inhabit both the mortal world and the fairy realm, or otherworld, it is an excellent familiar, especially if your goals include trance working, astral projection, lucid dreaming, meditation, scrying, or effecting a change of most any kind.

Many Native Americans believe dragonflies are willing familiars because they embody the souls of the dead. In the Tibetan and Taoist traditions, the dragonfly represents spirit or quintessence, believed to be the fifth element. But dragonflies make good familiars because they are akin to all elements: earth, air, fire, water, and spirit.

Female dragonflies lay their eggs in the moist earth. When the eggs hatch, they live as nymphs in the water, undergoing as many as twelve stages of development. This may take a single season, or up to five years to complete. Each individual decides when the time for metamorphosis is right. Adult dragonflies spend most of their lives in the air, depending on the fire of the Sun for warmth. When the dragonfly dies, it returns to the earth and the cycle is complete.

If you would like to invite the dragonfly into your life as a magical companion, you may want to start with a visit to your favorite bookseller or search engine. Once you've learned about the many species and vast range of colors (one for every ritual and magical purpose), sizes, habits, and habitats, as well as which species are active seasonally, you can summon them through meditation or lucid dreaming.

To this end, you may want to fashion a small dream pillow decorated with dragonfly motifs and filled with buckwheat or rice. Focus on the pillow as you meditate or put it next to or under your regular pillow as you sleep. When you conjure the image of the dragonfly, conjure him larger than life. Have him hover in slow motion to give you time to appreciate his attributes.

If you are artistic, you may wish to create a mandala or sand painting. The dragonfly is a recurring meditative focus in mandalas and ritual sand paintings in the Tibetan and Native American traditions respectively. Both are tools of positive change and spiritual growth. Yours needn't be elaborate. Some tag board, glue, and colored sand are all you need, besides a strong focus on your intent.

If you are trying to effect a change in your life, creative visualization is the key. You may find these lines from Alfred Lord Tennyson's poem, "The Two Visitors," helpful. They are a striking description of the metamorphosis of nymph to adult dragonfly.

> *An inner impulse rent the veil*
> *Of his old husk: from head to tail*
> *Came out clear plates of sapphire mail.*
> *He dried his wings: like gauze they grew;*
> *Thro' crofts and pastures wet with dew*
> *A living flash of light he flew.*

To create a further bond, you may want to observe your dragonfly familiar in your pal's natural environment. But if you aren't one to journey out to the lakes, ponds, streams, wastewater treatment plants, or other watery places where dragonflies roam in the wild, you may consider creating a habitat for them in your own back yard. Many field guides, as well as the National Wildlife Federation and the British Dragonfly Society, among others, give good advice for creating a dragonfly pond.

In general, you need to provide a small body of water, a variety of plants such as rushes and cattails, and plenty of rocks so that the adults can bask in the Sun. Just which types of plants and how large a pond you should create will be determined by the species of dragonflies that live in your area.

Don't forget that dragonfly territory is also the favorite haunt of fairies, so it might be a good idea to brush up on your fairy lore as well. As a rudimentary guide, you may associate adult dragonflies with sylphs and salamanders, who are also creatures of the air and fire respectively, while dragonfly eggs and nymphs can be associated with gnomes, or brownies, who are spirits of the earth, and undines, who are water spirits.

Much can be learned from the dragonfly of transformation, insight, and constancy. An association with them has always proven to be beneficial to humans. Early man knew that the presence of dragonflies and their nymphs in a body of water meant that the water was safe to drink and that the environment was healthy. With modern degradation of aquatic habitats, their presence is even more to be desired.

Whether or not a magical tradition is a part of your life, there is no doubt that the dragonfly is a powerful force of nature. It is no wonder that these charming, yet fierce and adaptable 300-million-year-old creatures appear in the art, literature, folklore, and magical traditions of almost every culture on the planet. They have become symbols of immortality and regeneration revered by humans worldwide.

Plan a Magical Community Event

by Boudica

Online forums have been a boon to those seeking individuals with common interests. For many, the Internet is the first place people realize they are not alone and can interact with other Pagans. But it can lead to a different kind of isolation, which is why I am always encouraging local Pagan Yahoo list owners to suggest to their membership/group to get out from behind the computer monitor, leave the house, and meet their fellow Pagans out in a social forum.

The problem most have is the actual planning and execution of such events. Where do we meet? What do we plan on doing? How often? Can we plan a big event?

At the local level, I usually try to discourage "big events." These can become costly very quickly and usually require long-term planning and a large planning committee. Most local groups do not have the cash or resources for large events. Considerations include renting a hall, putting a deposit on that hall, insurance to cover any "incidents" that may occur, food costs, decoration costs, door prizes . . . the list goes on and on.

One local organizer asked me about the possibility of having an author lecture at the event. I asked if they were willing to pay for that author's transportation, food, and lodging or stay with someone who could offer a bed and meals. Of course, the organizer lived in a one-bedroom apartment and couldn't think of anyone else who could really handle that responsibility. Besides that, many authors are booked almost two years in advance. This person was looking for an event in two months. While it can be done, it is time consuming. Also, arrangements have to be made short term, and you lose any possibility of travel discounts and early booking discounts at hotels and motels.

These kinds of events can run thousands of dollars. Planning is critical and one blunder can spell disaster. Leaving out an important element can end up costing yourself, your family, and your friends a lot of money.

The KIS principle (Keep It Simple) is encouraged when it comes to local community events. I would like to go over some of the more successful formats for community events, and then offer some of my own experiences and observations.

However, the very first thing I am going to do is issue a warning. Always hold these events in a public place. Always! You never know who is going to show up and you do not want to invite Jack the Ripper into your home. The Internet chat rooms or email groups may offer you a place to talk to others, but you never know who is on the other end of the monitor. Trust me, the Pagan community has its share of nutters, rapists, and molesters or, as I like to call them—community predators. Never meet anyone for the first few times when you are alone or in a private, secluded place.

When, Where, and How?

The most successful and the most inexpensive of the community gatherings is the Pagan Day/Night Out (PDO/PNO). These are usually held in a local bookstore like Barnes & Noble or Borders. Pagan folks can meet in the coffee shop in these stores for beverages and conversation, then retreat to the book section that interests them the most. These are low cost/no cost, public, and indoors, so weather is never a problem.

The same can be said for the Denny's PDO/PNO. With inexpensive meals, ice cream, and appetizers, Denny's is an alternative many folks opt for when there isn't a local bookstore. Starbucks coffee shops also offer a sheltered public location for PDO/PNOs, many having public access wireless connections for your laptop. And, of course, any good local diner or restaurant is fine if your group has a few bucks to spend.

Kids always present a challenge. Where can you meet where the kids can run around and have a good time as well? And it has to be affordable. I recommend two places—McDonald's and Burger King, especially the ones with playgrounds attached, and your local mall's food court or play area. Many malls provide a play area for kids and again, this offers you no-to low-cost shelter from the weather in a public area.

All of these areas offer you an environment where you can comfortably sit and talk for a minimal cost, so the list owner does not have to put up any money. Another consideration is that these places are local to most areas, which minimizes the cost of transportation. However, these suggested meeting places are simply guidelines. If you know your local burger joint is not someplace you want to hang out, then look for an alternative. There are food places unique to some areas that offer better facilities or food, so it is up to you as the organizer to decide what is the best for your group. A good practice is to always check the place out beforehand personally.

A key element to these kinds of events is "how often" and "what time?" To be honest, this mostly depends on your group. When do most people work? How many have children? When are most of your folks available? What kind of venue is going to suit them economically and culturally? A vegan group is not going to take too well to having their kids meet at Burger King. People are not going to have the time to meet every week either. (Even if they do, meeting every week takes away the uniqueness of these events. And you are not going to be able to please everyone or accommodate everyone's schedules.)

Most email groups offer a "poll" feature so you can ask all your members what would be best for them. From this you will get the demographics you need to plan these events out.

I recommend holding an event once each month, but varying the time to accommodate most members. On alternating months, schedule a daytime event for parents with children and an evening meeting for adults.

During summertime, we look to get outdoors as much as we can, so it is appropriate to find some alternative meeting places where we can really appreciate those things Pagans hold dear. Here are a few ideas:

Your local botanical garden. Most towns have a town park or area where they keep botanical specimens. This kind of event is a "brown bag garden PDO." You suggest to all members that they bring a lunch for themselves and their kids, and you meet at the local botanical garden or city/town park. Most of these areas do not require reservations, are open to the public with a small or no admission fee, and provide a great area for the kids to run around during your discussions.

City parks offer a similar environment, with many having the added bonus of playgrounds and picnic areas. Again, it is a public area, and open until dusk so you can arrange it for outings after school or on weekends.

State and county parks are another good alternative. My group holds our summer picnics at one of our local state parks. Check to make sure the park isn't holding its own event the day you plan yours, as parking, facilities, and more could be closed or taken by that event. We check the online calendar, and also call ahead to make sure we can use the facility. If the park knows we are coming, in many instances the area has been mowed just before our visit.

Beaches are another alternative for summer fun. Bring SPF 30 (sun block), drink plenty of water, bring your own food, and swim at your own risk. Make sure everyone understands that they are responsible for their own children if you make this a kid's event.

In all instances, leave the area cleaner than you found it. An old camping rule—if you pack it in, pack it out with you. We bring garbage bags with us, and we have the kids patrol the area before we leave to make sure it is all cleaned up. I usually arrive early and pick up whatever was left by the last party. As a leader, a good rule is to never ask your group to do something you would not do yourself.

Conflict Management/Saying No

Again, children can become an issue. Some parents see a community event as a chance to "share the load." A polite word will make it clear this is not going to be the case. And other issues will arise. As you gather experience, you will learn that you have to be tough and say, no, sorry, we are not going to babysit your kids for you. Or sorry, there were complaints about your behavior at our last event; we ask that you do not join us. Remember, it is OK to say "no."

You may not like having to do this, but, consider—if this person came on your list and started trolling, wouldn't you kick him or her off? Well, the same holds true here. You are looking at the comfort level of an entire community, not one individual or family. It takes a tough person to handle the types of situations that may arise. But believe me, by saying "no" to one person you will garner the respect of the rest of the group. Chances are if you didn't like that person's behavior, others didn't either.

Starting a community list may be fun at first, but it brings with it some very major responsibilities. You are not just starting a Yahoo list, you are giving birth to a community, which may, or may not, have been there before you started. This is not just a chat line, it is a lifeline in many cases as well as a communication tool for your community.

Often "networking opportunities" or "community events" will be laced with personality conflicts and personal issues. The worst-case scenarios are local "Witch wars." Even at the most basic community event, you will have drama queens, spit fights, and the he said/she said junk that comes with all communities—not just the Pagan community. It is going to take experience to sort out which members will provide drama and issues and which ones will be the movers and shakers who will help you grow your community.

However, be assured you will survive it. And you will come out of it with all your body parts intact. That is why I always suggest KIS—start small. Keep It Simple!

In about ten years you may be able to grow your community together well enough to afford one of those big events. But will you really want to take on all that hassle? And expense? And planning? Only time will tell. But for those really magical community events, keep the planning to a minimum, offer a safe, open, public place to meet, and just sit back and watch people connect naturally. After all, once the meeting gets going, your job is done if you did it right. Now you can just sit back and enjoy the event like everyone else.

The Myth and Meaning of Pegasus

by Ember

The image of Pegasus, the white, winged stallion of Greek mythology, remains one of our most popular symbols. The myth behind this legendary creature reveals many layers of meaning that explain why Pegasus is so important to humanity and helps us find ways to incorporate the symbol of Pegasus into our lives and spiritual practice.

The story of Pegasus begins with Medusa, a beautiful mortal woman who had long, magnificent hair and often bragged that she was more beautiful than the goddess Athena. Poseidon discovered Medusa worshipping in Athena's temple and seduced her. Athena was outraged at this desecration of her temple and, as punishment, turned Medusa into the figure that most people are familiar with—a horrible creature with living snakes for hair and a gaze that would turn anyone who looked upon her to stone. The myths vary as to her actual appearance. Some stories say she was hideous, others say her face was still lovely, but that to look in her eyes was to be doomed. She became the only mortal of the three Gorgons.

The moment that brings about the birth of Pegasus occurs when the Greek hero Perseus is summoned to kill Medusa. King Polydectes challenged his subject to retrieve Medusa's head, hoping Perseus would perish in the deed. But when Athena discovered what Perseus was setting out to do, she and Hermes offered assistance. They helped Perseus obtain special weapons including a magical sword and helmet, a polished shield, and winged sandals. Perseus used the shield to view only Medusa's reflection and he succeeded in beheading her.

Medusa's blood ran into the sea, mixed with the sea foam, and Pegasus burst forth from the water. Some versions of the myth state that Pegasus sprang from Medusa's neck, as well as another creature, a monster called Chrysaor. Still other versions claim Medusa was pregnant when Perseus killed her.

Pegasus was placed in the care of the Nine Muses on Mount Helicon, which is how he earned his reputation for inspiring the creative arts. During a singing contest on Mount Helicon, the mountain swelled in size and, on Poseidon's order, Pegasus struck the mountain with his hoof to return it to normal. When his hoof struck the ground, the spring Hippocrene welled up, becoming sacred to the Nine Muses. It was said to be a magical spring and that anyone who drank its waters would be given the gift of poetry.

Pegasus' next encounter with a hero comes when the young man Bellerophon was given the task of slaying the dreaded Chimera—a monster that was a combination of goat, lion, and dragon. Bellerophon was told that the answer to defeating the monster would come to him if he slept in Athena's temple. When he did this, Athena came to him in a dream showing him the well of Pirene where Pegasus liked to drink and a golden bridle that could be used to tame him. When Bellerophon awoke he found the bridle and set off to find the winged steed. The bridle indeed allowed him to capture Pegasus and become his master. Bellerophon, with the aid of Pegasus, was successful in killing the Chimera, and he rode Pegasus in many adventures. But following all his heroic deeds and successes, Bellerophon became overconfident. He thought he was worthy of joining the gods on Mount Olympus and attempted to fly Pegasus to the top. To punish Bellerophon for his arrogance by "knocking him off his high horse," Zeus sent an insect to sting Pegasus. When Bellerophon was thrown to the ground and was blinded and crippled, his story and adventures ended. He lived out his life wandering alone and unknown.

Pegasus took his place with the gods, serving Zeus by becoming the carrier of his lightning bolts. Eventually Pegasus was given a place of honor in the sky as a constellation.

Symbols Originate

There are many layers of meaning associated with the Pegasus myth. Because of Pegasus' origins, sired by Poseidon, rising from the sea, he can be considered a kind of "sea horse." In Greek mythology, a hippocampus was a sea horse that Gods of the Sea would ride. *Hippo* is Greek for "horse." *Campos* means "sea animal or sea monster." There is a part of the human brain called the hippocampus, which is responsible for creating and storing memories—named for its shape that resembles a seahorse. Also, Pegasus is linked to the muses, and the mother of the muses is Mnemosyne, the goddess of memory. These connections and references to the mind and memory help explain why Pegasus is a symbol of inspiration and writing, especially poetry and other forms of creative expression.

Poseidon, god of the sea, is recognized as the father of Pegasus, one reason for the association of Pegasus with water. Poseidon is also often associated with bulls and horses. The name Pegasus is also derived from water: the Greek *pege* means "spring." The sacred spring that Pegasus causes to flow, Hippocrene, literally means "horse-fountain," *krene* meaning fountain. Water is symbolic of the womb and rebirth and whether conceived within Medusa's body or at the moment her blood mixed with the sea foam, Pegasus is born from both of them—carrying with him the symbolism of water and a kind of redemption or freedom, since he was born when Medusa was freed from the burden of her cursed body. Even the capture of Pegasus occurred while he was drinking from a well and his later task of carrying Zeus' thunderbolts links him to storms.

Another action Pegasus can characterize is the flight of the soul, the ability to take wing and soar. A horse is often used to symbolize strength and virility—adding wings gives that form a greater power—strength and endurance paired with the ability to reach heights that are normally impossible to attain. Wings have often been used to represent prayer and contemplation so Pegasus has often been used as a spiritual symbol.

There is another message in the tale of Pegasus—the tendency of humans to overextend themselves or believe they are invincible. Despite his heroic deeds, Bellerophon goes too far and faces a rude awakening. His confidence that he could "fly over anything" proved to be his downfall. He did not achieve his successes on his own and foolishly thought he had power over the beast—perhaps he did not consider that this creature was a gift and blessing to him. Pegasus surpasses human folly by rising to the heavens while Bellerophon falls, learning a lesson in humility. Pegasus rises as an ideal—representing freedom and the flight of both the mind and the soul.

A Multifaceted Myth

There are many interpretations of the Pegasus myth. A creature ridden by heroes and in service to gods represents many levels of the plights and pleasures of mankind: dreams, escape, fantasy, knowledge, glory, homage, immortality, innocence, and transcendence. These passages, in whatever form, are part of all human life. Focus on the image of Pegasus for creativity, intellectual pursuits, spiritual awakening, overcoming obstacles, and transcending various levels of awareness. The image of Pegasus can also be used to represent the elements of air and water.

The birth of Pegasus represents a kind of redemption, being brought forth from a curse and, in turn, creating a spring of creativity, helping to achieve heroic successes, and in the end, becoming free and honored for his contributions. Strong and powerful, yet light as air, he is able to move between Earth and the Heavens, able to transcend. And these are the gifts of Pegasus—the ability to transform, to lift the spirit, and to "drink from the fountain." Pegasus is appropriately the symbol of the poet, the artist, the dreamer—or anyone who strives to reach new heights.

Mystery Cults

by Bryony Dwale

The desire of people to connect their lives with the greater divine power was seen in the popularity of the mystery cults, in which the initiates found assurance of a better future. By 50 BCE, the Roman Empire stretched from Italy to Gaul to Egypt, thanks to Julius Caesar. The empire was vast, incorporating millions of people. Thus, new deities started to leak into Roman society, much to the dismay of the Roman authorities, who were distrustful of cultic practices and deities that appeared to endorse political loyalties to something other than Rome.

Nonetheless, the Roman traditional religion still held great meaning. However, the influx of immigrants who made up a large percentage of the population often found comfort in a more personal, universal god. Sharing the mysteries of an initiation rite helped individuals create a sense of community and belonging. Deities like Mithras and Isis promised protection in this life, salvation in the next, and a personal connection with a powerful universal deity who was not limited to one city or country.

As Rome extended its empire, a greater variety of gods became available to worship and assimilate into society. One group came from Egypt, such as Anubis the jackal-headed god; and a mother, father, and son: Isis, Osiris, and Horus. In Egypt, Isis was a fertility goddess, but to the Romans she was the Earth Mother serving as goddess of life and protection. Despite tense relations in Cleopatra's Egypt, these gods found assimilation in Rome.

There were, however, several attempts to suppress the Isis movement. Isis was closely associated with the Ptolemaic dynasty. Regardless of the animosity with Egypt, the Cult of Isis became popular with groups of poorer freedmen and women in the city toward the end of the Republic. Shrines were destroyed by orders of the Senate in spite of her popularity and kept outside of the city until Caligula admitted them back into Rome in 37 AD.

The mysteries of Isis rapidly became identified with the Roman goddesses such as Demeter/Ceres, the goddess of the corn. Isis had some similarities to the Eleusianian Mysteries of Greece, which gave enlightenment about the afterlife and triumph over influence of the night. Several other goddesses were assimilated with Isis. Tyche, the goddess who usually retains the affairs of mortals is practically a twin; however, Isis can be distinguished in statues by her headdress; sometimes showing the Sun's disc rounded by a crescent Moon or cow's horns.

While the Cult of Isis was popular among women, by the second century AD there was a cult rising in popularity with men—especially soldiers—and women were forbidden. This cult was called Mithras.

Strongly associated with astrology and having links to Persian Zoroastrianism, which stresses dualism in life (the conflict between light and darkness), Mithraism is best known in its form developed in the later Roman Empire. Mithraism is an initiatory religion—information is passed from initiate to initiate. It was not based on any scripture, so there is little documentation. As such, reconstructing this religion's daily workings and beliefs is difficult.

Rituals were secret and limited to only men. There seemed to be elaborate and moving rituals including a form of baptism. There was a promise of life after death. In every temple, cave, or other place of honor was a representation of Mithras killing a bull. Rites were celebrated in small caves with feasts held within the cave. Astrological signs adorned the cave walls. At the end of the cave there was usually a statue of Mithras slaying a bull. There were seven initiation rites: Raven, Nymphus (bride), soldier, and all the way up to Lion. After that there were three more grades: the Persian, the Sun runner, and the Father. Each grade was protected by different plants and gods.

The cult carried a number of myths, one regularly illustrated is Mithras slaying a bull. The bull was the first living thing created by Ahuramazda, the light. Mithras grabbed the horns of the bull and wrestled it to the ground. Mithras took the bull to an underground cave where the bull escaped. The Sun, the chief messenger of Ahuramazda, sent a raven to follow the bull. Mithras supported the light, so Ahuramazda guided Mithras to the bull's location, where the slaying occurred. The bull's blood spilled and animals and plant life were created, the darkness sent his servants to drink up the lifeblood, but the lifeblood had already spread throughout the world.

In the end, Ahuramazda and Mithras took authority over the light. The Sun made a covenant with Mithras before whom he bowed and by whom he crowned. The Sun and Mithras held a ceremonial feast, and then parted.

The importance of the Sun in Mithraism seemed to encourage the cult's popularity. The Sun equaled justice and redemption. The men gained a sense of fraternity, a code of ethics, and secrecy. The initiates adhered to an ethical code that advocated behaving well and abstaining from any misconduct. This cult was believed to be started by Zoroaster. So Mithraism and Zoroastrianism share the important attributes such as dualism: light and darkness.

Though little is known about Zoroaster, a.k.a. Zarathustra, not even the date of his birth, his works endured long afterward. Zoroaster was met with coldness; if not for Darius, the Persian King (who converted to Zoroastrianism), then Zoroastrianism could have died out. And although the royal family did not impose the beliefs on their subjects, Zoroastrianism even survived the fall of the Persian Empire. The lasting impact is a testament to the message Zoroaster preached, a novel concept of divinity and human life (like Mithraism).

Zoroaster also believed that dualism was extremely important. Zoroaster emphasized the individual's responsibility to pick which side to join—a life of good behavior and truthful dealings, or a life of wickedness and lies. The emphasis on free will must rely on an individual's conscience. The decision, however, is crucial because there would be a time of reckoning. Good would triumph over evil. Good, also called Ahuramazda (again just like Mithras), would judge righteously.

The last judgment was linked to the notion of a divine kingdom after death for those who had lived according to good and truth. They would be allowed to accompany Ahuramazda to a life of eternal truth. Zoroaster called this eternal life the "House of Song," and the "Abode of Good Thought." Those who were lucky could find a place with Ahuramazda forever, and ultimately immortality. Those deemed wicked and liars were denied this immortality and would be condemned to eternal pain, darkness, and punishment. Zoroaster thus encouraged every person to follow Ahuramazda so that the darkness (Angra-Mainyu) would consequently be defeated and as a result good would reign.

The Mystery Cults found popularity because it gave home and comfort to women, the poor, and the general population when there was none before. The universal deities were not limited to any country, nation, province, or city. Zoroastrianism, Mithraism, and Isian beliefs provided a personal connection with a divine higher power, which people desired and enjoyed having.

The Magic of Objects in Suspension

by Janina Renée

As I sit here and write, my eye is drawn to the crystalline snow fairies, colored glass Moons and stars, and other Sun catchers that dangle in my window. In this very human impulse for suspending baubles in windows and other openings in our homes, as well as from trees and poles outdoors, intuitive magical traditions are at play.

With the recent popularity of the Chinese art of placement, feng shui, many people are aware of the practice of hanging wind chimes and other ornaments whose motion stimulates the circulation of chi, the life energy that flows through bodies, buildings, and landscapes. However, hanging objects have also been used as charms to deflect the evil eye, as playthings for the elemental forces of air, and as votive offerings to gods and spirits.

The practice of making votive offerings to deities goes way back; a favorite method was to hang them from trees. Many ancient religious cults kept sacred groves in which certain trees might be dedicated to the deities: for example, the oak represented the father of the gods, and the linden, with its heart-shaped leaves and fragrant flowers that attract honeybees, was sacred to the love goddess. To honor the deities, people often hung ribbons or decorative objects on these trees. Of course, very old, large, and interestingly shaped trees could attract offerings in their own right because of their "numen," or store of mystical force. An example of such practices is a Bronze Age site in Bohemia, where thousands of fired-clay pendants were found scattered in a twenty-square meter area, suggesting that they all hung from a sacred tree.

Suspended votive objects were very much a part of the Greco-Roman festival culture and came to be known as "oscilla" (singular, "oscillum"). From this, we get our word "oscillation," which refers to something that swings, but the root is from *os*, meaning a "face," because these pendant objects so often took the form of masks of gods, satyrs, or generalized human faces. Some were miniature, others nearly life-sized, but they were different from masks used by actors. Oscilla could also be puppets or other types of effigies. As these pendants are sometimes found in tombs and temples, some might have been votive offerings.

The practice of hanging oscilla from vines and trees was important to gods and festivals tied to horticulture and viticulture, so masks of Dionysius/Bacchus or other appropriate deities were hung at the Greek Anthesteria and the Roman Liberalia, Sementivae Feriae, Paganalia, and Feriae Latinae; in the cult of Demeter Malaphoros, people hung their loom weights from trees to stimulate agricultural production. Some of these festivals also involved ritual swinging: people swung the miniature effigies, and in some cases, maidens played games on swings. In something of a feng shui effect, the swinging motion was believed to purify the air, (which is why it was prescribed to dispel curses). It was probably also a form of sympathetic magic to show the crops how high they should grow.

Another type of votive pendant was used at the Roman Compitalia, a festival usually held in January that honored the Lares—the ancestral spirits and spirits attached to lands and households. People built shrines at crossroads and boundaries, where landowners hung wooden and woolen effigies to represent members of their households. In the way that some historians dismiss so many old customs as vestiges of human sacrifice, it has been suggested that the effigies served as substitute offerings to the spirits. However, these displays could have also been a way for everyone in the family and community to be represented, making a statement of unity as the human community saluted the community of spirits.

At the Sigillaria, (the sixth and seventh days of the Saturnalia in mid-December), little earthenware masks and pendant figurines were sold in shops as gifts for children, and to be hung on evergreen trees. Because of the lapse in centuries, there is probably not a direct link to the practice of hanging Christmas ornaments, but it shows how certain customs recur because they are psychologically satisfying.

Other Charming Uses

Hanging ornaments were not limited to festivals, but were common home decorations. In the case of the Greco-Roman oscilla,

discs of marble, wood, ceramic, metal, or plaster featuring faces of gods or scenes from mythology were typically hung between columns and other openings in houses and gardens.

In addition to purifying the air, as mentioned earlier, some decorations have a protective function. In many different cultures, masks and plaques with staring faces are thought to give evil spirits—as well as human intruders—the feeling of being watched. Images of staring faces are also used to stymie the evil eye, which is why the head of the Medusa (known as the "gorgoneion"), was a popular theme in ancient decoration.

In the Mediterranean, where the evil eye belief is strongest, many of the delightful ornaments used are still found. Blue-glass eye beads are used in jewelry, but also as larger ornaments to be hung in cars and houses; in Turkey, these popular amulets are known as "nazar boncugu" or "bonjuk." (Blue is common for protective objects, possibly because as the coolest color, it counteracts the withering heat that the evil eye projects.) Fish amulets are also protective because fish always have their eyes open. Pendants in the form of an outspread hand (known to Jews as the Hamsa hand, and to Muslims as the Hand of Fatima) suggests the action of stretching out the hand to block the stare; some of these hands also feature an eye or a fish in the center of the palm.

The staring-eye image aggressively mirrors back the powers of the evil eye, but other curious objects neutralize its power by attracting the first glance—the potent glance. Such amulets include tassels, knots, cowrie shells, silver charms called "sirenas," which are crowned mermaids riding seahorses with little bells hanging from them, and different types of chimaeras, which are fanciful composite creatures. This capacity to deflect the glance was also the purpose of the glass Witch balls, which were once hung from chains in homes and shops in Britain. Other Witch balls were hollow with an opening so that scraps of threads could be stuffed into them; the swirl pattern made by the colored threads would draw in the gaze.

Amuletic uses aside, there is just something playful about little charms that swing in the breeze. It could be said that such objects make visible the spirits of the air, and to be made visible is a form of blessing. (And in the case of wind chimes, the air is also given a voice.) Consequently, the next time you pass some dangling wind chimes, Sun catchers, or twirlers, give them a little push, with the wish that all good spirits enjoy their play.

A Samhain Visitation:
Connecting with Our Ancestors

by Michelle Skye

As Samhain nears, there is a delicious crackle in the air, a suppressed energy that tickles the subconscious and begs to be explored. Psychic fairs pop up all over the landscape and the supernatural seems but a hands-breadth away. Witches and ghosts and skeletons arrive on the doorstep, ready to decorate our humdrum lives, reminding us that the otherworld is closer than it might appear. Magic and mysticism is celebrated everywhere. It is the time of the Witch.

Yet, at the heart of the Samhain holiday, at its very root, is death. At this time of the year, the world is sliding into darkness. The earth lies fallow, resting after the hard harvest work. Plants and flowers die. Animals begin the long climb into hibernation. Is it any wonder that we hold our own sacred dead, our ancestors, at the very heart of the celebration? As the Earth and the Sun begin their descent into darkness, our minds naturally ponder our own mortality and remember loved ones who have gone before us into the great beyond.

Death is a fact of life. We all die. Yet, we all live on in our children, our nieces and nephews, our blood kin that succeed our mortal time on this Earth. We live on in their memories and stories, in their quirky habits and crooked smiles. We are honored not just through their remembrance of us but also through the living of their lives. We are a part of their soul memory, housed in the tiny structures that form the building blocks of life. We are always a part of them (whether they know it or not).

So as the days grow shorter and the Crone goddess stirs her cauldron of life-death-and-rebirth, it is time to heed the song that sings just under the surface of our consciousness. Our blood kin wait beyond the veil, ready to aid us, to heal and comfort us, to lend us strength. And if they have been reincarnated already, their knowledge and wisdom flow through our veins, if only we silence our chatter and listen.

The following activity forces you to slow down in order to truly and deeply connect to your personal ancestors. It compels you to unite with those in your life who have passed on and to invite them, once again, into your life. Since the activity pushes you to look death squarely in the face, it would be easy to rush through it without giving it the necessary thought and attention. But resist this notion. Allow yourself the time to slow down and welcome your ancestors back into your life.

You will need to purchase a candle for each of your remembered relatives who you wish to honor. This part sounds simple, but is crucial to your overall experience. Each candle must remind you of your relative, in color and/or scent. Many candle companies produce fragrant candles for every occasion. Traditionally, I find their scents to be somewhat overwhelming, but in this ritual activity, you are luring the spirits of your relatives closer to you, in heart as well as body. Powerful scents help to connect this world with the otherworld and will create a welcoming atmosphere for your ancestors in your home.

Choosing the scent of the candles is my favorite part of this activity and should be done with reverence and intent. Don't rush out on October 29 to purchase your candles. Begin thinking about your relatives in the beginning of October and research different candle companies for just the right scent. Think of finding just the right candle as an elaborate scavenger hunt. Look and listen, keeping an open mind. Do not become fixated on one specific idea for your relatives. Rather, allow your ancestors to direct you to the appropriate scents and colors. I still remember the excitement and love I felt when I stumbled across a candle called Green Grass, a scent especially evocative of my grandfather who, in his later years, constantly mowed the grass to "get out of the house."

Once you have purchased your candles, set aside a time (a week or so before Samhain) when you can spend about an hour alone. Performing this part of the ritual at night will aid you in connecting with your ancestors, as the night is often a time associated with spirits. The evening hours are also usually quieter and calmer than the daytime so you will undoubtedly find it easier to quiet your mind and stay focused on your goal. However, if you

simply have no free time in the evening, with the right intention and focus, this part of the activity can be done anytime during the day. Set up sacred space by lighting incense and playing your favorite meditative music. You can visualize a protective circle around you, but I have found that a formal circle is not necessary as long as you have the right mindset and are able to alter your perceptions in order to contact and be open to the otherworld.

Be sure to spend some time breathing deeply before you begin any ritualized activity. Since you will be working with energies outside the earth realm, it is a good idea to ground and center as well. Simply visualize your spine lengthening and forming an underground root system. Breathe the Earth's energy into your body and breathe out any stress, anxiety and negativity, using the root system of your spine. (Be sure to ask Mother Earth to transmute your negative energy into positive energy.) Once you feel very relaxed and filled with the Earth's energy, visualize a white ball of energy descending from the cosmos. Feel it enter your head and travel down your spine, aligning all of your energy centers. When it reaches the bottom of your spine, allow the white ball to travel back up your spine and leave your head, bathing you in protective and stimulating white light. You are now connected to the energy of Mother Earth and Father Sky. You are grounded and centered, and should feel relaxed and energized.

Take each candle in turn and hold it in your hand. Smell the candle and, with your eyes closed, visualize your ancestor. See your relative doing a simple task. Hear the words of her voice. Feel the breath of those words. Sense the power of the breath and allow it into yourself. In your mind, replay all the wonderful (and perhaps challenging) aspects of your relationship with your ancestor. Take as much time as you need to truly conjure your ancestor's spirit from within yourself. This may be a very emotional experience so give yourself the freedom to express any feelings and sentiments. When you feel ready, inscribe the name of your relative on the candle, using one of your ritual tools or a regular knife that you have cleansed with sacred water or herbs, and then anoint the candle with sacred oil. (Any oil can be sacred if you will it to be so. Don't feel obliged to purchase or make specific magical, spiritual oil. You can just as easily use the olive oil in your kitchen cabinet.)

The type of candle and candleholder you use will depend on the way you wish to honor your ancestors. If you are fortunate enough to live near the gravesites of your relatives, I recommend placing the candles at the actual gravestone on the night of Samhain. Votive candles will work best for this situation and the holder should be fairly deep to protect the fragile flame from wind. I usually burn my candles for a week before the holiday to make sure they are deep enough in the candleholder to withstand the elements. A little before sunset, go to the gravesites of your relatives. Be sure to bring your candles, a candleholder, a lighter, an apple for each relative (the traditional Celtic food of the dead), a sharp knife, and some bright and showy flowers. Chrysanthemums and marigolds are the traditional flowers of the Day of the Dead in Mexico, so you might consider buying them or purchasing flowers that most remind you of your relatives. At each gravesite, honor your ancestor with a few words and place some of the flowers on the ground. (If you live in a warm climate, consider bringing live plants with you and plant them in the ground.) Light the candle, then cut one apple in half, around the middle, revealing the star pattern. Leave all the lit candles, the apples, and the flowers at the gravesites and collect the candleholders the following day.

If you do not have access to the gravesites of your ancestors, set up your candles on your ritual altar or in a place of special significance for you. You can light your candles ahead of time or wait until Samhain to light them for the very first time. I personally like to light my candles in remembrance for several days ahead of time, making sure there is enough wax so that the candle burns throughout the night of Samhain. (Or at least, until you go to bed!) Again, be sure to offer flowers and food to your dead relatives by purchasing flowers and cutting an apple in half for each ancestor you are honoring. If you'd like to include pictures or mementos of your relatives, place those on your altar as well.

Through this simple act of remembrance, you are honoring all those who have gone before you; the people whose essence resides in your physical body, whose words shape your sense of self, whose spirits skim along the edges of your intuition. Your ancestors are a powerful source of solace and well-being. They spring eternal in the movements of your hands, the thoughts in your mind, and the emotions of your heart. They have experienced the shifts in seasons, the ebb and flow of life, the joys, the sorrows, the achievements and defeats. Learn from them. Their hands reach to you through the mists, ready and willing to join with yours. They are a part of you. Welcome them home.

Almanac Section

Calendar

Time Changes

Lunar Phases

Moon Signs

Full Moons

Sabbats

World Holidays

Incense of the Day

Color of the Day

Almanac Listings

In these listings you will find the date, day, lunar phase, Moon sign, color and incense for the day, and festivals from around the world.

The Date

The date is used in numerological calculations that govern magical rites.

The Day

Each day is ruled by a planet that possesses specific magical influences:

MONDAY (MOON): Peace, sleep, healing, compassion, friends, psychic awareness, purification, and fertility.

TUESDAY (MARS): Passion, sex, courage, aggression, and protection.

WEDNESDAY (MERCURY): The conscious mind, study, travel, divination, and wisdom.

THURSDAY (JUPITER): Expansion, money, prosperity, and generosity.

FRIDAY (VENUS): Love, friendship, reconciliation, and beauty.

SATURDAY (SATURN): Longevity, exorcism, endings, homes, and houses.

SUNDAY (SUN): Healing, spirituality, success, strength, and protection.

The Lunar Phase

The lunar phase is important in determining the best times for magic.

THE WAXING MOON (from the New Moon to the Full) is the ideal time for magic to draw things toward you.

THE FULL MOON is the time of greatest power.

THE WANING MOON (from the Full Moon to the New) is a time for study, meditation, and little magical work (except magic designed to banish harmful energies).

The Moon's Sign

The Moon continuously "moves" through the zodiac, from Aries to Pisces. Each sign possesses its own significance.

ARIES: Good for starting things, but lacks staying power. Things occur rapidly, but quickly pass. People tend to be argumentative and assertive.

TAURUS: Things begun now last the longest, tend to increase in value, and become hard to alter. Brings out appreciation for beauty and sensory experience.

GEMINI: Things begun now are easily changed by outside influence. Time for shortcuts, communication, games, and fun.

CANCER: Stimulates emotional rapport between people. Pinpoints need, supports growth and nurturance. Tends to domestic concerns.

LEO: Draws emphasis to the self, central ideas or institutions, away from connections with others and other emotional needs. People tend to be melodramatic.

VIRGO: Favors accomplishment of details and commands from higher up. Focuses on health, hygiene, and daily schedules.

LIBRA: Favors cooperation, social activities, beautification of surroundings, balance, and partnership.

SCORPIO: Increases awareness of psychic power. Precipitates psychic crises and ends connections thoroughly. People tend to brood and become secretive.

SAGITTARIUS: Encourages flights of imagination and confidence. This is an adventurous, philosophical, and athletic Moon sign. Favors expansion and growth.

CAPRICORN: Develops strong structure. Focus on traditions, responsibilities, and obligations. A good time to set boundaries and rules.

AQUARIUS: Rebellious energy. Time to break habits and make abrupt change. Personal freedom and individuality is the focus.

PISCES: The focus is on dreaming, nostalgia, intuition, and psychic impressions. A good time for spiritual or philanthropic activities.

Color and Incense

The color and incense for the day are based on information from *Personal Alchemy* by Amber Wolfe, and relate to the planet that rules each day. This information can be taken into consideration along with other factors when planning works of magic or when blending magic into mundane life. Please note that the incense selections are not hard-and-fast. If you can not find or do not like the incense listed for the day, choose a similar scent that appeals to you.

Festivals and Holidays

Festivals are listed throughout the year. The exact dates of many of these ancient festivals are difficult to determine; prevailing data has been used.

Time Changes

The times and dates of all astrological phenomena in this almanac are based on **Eastern Standard Time (EST)**. If you live outside of EST, you will need to make the following changes:

PACIFIC STANDARD TIME: Subtract three hours.

MOUNTAIN STANDARD TIME: Subtract two hours.

CENTRAL STANDARD TIME: Subtract one hour.

ALASKA/HAWAII: Subtract five hours.

DAYLIGHT SAVING TIME: Add an hour. In 2005, Congress extended the length of Daylight Saving Time by one month, effective in 2007. Daylight Saving Time now runs from March 9, 2008 to November 2, 2008.

2008 Sabbats and Full Moons

January 22	Full Moon 8:35 am
February 2	Imbolc
February 20	Full Moon 10:30 pm
March 21	Full Moon 2:40 pm
March 20	Ostara (Spring Equinox)
April 20	Full Moon 6:25 am
May 1	Beltane
May 19	Full Moon 10:11 pm
June 18	Full Moon 1:30 pm
June 20	Litha (Summer Solstice)
July 18	Full Moon 3:59 pm
August 1	Lammas
August 16	Full Moon 5:16 pm
September 15	Full Moon 5:13 am
September 22	Mabon (Fall Equinox)
October 14	Full Moon 4:02 pm
October 31	Samhain
November 13	Full Moon 1:17 am
December 12	Full Moon 11:37 am
December 21	Yule (Winter Solstice)

January

1 Tuesday
New Year's Day • Kwanzaa ends
Waning Moon
Moon Phase: Fourth Quarter
Color: Maroon

Moon Sign: Libra
Moon enters Scorpio 8:32 pm
Incense: Geranium

2 Wednesday
First Writing (Japanese)
Waning Moon
Moon Phase: Fourth Quarter
Color: White

Moon Sign: Scorpio
Incense: Lavender

3 Thursday
St. Genevieve's Day
Waning Moon
Moon Phase: Fourth Quarter
Color: Purple

Moon Sign: Scorpio
Incense: Nutmeg

4 Friday
Frost Fairs on the Thames
Waning Moon
Moon Phase: Fourth Quarter
Color: Coral

Moon Sign: Scorpio
Moon enters Sagittarius 9:13 am
Incense: Orchid

5 Saturday
Epiphany Eve
Waning Moon
Moon Phase: Fourth Quarter
Color: Indigo

Moon Sign: Sagittarius
Incense: Magnolia

6 Sunday
Epiphany
Waning Moon
Moon Phase: Fourth Quarter
Color: Orange

Moon Sign: Sagittarius
Moon enters Capricorn 8:43 pm
Incense: Eucalyptus

7 Monday
Rizdvo (Ukrainian)
Waning Moon
Moon Phase: Fourth Quarter
Color: Gray

Moon Sign: Capricorn
Incense: Hyssop

☽ **Tuesday**
Midwives' Day
Waning Moon
Moon Phase: New Moon 6:37 am
Color: White

Moon Sign: Capricorn
Incense: Cedar

9 **Wednesday**
Islamic New Year
Waxing Moon
Moon Phase: First Quarter
Color: Yellow

Moon Sign: Capricorn
Moon enters Aquarius 6:13 am
Incense: Honeysuckle

10 **Thursday**
Business God's Day (Japanese)
Waxing Moon
Moon Phase: First Quarter
Color: Green

Moon Sign: Aquarius
Incense: Mulberry

11 **Friday**
Carmentalia (Roman)
Waxing Moon
Moon Phase: First Quarter
Color: Pink

Moon Sign: Aquarius
Moon enters Pisces 1:44 pm
Incense: Vanilla

12 **Saturday**
Revolution Day (Tanzanian)
Waxing Moon
Moon Phase: First Quarter
Color: Blue

Moon Sign: Pisces
Incense: Pine

13 **Sunday**
Twentieth Day (Norwegian)
Waxing Moon
Moon Phase: First Quarter
Color: Yellow

Moon Sign: Pisces
Moon enters Aries 7:23 pm
Incense: Almond

14 **Monday**
Feast of the Ass (French)
Waxing Moon
Moon Phase: First Quarter
Color: Lavender

Moon Sign: Aries
Incense: Clary sage

○ **Tuesday**
Birthday of Martin Luther King, Jr. (actual)   Moon Sign: Aries
Waxing Moon   Moon enters Taurus 11:13 pm
Moon Phase: Second Quarter 2:46 pm   Incense: Bayberry
Color: Black

16 **Wednesday**
Apprentices Day   Moon Sign: Taurus
Waxing Moon   Incense: Marjoram
Moon Phase: Second Quarter
Color: Topaz

17 **Thursday**
St. Anthony's Day (Mexican)   Moon Sign: Taurus
Waxing Moon   Incense: Myrrh
Moon Phase: Second Quarter
Color: Turquoise

18 **Friday**
Assumption Day   Moon Sign: Taurus
Waning Moon   Moon enters Gemini 1:30 am
Moon Phase: Second Quarter   Incense: Rose
Color: Rose

19 **Saturday**
Kitchen God Feast (Chinese)   Moon Sign: Gemini
Waxing Moon   Incense: Patchouli
Moon Phase: Second Quarter
Color: Brown

20 **Sunday**
Breadbasket Festival (Portuguese)   Moon Sign: Gemini
Waxing Moon   Moon enters Cancer 3:05 am
Moon Phase: Second Quarter   Sun enters Aquarius 11:43 am
Color: Gold   Incense: Marigold

21 **Monday**
Birthday of Martin Luther King, Jr. (observed)   Moon Sign: Cancer
Waxing Moon   Incense: Rosemary
Moon Phase: Second Quarter
Color: White

January

⊙ **Tuesday**
St. Vincent's Day (French)
Waxing Moon
Moon Phase: Full Moon 8:35am
Color: Scarlet

Moon Sign: Cancer
Moon enters Leo 5:20 am
Incense: Ylang ylang

---

23 **Wednesday**
St. Ildefonso's Day
Waning Moon
Moon Phase: Third Quarter
Color: Brown

Moon Sign: Leo
Incense: Lilac

---

24 **Thursday**
Alasitas Fair (Bolivian)
Waning Moon
Moon Phase: Third Quarter
Color: Purple

Moon Sign: Leo
Moon enters Virgo 9:48 am
Incense: Clove

---

25 **Friday**
Burns' Night (Scottish)
Waning Moon
Moon Phase: Third Quarter 6:01 pm
Color: Coral

Moon Sign: Virgo
Incense: Thyme

---

26 **Saturday**
Republic Day (Indian)
Waning Moon
Moon Phase: Third Quarter
Color: Indigo

Moon Sign: Virgo
Moon enters Libra 5:35 pm
Incense: Sandalwood

---

27 **Sunday**
Vogelgruff (Swiss)
Waning Moon
Moon Phase: Third Quarter
Color: Amber

Moon Sign: Libra
Incense: Juniper

---

28 **Monday**
St. Charlemagne's Day
Waning Moon
Moon Phase: Third Quarter
Color: Silver

Moon Sign: Libra
Incense: Lily

29 Tuesday
Australia Day
Waning Moon
Moon Phase: Third Quarter
Color: Gray

Moon Sign: Libra
Moon enters Scorpio 4:35 am
Incense: Basil

◖ Wednesday
Three Hierarchs' Day (Eastern Orthodox)
Waning Moon
Moon Phase: Fourth Quarter 12:03 am
Color: Yellow

Moon Sign: Scorpio
Incense: Bay laurel

---

31 Thursday
Independence Day (Nauru)
Waning Moon
Moon Phase: Fourth Quarter
Color: Crimson

Moon Sign: Scorpio
Moon enters Sagittarius 5:08 pm
Incense: Jasmine

Fairies of the UK

In the United Kingdom there is a type of fairy called Spriggans. This particular fairy is dour, ugly, and grotesque. They are quite small but have the ability to inflate themselves into monstrous forms which allow humans to believe Spriggans are ghosts of old giants. Additionally, Spriggans are guardians of hill treasure as well as a band of villains and skilled thieves. They can rob human houses and cause whirlwinds that destroy corn fields and infect crops while causing all kinds of other unpleasant mischief.

Hyter Sprites are shape-shifting fairies from eastern England. They most frequently take the form of birds.

—Bryony Dwale

February

1   Friday
St. Brigid's Day (Irish)   Moon Sign: Sagittarius
Waning Moon   Incense: Violet
Moon Phase: Fourth Quarter
Color: Purple

2   Saturday
Imbolc • Groundhog Day   Moon Sign: Sagittarius
Waning Moon   Incense: Sage
Moon Phase: Fourth Quarter
Color: Black

3   Sunday
St. Blaise's Day   Moon Sign: Sagittarius
Waning Moon   Moon enters Capricorn 4:52 am
Moon Phase: Fourth Quarter   Incense: Hyacinth
Color: Gold

4   Monday
Independence Day (Sri Lankan)   Moon Sign: Capricorn
Waning Moon   Incense: Narcissus
Moon Phase: Fourth Quarter
Color: Lavender

5   Tuesday
Mardi Gras   Moon Sign: Capricorn
Waning Moon   Moon enters Aquarius 2:10 pm
Moon Phase: Fourth Quarter   Incense: Ginger
Color: Red

☽   Wednesday
Ash Wednesday   Moon Sign: Aquarius
Waning Moon   Incense: Lilac
Moon Phase: New Moon 10:44 pm
Color: Topaz

7   Thursday
Chinese New Year (rat)   Moon Sign: Aquarius
Waxing Moon   Moon enters Pisces 8:46 pm
Moon Phase: First Quarter   Incense: Apricot
Color: Turquoise

February

8 **Friday**
Mass for Broken Needles (Japanese)
Waxing Moon
Moon Phase: First Quarter
Color: Coral

Moon Sign: Pisces
Incense: Cypress

---

9 **Saturday**
St. Marion's Day (Lebanese)
Waxing Moon
Moon Phase: First Quarter
Color: Brown

Moon Sign: Pisces
Incense: Rue

---

10 **Sunday**
Gasparilla Day (Florida)
Waxing Moon
Moon Phase: First Quarter 4:51 pm
Color: Yellow

Moon Sign: Pisces
Moon enters Aries 1:17 am
Incense: Frankincense

---

11 **Monday**
Foundation Day (Japanese)
Waxing Moon
Moon Phase: First Quarter
Color: Ivory

Moon Sign: Aries
Incense: Hyssop

---

12 **Tuesday**
Lincoln's Birthday (actual)
Waxing Moon
Moon Phase: First Quarter
Color: White

Moon Sign: Aries
Moon enters Taurus 4:34 am
Incense: Cinnamon

☽ **Wednesday**
Parentalia (Roman)
Waxing Moon
Moon Phase: Second Quarter 10:33 pm
Color: Brown

Moon Sign: Taurus
Incense: Lavender

---

14 **Thursday**
Valentine's Day
Waxing Moon
Moon Phase: Second Quarter
Color: Purple

Moon Sign: Taurus
Moon enters Gemini 7:19 am
Incense: Carnation

February

15 **Friday**
Lupercalia (Roman)
Waxing Moon
Moon Phase: Second Quarter
Color: Pink

Moon Sign: Gemini
Incense: Yarrow

16 **Saturday**
Fumi-e (Japanese)
Waxing Moon
Moon Phase: Second Quarter
Color: Gray

Moon Sign: Gemini
Moon enters Cancer 10:12 am
Incense: Ivy

17 **Sunday**
Quirinalia (Roman)
Waxing Moon
Moon Phase: Second Quarter
Color: Orange

Moon Sign: Cancer
Incense: Almond

18 **Monday**
Presidents' Day (observed)
Waxing Moon
Moon Phase: Second Quarter
Color: Silver

Moon Sign: Cancer
Moon enters Leo 1:51 pm
Incense: Neroli

19 **Tuesday**
Pero Palo's Trial (Spanish)
Waxing Moon
Moon Phase: Second Quarter
Color: Gray

Moon Sign: Leo
Sun enters Pisces 1:49 am
Incense: Bayberry

☻ **Wednesday**
Installation of the new Lama (Tibetan)
Waxing Moon
Moon Phase: Full Moon 10:30 pm
Color: Yellow

Moon Sign: Leo
Moon enters Virgo 7:06 pm
Incense: Honeysuckle

21 **Thursday**
Feast of Lanterns (Chinese)
Waning Moon
Moon Phase: Third Quarter
Color: Green

Moon Sign: Virgo
Incense: Balsam

22 **Friday**
Caristia (Roman)
Waning Moon
Moon Phase: Third Quarter
Color: White

Moon Sign: Virgo
Incense: Alder

---

23 **Saturday**
Terminalia (Roman)
Waning Moon
Moon Phase: Third Quarter
Color: Blue

Moon Sign: Virgo
Moon enters Libra 2:44 am
Incense: Sandalwood

---

24 **Sunday**
Regifugium (Roman)
Waning Moon
Moon Phase: Third Quarter 2:56 am
Color: Amber

Moon Sign: Libra
Incense: Heliotrope

---

25 **Monday**
Saint Walburga's Day (German)
Waning Moon
Moon Phase: Third Quarter
Color: White

Moon Sign: Libra
Moon enters Scorpio 1:05 pm
Incense: Clary sage

---

26 **Tuesday**
Zamboanga Festival (Filipino)
Waning Moon
Moon Phase: Third Quarter
Color: Black

Moon Sign: Scorpio
Incense: Geranium

---

27 **Wednesday**
Threepenny Day
Waning Moon
Moon Phase: Third Quarter
Color: Topaz

Moon Sign: Scorpio
Incense: Marjoram

○ **Thursday**
Kalevala Day (Finnish)
Waning Moon
Moon Phase: Fourth Quarter 9:18 pm
Color: Crimson

Moon Sign: Scorpio
Moon enters Sagittarius 1:22 am
Incense: Mulberry

March

29 Friday
Leap Day
Waning Moon
Moon Phase: Fourth Quarter
Color: Rose

Moon Sign: Sagittarius
Incense: Mint

---

1 Saturday
Matronalia (Roman)
Waning Moon
Moon Phase: Fourth Quarter
Color: Indigo

Moon Sign: Sagittarius
Moon enters Capricorn 1:33 pm
Incense: Pine

---

2 Sunday
St. Chad's Day (English)
Waning Moon
Moon Phase: Fourth Quarter
Color: Yellow

Moon Sign: Capricorn
Incense: Juniper

---

3 Monday
Doll Festival (Japanese)
Waning Moon
Moon Phase: Fourth Quarter
Color: Lavender

Moon Sign: Capricorn
Moon enters Aquarius 11:24 pm
Incense: Neroli

---

4 Tuesday
St. Casimir's Day (Polish)
Waning Moon
Moon Phase: Fourth Quarter
Color: Maroon

Moon Sign: Aquarius
Incense: Basil

---

5 Wednesday
Isis Festival (Roman)
Waning Moon
Moon Phase: Fourth Quarter
Color: Yellow

Moon Sign: Aquarius
Incense: Marjoram

---

6 Thursday
Alamo Day
Waning Moon
Moon Phase: Fourth Quarter
Color: Green

Moon Sign: Aquarius
Moon enters Pisces 5:53 am
Incense: Clove

March

🌙 **Friday**
Bird and Arbor Day
Waning Moon
Moon Phase: New Moon 12:14 pm
Color: Purple

Moon Sign: Pisces
Incense: Rose

---

8 Saturday
International Women's Day
Waxing Moon
Moon Phase: First Quarter
Color: Brown

Moon Sign: Pisces
Moon enters Aries 9:23 am
Incense: Magnolia

---

9 Sunday
Daylight Saving Time begins
Waxing Moon
Moon Phase: First Quarter
Color: Gold

Moon Sign: Aries
Incense: Eucalyptus

---

10 Monday
Tibet Day
Waxing Moon
Moon Phase: First Quarter
Color: Ivory

Moon Sign: Aries
Moon enters Taurus 12:13 pm
Incense: Lily

---

11 Tuesday
Feast of Gauri (Hindu)
Waxing Moon
Moon Phase: First Quarter
Color: Gray

Moon Sign: Taurus
Incense: Cedar

---

12 Wednesday
Receiving the Water (Buddhist)
Waxing Moon
Moon Phase: First Quarter
Color: White

Moon Sign: Taurus
Moon enters Gemini 1:54 pm
Incense: Bay laurel

---

13 Thursday
Purification Feast (Balinese)
Waxing Moon
Moon Phase: First Quarter
Color: Purple

Moon Sign: Gemini
Incense: Myrrh

March

☽ Friday
Mamuralia (Roman)
Waxing Moon
Moon Phase: Second Quarter 6:45 am
Color: Coral

Moon Sign: Gemini
Moon enters Cancer 4:37 pm
Incense: Thyme

---

15 Saturday
Phallus Festival (Japanese)
Waxing Moon
Moon Phase: Second Quarter
Color: Blue

Moon Sign: Cancer
Incense: Patchouli

---

16 Sunday
Palm Sunday
Waxing Moon
Moon Phase: Second Quarter
Color: Orange

Moon Sign: Cancer
Moon enters Leo 9:04 pm
Incense: Marigold

---

17 Monday
St. Patrick's Day
Waxing Moon
Moon Phase: Second Quarter
Color: Silver

Moon Sign: Leo
Incense: Rosemary

---

18 Tuesday
Sheelah's Day (Irish)
Waxing Moon
Moon Phase: Second Quarter
Color: Black

Moon Sign: Leo
Incense: Bayberry

---

19 Wednesday
St. Joseph's Day (Sicilian)
Waxing Moon
Moon Phase: Second Quarter
Color: Brown

Moon Sign: Leo
Moon enters Virgo 3:25 am
Incense: Honeysuckle

---

20 Thursday
Ostara • Spring Equinox
Waxing Moon
Moon Phase: Second Quarter
Color: Turquoise

Moon Sign: Virgo
Sun enters Aries 1:48 am
Incense: Jasmine

☺ **Friday**
Purim • Good Friday
Waxing Moon
Moon Phase: Full Moon 2:40 pm
Color: Pink

Moon Sign: Virgo
Moon enters Libra 11:45 am
Incense: Orchid

---

22 **Saturday**
Hilaria (Roman)
Waning Moon
Moon Phase: Third Quarter
Color: Gray

Moon Sign: Libra
Incense: Sage

---

23 **Sunday**
Easter
Waning Moon
Moon Phase: Third Quarter
Color: Amber

Moon Sign: Libra
Moon enters Scorpio 10:06 pm
Incense: Frankincense

---

24 **Monday**
Day of Blood (Roman)
Waning Moon
Moon Phase: Third Quarter
Color: Gray

Moon Sign: Scorpio
Incense: Narcissus

---

25 **Tuesday**
Tichborne Dole (English)
Waxing Moon
Moon Phase: Third Quarter
Color: Red

Moon Sign: Scorpio
Incense: Ylang ylang

---

26 **Wednesday**
Prince Kuhio Day (Hawaiian)
Waning Moon
Moon Phase: Third Quarter
Color: Topaz

Moon Sign: Scorpio
Moon enters Sagittarius 10:11 am
Incense: Lilac

---

27 **Thursday**
Smell the Breezes Day (Egyptian)
Waning Moon
Moon Phase: Third Quarter
Color: Crimson

Moon Sign: Sagittarius
Incense: Clove

March
♈

28 Friday
Oranges and Lemons Service (English)   Moon Sign: Sagittarius
Waning Moon   Moon enters Capricorn 10:43 pm
Moon Phase: Third Quarter   Incense: Vanilla
Color: White

☽ Saturday
St. Eustace's Day   Moon Sign: Capricorn
Waning Moon   Incense: Rue
Moon Phase: Fourth Quarter 5:47 pm
Color: Black

30 Sunday
Seward's Day (Alaskan)   Moon Sign: Capricorn
Waning Moon   Incense: Hyacinth
Moon Phase: Fourth Quarter
Color: Orange

31 Monday
The Borrowed Days (Ethiopian)   Moon Sign: Capricorn
Waning Moon   Moon enters Aquarius 9:34 am
Moon Phase: Fourth Quarter   Incense: Hyssop
Color: Lavender

Fairies of Scotland

In Scotland, Ghillie Dhu is a solitary, yet malevolent, fairy who inhabits birch trees. Ghillie Dhu's clothes are made of leaves and moss so as to camouflage themselves.

The Blue Men of Munich are blue sea creatures living around the Scottish Isles. These particular fairies cause unexpected storms and shipwrecks. The sailors who encounter them can win contests involving rhymes.

—Bryony Dwale

April

1 Tuesday
April Fools' Day
Waning Moon
Moon Phase: Fourth Quarter
Color: White

Moon Sign: Aquarius
Incense: Ginger

2 Wednesday
The Battle of Flowers (French)
Waning Moon
Moon Phase: Fourth Quarter
Color: Brown

Moon Sign: Aquarius
Moon enters Pisces 4:55 pm
Incense: Lavender

3 Thursday
Thirteenth Day (Iranian)
Waning Moon
Moon Phase: Fourth Quarter
Color: Green

Moon Sign: Pisces
Incense: Apricot

4 Friday
Megalesia (Roman)
Waning Moon
Moon Phase: Fourth Quarter
Color: Pink

Moon Sign: Pisces
Moon enters Aries 8:27 pm
Incense: Mint

5 Saturday
Tomb-Sweeping Day (Chinese)
Waning Moon
Moon Phase: New Moon 11:55 pm
Color: Blue

Moon Sign: Aries
Incense: Ivy

6 Sunday
Chakri Day (Thai)
Waxing Moon
Moon Phase: First Quarter
Color: Yellow

Moon Sign: Aries
Moon enters Taurus 9:19 pm
Incense: Almond

7 Monday
Festival of Pure Brightness (Chinese)
Waxing Moon
Moon Phase: First Quarter
Color: Gray

Moon Sign: Taurus
Incense: Rosemary

8 Tuesday
Buddha's Birthday
Waxing Moon
Moon Phase: First Quarter
Color: Black

Moon Sign: Taurus
Moon enters Gemini 9:27 pm
Incense: Cinnamon

9 Wednesday
Valour Day (Filipino)
Waxing Moon
Moon Phase: First Quarter
Color: Yellow

Moon Sign: Gemini
Incense: Lilac

10 Thursday
The Tenth of April (English)
Waxing Moon
Moon Phase: First Quarter
Color: Turquoise

Moon Sign: Gemini
Moon enters Cancer 10:43 pm
Incense: Balsam

11 Friday
Heroes Day (Costa Rican)
Waxing Moon
Moon Phase: First Quarter
Color: White

Moon Sign: Cancer
Incense: Yarrow

☾ Saturday
Cerealia (Roman)
Waxing Moon
Moon Phase: Second Quarter 2:32 pm
Color: Indigo

Moon Sign: Cancer
Incense: Sage

13 Sunday
Thai New Year
Waxing Moon
Moon Phase: Second Quarter
Color: Amber

Moon Sign: Cancer
Moon enters Leo 2:29 am
Incense: Juniper

14 Monday
Sanno Festival (Japanese)
Waxing Moon
Moon Phase: Second Quarter
Color: Lavender

Moon Sign: Leo
Incense: Clary sage

April

15 Tuesday
Plowing Festival (Chinese)
Waxing Moon
Moon Phase: Second Quarter
Color: Gray

Moon Sign: Leo
Moon enters Virgo 9:06 am
Incense: Basil

---

16 Wednesday
Zurich Spring Festival (Swiss)
Waxing Moon
Moon Phase: Second Quarter
Color: White

Moon Sign: Virgo
Incense: Honeysuckle

---

17 Thursday
Yayoi Matsuri (Japanese)
Waxing Moon
Moon Phase: Second Quarter
Color: Purple

Moon Sign: Virgo
Moon enters Libra 6:10 pm
Incense: Carnation

---

18 Friday
Flower Festival (Japanese)
Waxing Moon
Moon Phase: Second Quarter
Color: Rose

Moon Sign: Libra
Incense: Alder

---

19 Saturday
Cerealia last day (Roman)
Waxing Moon
Moon Phase: Second Quarter
Color: Black

Moon Sign: Libra
Sun enters Taurus 12:51 pm
Incense: Patchouli

☺ Sunday
Passover begins
Waxing Moon
Moon Phase: Full Moon 6:25 am
Color: Gold

Moon Sign: Libra
Moon enters Scorpio 5:00 am
Incense: Heliotrope

---

21 Monday
Tiradentes Day (Brazilian)
Waning Moon
Moon Phase: Third Quarter
Color: White

Moon Sign: Scorpio
Incense: Lily

April

22 Tuesday
Earth Day
Waning Moon
Moon Phase: Third Quarter
Color: Red

Moon Sign: Scorpio
Moon enters Sagittarius 5:07 pm
Incense: Geranium

23 Wednesday
St. George's Day (English)
Waning Moon
Moon Phase: Third Quarter
Color: Topaz

Moon Sign: Sagittarius
Incense: Bay laurel

24 Thursday
St. Mark's Eve
Waning Moon
Moon Phase: Third Quarter
Color: White

Moon Sign: Sagittarius
Incense: Nutmeg

25 Friday
Orthodox Good Friday
Waning Moon
Moon Phase: Third Quarter
Color: Coral

Moon Sign: Sagittarius
Moon enters Capricorn 5:47 am
Incense: Violet

26 Saturday
Arbor Day
Waning Moon
Moon Phase: Third Quarter
Color: Gray

Moon Sign: Capricorn
Incense: Ivy

27 Sunday
Orthodox Easter • Passover ends
Waning Moon
Moon Phase: Third Quarter
Color: Orange

Moon Sign: Capricorn
Moon enters Aquarius 5:27 pm
Incense: Eucalyptus

◐ Monday
Floralia (Roman)
Waning Moon
Moon Phase: Fourth Quarter 10:12 am
Color: Silver

Moon Sign: Aquarius
Incense: Neroli

April

29 Tuesday
Green Day (Japanese)
Waning Moon
Moon Phase: Fourth Quarter
Color: Scarlet

Moon Sign: Aquarius
Incense: Cedar

---

30 Wednesday
Walpurgis Night • May Eve
Waning Moon
Moon Phase: Fourth Quarter
Color: Brown

Moon Sign: Aquarius
Moon enters Pisces 2:11 am
Incense: Marjoram

Welsh and Irish Fairies

The Gwrargedd Annwn are Welsh fairies. They are beautiful water fairies who live in palaces under water. They are kind to children with no money and to mothers. Occasionally, they can take mortals for husbands.

The Coblynau are Welsh mine fairies. These fairies protect and help miners unless, of course, angered.

On the Isle of Man, the Leanan Sidhe is a blood-sucking vampire woman, but in Ireland she's the muse for poets.

In Ireland there is a fairy called the Ballybog. They are small brown fairies that live in the peat bogs. They are appeased with offerings to allow peat to be cut for fuel.

—Bryony Dwale

May

1 **Thursday**
Beltane • May Day
Waning Moon
Moon Phase: Fourth Quarter
Color: Purple

Moon Sign: Pisces
Incense: Mulberry

---

2 **Friday**
Big Kite Flying (Japanese)
Waning Moon
Moon Phase: Fourth Quarter
Color: White

Moon Sign: Pisces
Moon enters Aries 6:51 am
Incense: Cypress

---

3 **Saturday**
Holy Cross Day
Waning Moon
Moon Phase: Fourth Quarter
Color: Black

Moon Sign: Aries
Incense: Sandalwood

---

4 **Sunday**
Bona Dea (Roman)
Waning Moon
Moon Phase: Fourth Quarter
Color: Yellow

Moon Sign: Aries
Moon enters Taurus 7:58 am
Incense: Frankincense

---

5 **Monday**
Cinco de Mayo (Mexican)
Waning Moon
Moon Phase: New Moon 8:18 am
Color: Ivory

Moon Sign: Taurus
Incense: Hyssop

---

6 **Tuesday**
Martyrs' Day (Lebanese)
Waxing Moon
Moon Phase: First Quarter
Color: Scarlet

Moon Sign: Taurus
Moon enters Gemini 7:17 am
Incense: Bayberry

---

7 **Wednesday**
Pilgrimage of St. Nicholas (Italian)
Waxing Moon
Moon Phase: First Quarter
Color: Brown

Moon Sign: Gemini
Incense: Lilac

8 **Thursday**
Liberation Day (French)
Waxing Moon
Moon Phase: First Quarter
Color: Turquoise

Moon Sign: Gemini
Moon enters Cancer 7:02 am
Incense: Myrrh

9 **Friday**
Lemuria (Roman)
Waxing Moon
Moon Phase: First Quarter
Color: Rose

Moon Sign: Cancer
Incense: Vanilla

10 **Saturday**
First Day of Bird Week (Japanese)
Waxing Moon
Moon Phase: First Quarter
Color: Blue

Moon Sign: Cancer
Moon enters Leo 9:10 am
Incense: Pine

☽ **Sunday**
Mother's Day
Waxing Moon
Moon Phase: Second Quarter 11:47 pm
Color: Orange

Moon Sign: Leo
Incense: Marigold

12 **Monday**
Florence Nightingale's Birthday
Waxing Moon
Moon Phase: Second Quarter
Color: Silver

Moon Sign: Leo
Moon enters Virgo 2:48 pm
Incense: Narcissus

13 **Tuesday**
Pilgrimage to Fatima (Portuguese)
Waxing Moon
Moon Phase: Second Quarter
Color: Gray

Moon Sign: Virgo
Incense: Ginger

14 **Wednesday**
Carabao Festival (Spanish)
Waxing Moon
Moon Phase: Second Quarter
Color: Topaz

Moon Sign: Virgo
Moon enters Libra 11:46 pm
Incense: Honeysuckle

May

---

15 Thursday
Festival of St. Dympna (Belgian)
Waxing Moon
Moon Phase: Second Quarter
Color: White

Moon Sign: Libra
Incense: Clove

---

16 Friday
St. Honoratus' Day
Waxing Moon
Moon Phase: Second Quarter
Color: Coral

Moon Sign: Libra
Incense: Orchid

---

17 Saturday
Norwegian Independence Day
Waxing Moon
Moon Phase: Second Quarter
Color: Indigo

Moon Sign: Libra
Moon enters Scorpio 10:59 am
Incense: Rue

---

18 Sunday
Las Piedras Day (Uruguayan)
Waxing Moon
Moon Phase: Second Quarter
Color: Amber

Moon Sign: Scorpio
Incense: Hyacinth

Monday
Pilgrimage to Treguier (French)
Waxing Moon
Moon Phase: Full Moon 10:11 pm
Color: Lavender

Moon Sign: Scorpio
Moon enters Sagittarius 11:18 pm
Incense: Clary sage

---

20 Tuesday
Pardon of the Singers (British)
Waning Moon
Moon Phase: Third Quarter
Color: Red

Moon Sign: Sagittarius
Sun enters Gemini 12:01 pm
Incense: Ylang ylang

---

21 Wednesday
Victoria Day (Canadian)
Waning Moon
Moon Phase: Third Quarter
Color: White

Moon Sign: Sagittarius
Incense: Lavender

May

22 Thursday
Heroes' Day (Sri Lankan)
Waning Moon
Moon Phase: Third Quarter
Color: Green

Moon Sign: Sagittarius
Moon enters Capricorn 11:55 am
Incense: Jasmine

23 Friday
Tubilustrium (Roman)
Waning Moon
Moon Phase: Third Quarter
Color: Pink

Moon Sign: Capricorn
Incense: Thyme

24 Saturday
Culture Day (Bulgarian)
Waning Moon
Moon Phase: Third Quarter
Color: Gray

Moon Sign: Capricorn
Moon enters Aquarius 11:51 pm
Incense: Magnolia

25 Sunday
Lady Godiva's Day
Waning Moon
Moon Phase: Third Quarter
Color: Gold

Moon Sign: Aquarius
Incense: Almond

26 Monday
Memorial Day (Observed)
Waning Moon
Moon Phase: Third Quarter
Color: White

Moon Sign: Aquarius
Incense: Lily

◐ Tuesday
St. Augustine of Canterbury's Day
Waning Moon
Moon Phase: Fourth Quarter 10:56 pm
Color: Black

Moon Sign: Aquarius
Moon enters Pisces 9:38 am
Incense: Cinnamon

28 Wednesday
St. Germain's Day
Waning Moon
Moon Phase: Fourth Quarter
Color: Yellow

Moon Sign: Pisces
Incense: Bay laurel

May

29 Thursday
Royal Oak Day (English)
Waning Moon
Moon Phase: Fourth Quarter
Color: Crimson

Moon Sign: Pisces
Moon enters Aries 3:52 pm
Incense: Carnation

---

30 Friday
Memorial Day (actual)
Waning Moon
Moon Phase: Fourth Quarter
Color: Purple

Moon Sign: Aries
Incense: Yarrow

---

31 Saturday
Flowers of May
Waning Moon
Moon Phase: Fourth Quarter
Color: Indigo

Moon Sign: Aries
Moon enters Taurus 6:18 pm
Incense: Patchouli

German and Russian Fairies

In southern Germany the Wichtlien announce the death of a miner by tapping three times. When a disaster is about to occur, the Wichtlien are heard digging, pounding, and imitating the miner's work.

The domovoi are male Russian elves. In modern times, they live in apartments. The females are called domovikha. They help with household chores.

—Bryony Dwale

June

♊

1   Sunday
National Day (Tunisian)
Waning Moon
Moon Phase: Fourth Quarter
Color: Yellow

Moon Sign: Taurus
Incense: Heliotrope

---

2   Monday
Rice Harvest Festival (Malaysian)
Waning Moon
Moon Phase: Fourth Quarter
Color: Gray

Moon Sign: Taurus
Moon enters Gemini 6:06 pm
Incense: Rosemary

☽   Tuesday
Memorial to Broken Dolls (Japanese)
Waning Moon
Moon Phase: New Moon 3:22 pm
Color: Red

Moon Sign: Gemini
Incense: Cedar

---

4   Wednesday
Full Moon Day (Burmese)
Waxing Moon
Moon Phase: First Quarter
Color: Yellow

Moon Sign: Gemini
Moon enters Cancer 5:16 pm
Incense: Honeysuckle

---

5   Thursday
Constitution Day (Danish)
Waxing Moon
Moon Phase: First Quarter
Color: Green

Moon Sign: Cancer
Incense: Myrrh

---

6   Friday
Swedish Flag Day
Waxing Moon
Moon Phase: First Quarter
Color: White

Moon Sign: Cancer
Moon enters Leo 6:00 pm
Incense: Alder

---

7   Saturday
St. Robert of Newminster's Day
Waxing Moon
Moon Phase: First Quarter
Color: Brown

Moon Sign: Leo
Incense: Ivy

June

8   Sunday
St. Medard's Day (Belgian)   Moon Sign: Leo
Waxing Moon   Moon enters Virgo 10:01 pm
Moon Phase: First Quarter 7:43 am   Incense: Juniper
Color: Orange

9   Monday
Shavuot   Moon Sign: Virgo
Waxing Moon   Incense: Hyssop
Moon Phase: First Quarter
Color: Lavender

◖   Tuesday
Time-Observance Day (Chinese)   Moon Sign: Virgo
Waxing Moon   Incense: Basil
Moon Phase: Second Quarter 11:03 am
Color: White

11   Wednesday
Kamehameha Day (Hawaiian)   Moon Sign: Virgo
Waxing Moon   Moon enters Libra 5:55 am
Moon Phase: Second Quarter   Incense: Marjoram
Color: Brown

12   Thursday
Independence Day (Filipino)   Moon Sign: Libra
Waxing Moon   Incense: Balsam
Moon Phase: Second Quarter
Color: Turquoise

13   Friday
St. Anthony of Padua's Day   Moon Sign: Libra
Waxing Moon   Moon enters Scorpio 4:53 pm
Moon Phase: Second Quarter   Incense: Mint
Color: Pink

14   Saturday
Flag Day   Moon Sign: Scorpio
Waxing Moon   Incense: Sage
Moon Phase: Second Quarter
Color: Gray

15 Sunday
Father's Day
Waxing Moon
Moon Phase: Second Quarter
Color: Gold

Moon Sign: Scorpio
Incense: Almond

---

16 Monday
Bloomsday (Irish)
Waxing Moon
Moon Phase: Second Quarter
Color: White

Moon Sign: Scorpio
Moon enters Sagittarius 5:19 am
Incense: Neroli

---

17 Tuesday
Bunker Hill Day
Waxing Moon
Moon Phase: Second Quarter
Color: Black

Moon Sign: Sagittarius
Incense: Geranium

Wednesday
Independence Day (Egyptian)
Waxing Moon
Moon Phase: Full Moon 1:30 pm
Color: White

Moon Sign: Sagittarius
Moon enters Capricorn 5:51 pm
Incense: Lavender

---

19 Thursday
Juneteenth
Waning Moon
Moon Phase: Third Quarter
Color: Purple

Moon Sign: Capricorn
Incense: Mulberry

---

20 Friday
Litha • Summer Solstice
Waning Moon
Moon Phase: Third Quarter
Color: Rose

Moon Sign: Capricorn
Sun enters Cancer 7:59 pm
Incense: Rose

---

21 Saturday
U.S. Constitution ratified
Waning Moon
Moon Phase: Third Quarter
Color: Blue

Moon Sign: Capricorn
Moon enters Aquarius 5:33 am
Incense: Pine

22 Sunday
Rose Festival (English)
Waning Moon
Moon Phase: Third Quarter
Color: Amber

Moon Sign: Aquarius
Incense: Eucalyptus

---

23 Monday
St. John's Eve
Waning Moon
Moon Phase: Third Quarter
Color: Silver

Moon Sign: Aquarius
Moon enters Pisces 3:32 pm
Incense: Narcissus

---

24 Tuesday
St. John's Day
Waning Moon
Moon Phase: Third Quarter
Color: Gray

Moon Sign: Pisces
Incense: Bayberry

---

25 Wednesday
Fiesta of Santa Orosia (Spanish)
Waning Moon
Moon Phase: Third Quarter
Color: Topaz

Moon Sign: Pisces
Moon enters Aries 10:49 pm
Incense: Bay laurel

 Thursday
Pied Piper Day (German)
Waning Moon
Moon Phase: Fourth Quarter 8:10 am
Color: White

Moon Sign: Aries
Incense: Nutmeg

---

27 Friday
Day of the Seven Sleepers (Islamic)
Waning Moon
Moon Phase: Fourth Quarter
Color: Purple

Moon Sign: Aries
Incense: Cypress

---

28 Saturday
Paul Bunyan Day
Waning Moon
Moon Phase: Fourth Quarter
Color: Indigo

Moon Sign: Aries
Moon enters Taurus 2:50 am
Incense: Magnolia

29 Sunday
St. Peter and Paul's Day   Moon Sign: Taurus
Waning Moon   Incense: Marigold
Moon Phase: Fourth Quarter
Color: Yellow

30 Monday
The Burning of the Three Firs (French)   Moon Sign: Taurus
Waning Moon   Moon enters Gemini 4:03 am
Moon Phase: Fourth Quarter   Incense: Clary sage
Color: Ivory

꧁✤꧂

Scandinavian Fairies

In Finland, the Tomtra are a less benevolent fairy. They are brownies and tend to torment residents into becoming tidy. If the humans fail, then the Tomtra will leave and take away the family luck. Thursdays are their sacred day of rest. The Tomtra are skilled fiddle players and are heard playing during old festival nights.

The Fossegrim are Norwegian water fairies. Their forms disappear into a mist that covers where their feet should be. They are guardians of waterfalls and fjords. Furthermore, they can play exquisite harp music. They also have enthralling voices, which enchant mortals. The Fossegrim can change quickly from male to female.

—Bryony Dwale

1 Tuesday
Canada Day
Waning Moon
Moon Phase: Fourth Quarter
Color: Scarlet

Moon Sign: Gemini
Incense: Ginger

---

2 Wednesday
Heroes' Day (Zambian)
Waning Moon
Moon Phase: New Moon 10:18 pm
Color: Yellow

Moon Sign: Gemini
Moon enters Cancer 3:53 am
Incense: Lilac

---

3 Thursday
Indian Sun Dance (Native American)
Waning Moon
Moon Phase: First Quarter
Color: Turquoise

Moon Sign: Cancer
Incense: Carnation

---

4 Friday
Independence Day
Waxing Moon
Moon Phase: First Quarter
Color: Coral

Moon Sign: Cancer
Moon enters Leo 4:15 am
Incense: Violet

---

5 Saturday
Tynwald (Nordic)
Waxing Moon
Moon Phase: First Quarter
Color: Blue

Moon Sign: Leo
Incense: Rue

---

6 Sunday
Khao Phansa Day (Thai)
Waxing Moon
Moon Phase: First Quarter
Color: Orange

Moon Sign: Leo
Moon enters Virgo 7:04 am
Incense: Heliotrope

---

7 Monday
Weaver's Festival (Japanese)
Waxing Moon
Moon Phase: First Quarter
Color: Gray

Moon Sign: Virgo
Incense: Narcissus

8   Tuesday
St. Elizabeth's Day (Portuguese)
Waxing Moon
Moon Phase: First Quarter
Color: White

Moon Sign: Virgo
Moon enters Libra 1:31 pm
Incense: Ylang ylang

---

9   Wednesday
Battle of Sempach Day (Swiss)
Waxing Moon
Moon Phase: First Quarter
Color: Brown

Moon Sign: Libra
Incense: Bay laurel

☽   Thursday
Lady Godiva Day (English)
Waxing Moon
Moon Phase: Second Quarter 12:35 am
Color: Green

Moon Sign: Libra
Moon enters Scorpio 11:35 pm
Incense: Clove

---

11   Friday
Revolution Day (Mongolian)
Waxing Moon
Moon Phase: Second Quarter
Color: Pink

Moon Sign: Scorpio
Incense: Yarrow

---

12   Saturday
Lobster Carnival (Nova Scotian)
Waxing Moon
Moon Phase: Second Quarter
Color: Black

Moon Sign: Scorpio
Incense: Sandalwood

---

13   Sunday
Festival of the Three Cows (Spanish)
Waxing Moon
Moon Phase: Second Quarter
Color: Gold

Moon Sign: Scorpio
Moon enters Sagittarius 11:50 am
Incense: Hyacinth

---

14   Monday
Bastille Day (French)
Waxing Moon
Moon Phase: Second Quarter
Color: Silver

Moon Sign: Sagittarius
Incense: Lily

July

15 Tuesday
St. Swithin's Day
Waxing Moon
Moon Phase: Second Quarter
Color: Black

Moon Sign: Sagittarius
Incense: Cedar

---

16 Wednesday
Our Lady of Carmel
Waxing Moon
Moon Phase: Second Quarter
Color: White

Moon Sign: Sagittarius
Moon enters Capricorn 12:20 am
Incense: Lavender

---

17 Thursday
Rivera Day (Puerto Rican)
Waxing Moon
Moon Phase: Second Quarter
Color: Purple

Moon Sign: Capricorn
Incense: Apricot

Friday
Gion Matsuri Festival (Japanese)
Waxing Moon
Moon Phase: Full Moon 3:59 pm
Color: Rose

Moon Sign: Capricorn
Moon enters Aquarius 11:40 am
Incense: Thyme

---

19 Saturday
Flitch Day (English)
Waning Moon
Moon Phase: Third Quarter
Color: Brown

Moon Sign: Aquarius
Incense: Ivy

---

20 Sunday
Binding of Wreaths (Lithuanian)
Waning Moon
Moon Phase: Third Quarter
Color: Yellow

Moon Sign: Aquarius
Moon enters Pisces 9:07 pm
Incense: Frankincense

---

21 Monday
National Day (Belgian)
Waning Moon
Moon Phase: Third Quarter
Color: Lavender

Moon Sign: Pisces
Incense: Clary sage

July

22 Tuesday
St. Mary Magdalene's Day
Waning Moon
Moon Phase: Third Quarter
Color: Gray

Moon Sign: Pisces
Sun enters Leo 6:55 am
Incense: Cinnamon

23 Wednesday
Mysteries of Santa Cristina (Italian)
Waning Moon
Moon Phase: Third Quarter
Color: Topaz

Moon Sign: Pisces
Moon enters Aries 4:22 am
Incense: Marjoram

24 Thursday
Pioneer Day (Mormon)
Waning Moon
Moon Phase: Third Quarter
Color: White

Moon Sign: Aries
Incense: Nutmeg

○ Friday
St. James' Day
Waning Moon
Moon Phase: Fourth Quarter 2:41 pm
Color: Purple

Moon Sign: Aries
Moon enters Taurus 9:14 am
Incense: Vanilla

26 Saturday
St. Anne's Day
Waning Moon
Moon Phase: Fourth Quarter
Color: Indigo

Moon Sign: Taurus
Incense: Patchouli

27 Sunday
Sleepyhead Day (Finnish)
Waning Moon
Moon Phase: Fourth Quarter
Color: Amber

Moon Sign: Taurus
Moon enters Gemini 11:55 am
Incense: Juniper

28 Monday
Independence Day (Peruvian)
Waning Moon
Moon Phase: Fourth Quarter
Color: Ivory

Moon Sign: Gemini
Incense: Rosemary

July

29   Tuesday
Pardon of the Birds (French)   Moon Sign: Gemini
Waning Moon   Moon enters Cancer 1:11 pm
Moon Phase: Fourth Quarter   Incense: Basil
Color: Red

---

30   Wednesday
Micmac Festival of St. Ann   Moon Sign: Cancer
Waning Moon   Incense: Honeysuckle
Moon Phase: Fourth Quarter
Color: Yellow

---

31   Thursday
Weighing of the Aga Khan   Moon Sign: Cancer
Waning Moon   Moon enters Leo 2:21 pm
Moon Phase: Fourth Quarter   Incense: Jasmine
Color: Crimson

South American Spirits

Duendes are Spanish, Mexican, and South American house spirits. Duendes are hostile to humans who inhabit homes. They look like small middle-aged women dressed in green who poke and prod residents with their long fingers at night. They are motivated by envy and it is said exorcism does not work because they are insistent.

In South America, Cururipur is a spirit of the rain forest and jungle. Cururipur is a guardian of wild creatures, in particular tortoises, whom he protects from hunters.

—Bryony Dwale

 **Friday**
Lammas
Waning Moon
Moon Phase: New Moon 6:12 am
Color: Rose

Moon Sign: Leo
Incense: Orchid

---

2 **Saturday**
Porcingula (Native American)
Waxing Moon
Moon Phase: First Quarter
Color: Brown

Moon Sign: Leo
Moon enters Virgo 4:59 pm
Incense: Pine

---

3 **Sunday**
Drimes (Greek)
Waxing Moon
Moon Phase: First Quarter
Color: Gold

Moon Sign: Virgo
Incense: Marigold

---

4 **Monday**
Cook Islands Constitution Celebration
Waxing Moon
Moon Phase: First Quarter
Color: Silver

Moon Sign: Virgo
Moon enters Libra 10:28 pm
Incense: Lily

---

5 **Tuesday**
Benediction of the Sea (French)
Waxing Moon
Moon Phase: First Quarter
Color: White

Moon Sign: Libra
Incense: Geranium

---

6 **Wednesday**
Hiroshima Peace Ceremony
Waxing Moon
Moon Phase: First Quarter
Color: Yellow

Moon Sign: Libra
Incense: Marjoram

---

7 **Thursday**
Republic Day (Ivory Coast)
Waxing Moon
Moon Phase: First Quarter
Color: Green

Moon Sign: Libra
Moon enters Scorpio 7:26 am
Incense: Apricot

August

○ **Friday**
Dog Days (Japanese)
Waxing Moon
Moon Phase: Second Quarter 4:20 pm
Color: White

Moon Sign: Scorpio
Incense: Alder

---

9 **Saturday**
Nagasaki Peace Ceremony
Waxing Moon
Moon Phase: Second Quarter
Color: Gray

Moon Sign: Scorpio
Moon enters Sagittarius 7:10 pm
Incense: Magnolia

---

10 **Sunday**
St. Lawrence's Day
Waxing Moon
Moon Phase: Second Quarter
Color: Yellow

Moon Sign: Sagittarius
Incense: Eucalyptus

---

11 **Monday**
Puck Fair (Irish)
Waxing Moon
Moon Phase: Second Quarter
Color: White

Moon Sign: Sagittarius
Incense: Neroli

---

12 **Tuesday**
Fiesta of Santa Clara
Waxing Moon
Moon Phase: Second Quarter
Color: Black

Moon Sign: Sagittarius
Moon enters Capricorn 7:42 am
Incense: Bayberry

---

13 **Wednesday**
Women's Day (Tunisian)
Waxing Moon
Moon Phase: Second Quarter
Color: Brown

Moon Sign: Capricorn
Incense: Bay laurel

---

14 **Thursday**
Festival at Sassari
Waxing Moon
Moon Phase: Second Quarter
Color: Turquoise

Moon Sign: Capricorn
Moon enters Aquarius 6:56 pm
Incense: Carnation

15 Friday
Assumption Day
Waxing Moon
Moon Phase: Second Quarter
Color: Pink

Moon Sign: Aquarius
Incense: Cypress

Saturday
Festival of Minstrels (European)
Waxing Moon
Moon Phase: Full Moon 5:16 pm
Color: Blue

Moon Sign: Aquarius
Incense: Sandalwood

---

17 Sunday
Feast of the Hungry Ghosts (Chinese)
Waning Moon
Moon Phase: Third Quarter
Color: Amber

Moon Sign: Aquarius
Moon enters Pisces 3:46 am
Incense: Almond

---

18 Monday
St. Helen's Day
Waning Moon
Moon Phase: Third Quarter
Color: Black

Moon Sign: Pisces
Incense: Hyssop

---

19 Tuesday
Rustic Vinalia (Roman)
Waning Moon
Moon Phase: Third Quarter
Color: Gray

Moon Sign: Pisces
Moon enters Aries 10:10 am
Incense: Basil

---

20 Wednesday
Constitution Day (Hungarian)
Waning Moon
Moon Phase: Third Quarter
Color: Topaz

Moon Sign: Aries
Incense: Lilac

---

21 Thursday
Consualia (Roman)
Waning Moon
Moon Phase: Third Quarter
Color: Green

Moon Sign: Aries
Moon enters Taurus 2:38 pm
Incense: Balsam

August

22 Friday
Feast of the Queenship of Mary (English)
Waning Moon
Moon Phase: Third Quarter
Color: Purple

Moon Sign: Taurus
Sun enters Virgo 2:02 pm
Incense: Rose

Saturday
National Day (Romanian)
Waning Moon
Moon Phase: Fourth Quarter 7:49 pm
Color: Black

Moon Sign: Taurus
Moon enters Gemini 5:48 pm
Incense: Sage

---

24 Sunday
St. Bartholomew's Day
Waning Moon
Moon Phase: Fourth Quarter
Color: Orange

Moon Sign: Gemini
Incense: Hyacinth

---

25 Monday
Feast of the Green Corn (Native American)
Waning Moon
Moon Phase: Fourth Quarter
Color: Lavender

Moon Sign: Gemini
Moon enters Cancer 8:18 pm
Incense: Narcissus

---

26 Tuesday
Pardon of the Sea (French)
Waning Moon
Moon Phase: Fourth Quarter
Color: Scarlet

Moon Sign: Cancer
Incense: Ginger

---

27 Wednesday
Summer Break (English)
Waning Moon
Moon Phase: Fourth Quarter
Color: Yellow

Moon Sign: Cancer
Moon enters Leo 10:51 pm
Incense: Lavender

---

28 Thursday
St. Augustine's Day
Waning Moon
Moon Phase: Fourth Quarter
Color: Purple

Moon Sign: Leo
Incense: Clove

29 Friday
St. John's Beheading   Moon Sign: Leo
Waning Moon   Incense: Mint
Moon Phase: Fourth Quarter
Color: Coral

☽ Saturday
St. Rose of Lima Day (Peruvian)   Moon Sign: Leo
Waning Moon   Moon enters Virgo 2:18 am
Moon Phase: New Moon 3:58 pm   Incense: Rue
Color: Indigo

---

31 Sunday
Unto These Hills Pageant (Cherokee)   Moon Sign: Virgo
Waxing Moon   Incense: Frankincense
Moon Phase: First Quarter
Color: Gold

~❦~

Fairies in North America

The Manitou are antlered fairies indigenous to the Algonquin tribe in eastern North America. The Manitou are said to practice drum magic.

The Native American male spirit is called Bokwus. This spirit is found in spruce forests in the vicinity of rushing water. They are distinguished by the fierce war paint on their faces and can seek to drown the unwary.

—Bryony Dwale

September

♍

1 Monday
Labor Day (observed)
Waxing Moon
Moon Phase: First Quarter
Color: Silver

Moon Sign: Virgo
Moon enters Libra 7:44 am
Incense: Rosemary

---

2 Tuesday
Ramadan begins
Waxing Moon
Moon Phase: First Quarter
Color: Gray

Moon Sign: Libra
Incense: Ylang ylang

---

3 Wednesday
Founder's Day (San Marino)
Waxing Moon
Moon Phase: First Quarter 10:32 pm
Color: Brown

Moon Sign: Libra
Moon enters Scorpio 4:02 pm
Incense: Honeysuckle

---

4 Thursday
Los Angeles' Birthday
Waxing Moon
Moon Phase: First Quarter
Color: Turquoise

Moon Sign: Scorpio
Incense: Nutmeg

---

5 Friday
Roman Circus
Waxing Moon
Moon Phase: First Quarter
Color: Pink

Moon Sign: Scorpio
Incense: Thyme

---

6 Saturday
The Virgin of Remedies (Spanish)
Waxing Moon
Moon Phase: First Quarter
Color: Blue

Moon Sign: Scorpio
Moon enters Sagittarius 3:11 am
Incense: Sage

☽ Sunday
Festival of the Durga (Hindu)
Waxing Moon
Moon Phase: Second Quarter 10:04 am
Color: Amber

Moon Sign: Sagittarius
Incense: Eucalyptus

September ♍

8 Monday
Birthday of the Virgin Mary
Waxing Moon
Moon Phase: Second Quarter
Color: Ivory

Moon Sign: Sagittarius
Moon enters Capricorn 3:45 pm
Incense: Clary sage

9 Tuesday
Chrysanthemum Festival (Japanese)
Waxing Moon
Moon Phase: Second Quarter
Color: Maroon

Moon Sign: Capricorn
Incense: Cinnamon

10 Wednesday
Festival of the Poets (Japanese)
Waxing Moon
Moon Phase: Second Quarter
Color: Topaz

Moon Sign: Capricorn
Incense: Bay laurel

11 Thursday
Coptic New Year
Waxing Moon
Moon Phase: Second Quarter
Color: White

Moon Sign: Capricorn
Moon enters Aquarius 3:19 am
Incense: Apricot

12 Friday
National Day (Ethiopian)
Waxing Moon
Moon Phase: Second Quarter
Color: Rose

Moon Sign: Aquarius
Incense: Vanilla

13 Saturday
The God's Banquet (Roman)
Waxing Moon
Moon Phase: Second Quarter
Color: Gray

Moon Sign: Aquarius
Moon enters Pisces 12:04 pm
Incense: Ivy

14 Sunday
Holy Cross Day
Waxing Moon
Moon Phase: Second Quarter
Color: Orange

Moon Sign: Pisces
Incense: Juniper

September ♍

☺ **Monday**
Birthday of the Moon (Chinese)
Waxing Moon
Moon Phase: Full Moon 5:13 am
Color: Lavender

Moon Sign: Pisces
Moon enters Aries 5:39 pm
Incense: Narcissus

---

16 **Tuesday**
Mexican Independence Day
Waning Moon
Moon Phase: Third Quarter
Color: Black

Moon Sign: Aries
Incense: Cedar

---

17 **Wednesday**
Von Steuben's Day
Waning Moon
Moon Phase: Third Quarter
Color: Yellow

Moon Sign: Aries
Moon enters Taurus 8:56 pm
Incense: Lavender

---

18 **Thursday**
Dr. Johnson's Birthday
Waning Moon
Moon Phase: Third Quarter
Color: Purple

Moon Sign: Taurus
Incense: Carnation

---

19 **Friday**
St. Januarius' Day (Italian)
Waning Moon
Moon Phase: Third Quarter
Color: White

Moon Sign: Taurus
Moon enters Gemini 11:17 pm
Incense: Yarrow

---

20 **Saturday**
St. Eustace's Day
Waning Moon
Moon Phase: Third Quarter
Color: Indigo

Moon Sign: Gemini
Incense: Rue

---

21 **Sunday**
Christ's Hospital Founder's Day (British)
Waning Moon
Moon Phase: Third Quarter
Color: Yellow

Moon Sign: Gemini
Incense: Heliotrope

September

○ **Monday**
Mabon • Fall Equinox
Waxing Moon
Moon Phase: Fourth Quarter 1:04 am
Color: Gray

Moon Sign: Gemini
Moon enters Cancer 1:48 am
Sun enters Libra 11:44 am
Incense: Neroli

---

23 **Tuesday**
Shubun no Hi (Chinese)
Waxing Moon
Moon Phase: Fourth Quarter
Color: White

Moon Sign: Cancer
Incense: Geranium

---

24 **Wednesday**
Schwenkenfelder Thanksgiving (Germ.-Amer.)
Waxing Moon
Moon Phase: Fourth Quarter
Color: Brown

Moon Sign: Cancer
Moon enters Leo 5:13 am
Incense: Lilac

---

25 **Thursday**
Doll's Memorial Service (Japanese)
Waxing Moon
Moon Phase: Fourth Quarter
Color: Green

Moon Sign: Leo
Incense: Mulberry

---

26 **Friday**
Feast of Santa Justina (Mexican)
Waxing Moon
Moon Phase: Fourth Quarter
Color: Purple

Moon Sign: Leo
Moon enters Virgo 9:52 am
Incense: Violet

---

27 **Saturday**
Saints Cosmas and Damian's Day
Waning Moon
Moon Phase: Fourth Quarter
Color: Blue

Moon Sign: Virgo
Incense: Patchouli

---

28 **Sunday**
Confucius' Birthday
Waning Moon
Moon Phase: Fourth Quarter
Color: Gold

Moon Sign: Virgo
Moon enters Libra 4:05 pm
Incense: Marigold

Monday
Michaelmas
Waning Moon
Moon Phase: New Moon 4:12 am
Color: Silver

Moon Sign: Libra
Incense: Hyssop

30 Tuesday
Rosh Hashanah
Waning Moon
Moon Phase: First Quarter
Color: Red

Moon Sign: Libra
Incense: Cinnamon

Fairies in Eastern Europe

Ieles are eastern European vampire fairies. They appear at night like a huge two-legged cat. They are associated with crossroads, traditional places of magical powers, and they lure their victims with enticing singing.

The Luume is a Lithuanian fairy often known to help the poor and orphans. She spins and weaves (kind of like the Grecian three fates) and rules over the fate of men. In Latvia she goes by the name of "White Lady."

In Portugal, the Moors are fairies who live in rocky hills above rivers and underground in palaces. They are powerful on the night of a Full Moon when you can hear their charming singing. Humans fear they would take away their children.

—Bryony Dwale

October

1   Wednesday
Armed Forces Day (South Korean)   Moon Sign: Libra
Waxing Moon   Moon enters Scorpio 12:26 am
Moon Phase: First Quarter   Incense: Marjoram
Color: Brown

---

2   Thursday
Ramadan ends   Moon Sign: Scorpio
Waxing Moon   Incense: Jasmine
Moon Phase: First Quarter
Color: Green

---

3   Friday
Moroccan New Year's Day   Moon Sign: Scorpio
Waxing Moon   Moon enters Sagittarius 11:14 am
Moon Phase: First Quarter   Incense: Mint
Color: Purple

---

4   Saturday
St. Francis' Day   Moon Sign: Sagittarius
Waxing Moon   Incense: Magnolia
Moon Phase: First Quarter
Color: Gray

---

5   Sunday
Republic Day (Portuguese)   Moon Sign: Sagittarius
Waxing Moon   Moon enters Capricorn 11:48 pm
Moon Phase: First Quarter   Incense: Almond
Color: Gold

---

6   Monday
Dedication of the Virgin's Crowns (English)   Moon Sign: Capricorn
Waxing Moon   Incense: Lily
Moon Phase: First Quarter
Color: Lavender

☾   Tuesday
Kermesse (German)   Moon Sign: Capricorn
Waxing Moon   Incense: Basil
Moon Phase: Second Quarter 5:04 am
Color: Maroon

October

8 Wednesday
Okunchi (Japanese)
Waxing Moon
Moon Phase: Second Quarter
Color: White

Moon Sign: Capricorn
Moon enters Aquarius 12:03 pm
Incense: Lavender

9 Thursday
Yom Kippur
Waxing Moon
Moon Phase: Second Quarter
Color: Purple

Moon Sign: Aquarius
Incense: Balsam

10 Friday
Health Day (Japanese)
Waxing Moon
Moon Phase: Second Quarter
Color: Pink

Moon Sign: Aquarius
Moon enters Pisces 9:31 pm
Incense: Cypress

11 Saturday
Medetrinalia (Roman)
Waxing Moon
Moon Phase: Second Quarter
Color: Brown

Moon Sign: Pisces
Incense: Pine

12 Sunday
National Day (Spanish)
Waxing Moon
Moon Phase: Second Quarter
Color: Amber

Moon Sign: Pisces
Incense: Frankincense

13 Monday
Columbus Day (observed)
Waxing Moon
Moon Phase: Second Quarter
Color: Ivory

Moon Sign: Pisces
Moon enters Aries 3:07 am
Incense: Hyssop

☻ Tuesday
Sukkot begins
Waxing Moon
Moon Phase: Full Moon 4:02 pm
Color: Black

Moon Sign: Aries
Incense: Ylang ylang

15 Wednesday
The October Horse (Roman)
Waning Moon
Moon Phase: Third Quarter
Color: Topaz

Moon Sign: Aries
Moon enters Taurus 5:31 am
Incense: Bay laurel

---

16 Thursday
The Lion Sermon (British)
Waning Moon
Moon Phase: Third Quarter
Color: White

Moon Sign: Taurus
Incense: Mulberry

---

17 Friday
Pilgrimage to Paray-le-Monial
Waning Moon
Moon Phase: Third Quarter
Color: Rose

Moon Sign: Taurus
Moon enters Gemini 6:25 am
Incense: Alder

---

18 Saturday
Brooklyn Barbeque
Waning Moon
Moon Phase: Third Quarter
Color: Black

Moon Sign: Gemini
Incense: Sandalwood

---

19 Sunday
Our Lord of Miracles Procession (Peruvian)
Waning Moon
Moon Phase: Third Quarter
Color: Orange

Moon Sign: Gemini
Moon enters Cancer 7:40 am
Incense: Hyacinth

---

20 Monday
Sukkot ends
Waning Moon
Moon Phase: Third Quarter
Color: Silver

Moon Sign: Cancer
Incense: Rosemary

○ Tuesday
Feast of the Black Christ
Waning Moon
Moon Phase: Fourth Quarter 7:54 am
Color: White

Moon Sign: Cancer
Moon enters Leo 10:35 am
Incense: Ginger

22   Wednesday
Goddess of Mercy Day (Chinese)   Moon Sign: Leo
Waning Moon   Sun enters Scorpio 9:08 pm
Moon Phase: Fourth Quarter   Incense: Honeysuckle
Color: Yellow

23   Thursday
Revolution Day (Hungarian)   Moon Sign: Leo
Waning Moon   Moon enters Virgo 3:40 pm
Moon Phase: Fourth Quarter   Incense: Clove
Color: Crimson

24   Friday
United Nations Day   Moon Sign: Virgo
Waning Moon   Incense: Rose
Moon Phase: Fourth Quarter
Color: White

25   Saturday
St. Crispin's Day   Moon Sign: Virgo
Waning Moon   Moon enters Libra 10:47 pm
Moon Phase: Fourth Quarter   Incense: Ivy
Color: Blue

26   Sunday
Quit Rent Ceremony (England)   Moon Sign: Libra
Waning Moon   Incense: Juniper
Moon Phase: Fourth Quarter
Color: Yellow

27   Monday
Feast of the Holy Souls   Moon Sign: Libra
Waning Moon   Incense: Clary sage
Moon Phase: Fourth Quarter
Color: Gray

☽   Tuesday
Ochi Day (Greek)   Moon Sign: Libra
Waning Moon   Moon enters Scorpio 7:47 am
Moon Phase: New Moon 7:14 pm   Incense: Cedar
Color: Red

29 Wednesday
Iroquois Feast of the Dead
Waxing Moon
Moon Phase: First Quarter
Color: Brown

Moon Sign: Scorpio
Incense: Lilac

---

30 Thursday
Meiji Festival (Japanese)
Waxing Moon
Moon Phase: First Quarter
Color: Turquoise

Moon Sign: Scorpio
Moon enters Sagittarius 6:41 pm
Incense: Myrrh

---

31 Friday
Halloween • Samhain
Waxing Moon
Moon Phase: First Quarter
Color: Coral

Moon Sign: Sagittarius
Incense: Orchid

Fairies of Africa

Yumboes are silver-haired fairies from Senegal in West Africa. The Yumboes hold moonlight revels. Their homes are exotic palaces beneath the hills.

In southern Africa, the fairy Abatwa is a small fairy who lives in anthills. Children and pregnant women are prone to see this particular fairy.

—Bryony Dwale

November

1 Saturday
All Saints' Day
Waxing Moon
Moon Phase: First Quarter
Color: Indigo

Moon Sign: Sagittarius
Incense: Sage

---

2 Sunday
Daylight Saving Time ends • All Soul's Day
Waxing Moon
Moon Phase: First Quarter
Color: Yellow

Moon Sign: Sagittarius
Moon enters Capricorn 6:13 am
Incense: Hyacinth

---

3 Monday
St. Hubert's Day (Belgian)
Waxing Moon
Moon Phase: First Quarter
Color: Silver

Moon Sign: Capricorn
Incense: Neroli

---

4 Tuesday
Election Day (general)
Waxing Moon
Moon Phase: First Quarter
Color: Maroon

Moon Sign: Capricorn
Moon enters Aquarius 7:01 pm
Incense: Cinnamon

☽ Wednesday
Guy Fawkes Night (British)
Waxing Moon
Moon Phase: Second Quarter 11:03 pm
Color: Topaz

Moon Sign: Aquarius
Incense: Lilac

---

6 Thursday
Leonard's Ride (German)
Waxing Moon
Moon Phase: Second Quarter
Color: Green

Moon Sign: Aquarius
Incense: Carnation

---

7 Friday
Mayan Day of the Dead
Waxing Moon
Moon Phase: Second Quarter
Color: White

Moon Sign: Aquarius
Moon enters Pisces 5:43 am
Incense: Vanilla

November

♏

8   Saturday
The Lord Mayor's Show (English)
Waxing Moon
Moon Phase: Second Quarter
Color: Brown

Moon Sign: Pisces
Incense: Rue

---

9   Sunday
Lord Mayor's Day (British)
Waxing Moon
Moon Phase: Second Quarter
Color: Orange

Moon Sign: Pisces
Moon enters Aries 12:26 pm
Incense: Heliotrope

---

10   Monday
Martin Luther's Birthday
Waxing Moon
Moon Phase: Second Quarter
Color: Ivory

Moon Sign: Aries
Incense: Lily

---

11   Tuesday
Veterans Day
Waxing Moon
Moon Phase: Second Quarter
Color: White

Moon Sign: Aries
Moon enters Taurus 3:05 pm
Incense: Bayberry

---

12   Wednesday
Tesuque Feast Day (Native American)
Waxing Moon
Moon Phase: Second Quarter
Color: Yellow

Moon Sign: Taurus
Incense: Lavender

☺   Thursday
Festival of Jupiter (Roman)
Waxing Moon
Moon Phase: Full Moon 1:17 am
Color: Crimson

Moon Sign: Taurus
Moon enters Gemini 3:11 pm
Incense: Apricot

---

14   Friday
The Little Carnival (Greek)
Waning Moon
Moon Phase: Third Quarter
Color: Rose

Moon Sign: Gemini
Incense: Rose

November ♏

15 Saturday
St. Leopold's Day
Waning Moon
Moon Phase: Third Quarter
Color: Blue

Moon Sign: Gemini
Moon enters Cancer 2:52 pm
Incense: Patchouli

---

16 Sunday
St. Margaret of Scotland's Day
Waning Moon
Moon Phase: Third Quarter
Color: Amber

Moon Sign: Cancer
Incense: Marigold

---

17 Monday
Queen Elizabeth's Day
Waning Moon
Moon Phase: Third Quarter
Color: Lavender

Moon Sign: Cancer
Moon enters Leo 4:07 pm
Incense: Narcissus

---

18 Tuesday
St. Plato's Day
Waning Moon
Moon Phase: Third Quarter
Color: Red

Moon Sign: Leo
Incense: Geranium

☽ Wednesday
Garifuna Day (Belizian)
Waning Moon
Moon Phase: Fourth Quarter 4:31 pm
Color: White

Moon Sign: Leo
Moon enters Virgo 8:12 pm
Incense: Marjoram

---

20 Thursday
Commerce God Ceremony (Japanese)
Waning Moon
Moon Phase: Fourth Quarter
Color: Turquoise

Moon Sign: Virgo
Incense: Nutmeg

---

21 Friday
Repentance Day (German)
Waning Moon
Moon Phase: Fourth Quarter
Color: Pink

Moon Sign: Virgo
Sun enters Sagittarius 5:44 pm
Incense: Yarrow

November

22 Saturday
St. Cecilia's Day
Waning Moon
Moon Phase: Fourth Quarter
Color: Black

Moon Sign: Virgo
Moon enters Libra 3:20 am
Incense: Ivy

23 Sunday
St. Clement's Day
Waning Moon
Moon Phase: Fourth Quarter
Color: Gold

Moon Sign: Libra
Incense: Eucalyptus

24 Monday
Feast of the Burning Lamps (Egyptian)
Waning Moon
Moon Phase: Fourth Quarter
Color: White

Moon Sign: Libra
Moon enters Scorpio 12:54 pm
Incense: Hyssop

25 Tuesday
St. Catherine of Alexandria's Day
Waning Moon
Moon Phase: Fourth Quarter
Color: Gray

Moon Sign: Scorpio
Incense: Basil

26 Wednesday
Festival of Lights (Tibetan)
Waning Moon
Moon Phase: Fourth Quarter
Color: Yellow

Moon Sign: Scorpio
Incense: Honeysuckle

☽ Thursday
Thanksgiving Day
Waning Moon
Moon Phase: New Moon 11:54 am
Color: Green

Moon Sign: Scorpio
Moon enters Sagittarius 12:14 am
Incense: Balsam

28 Friday
Day of the New Dance (Tibetan)
Waxing Moon
Moon Phase: First Quarter
Color: Purple

Moon Sign: Sagittarius
Incense: Mint

29 Saturday
Tubman's Birthday (Liberian)　　　　　Moon Sign: Sagittarius
Waxing Moon　　　　Moon enters Capricorn 12:48 pm
Moon Phase: First Quarter　　　　　　Incense: Sandalwood
Color: Blue

30 Sunday
St. Andrew's Day　　　　　　　　　Moon Sign: Capricorn
Waxing Moon　　　　　　　　　　　　Incense: Juniper
Moon Phase: First Quarter
Color: Yellow

Fairies of Italy and Japan

In Italy, the Folletti are benign female fairies of the air. They can shape-shift into butterflies and travel on the wind. When traveling on the wind they can sometimes cause dust clouds.

Gianes are solitary Italian Wood Elves. They are famed for their weaving ability and divination by using the movement of a spinning wheel to create images. Mortals try to use this form of divination to invoke the wisdom of the Gianes.

Tengu are Japanese winged woodland fairies. They carry fans made of feathers. They can shape-shift into woodland animals. The Tengu have little contact with humans.

—Bryony Dwale

December

1 Monday
Big Tea Party (Japanese)
Waxing Moon
Moon Phase: First Quarter
Color: Lavender

Moon Sign: Capricorn
Incense: Lily

2 Tuesday
Republic Day (Laotian)
Waxing Moon
Moon Phase: First Quarter
Color: Gray

Moon Sign: Capricorn
Moon enters Aquarius 1:44 am
Incense: Cedar

3 Wednesday
St. Francis Xavier's Day
Waxing Moon
Moon Phase: First Quarter
Color: Brown

Moon Sign: Aquarius
Incense: Bay laurel

4 Thursday
St. Barbara's Day
Waxing Moon
Moon Phase: First Quarter
Color: Green

Moon Sign: Aquarius
Moon enters Pisces 1:23 pm
Incense: Jasmine

☽ Friday
Eve of St. Nicholas' Day
Waxing Moon
Moon Phase: Second Quarter 4:25 pm
Color: White

Moon Sign: Pisces
Incense: Violet

6 Saturday
St. Nicholas' Day
Waxing Moon
Moon Phase: Second Quarter
Color: Indigo

Moon Sign: Pisces
Moon enters Aries 9:44 pm
Incense: Pine

7 Sunday
Burning the Devil (Guatemalan)
Waxing Moon
Moon Phase: Second Quarter
Color: Amber

Moon Sign: Aries
Incense: Frankincense

December

8 **Monday**
Feast of the Immaculate Conception
Waxing Moon
Moon Phase: Second Quarter
Color: White

Moon Sign: Aries
Incense: Rosemary

---

9 **Tuesday**
St. Leocadia's Day
Waxing Moon
Moon Phase: Second Quarter
Color: Maroon

Moon Sign: Aries
Moon enters Taurus 1:52 am
Incense: Ginger

---

10 **Wednesday**
Nobel Day
Waxing Moon
Moon Phase: Second Quarter
Color: Yellow

Moon Sign: Taurus
Incense: Honeysuckle

---

11 **Thursday**
Pilgrimage at Tortugas
Waxing Moon
Moon Phase: Second Quarter
Color: Turquoise

Moon Sign: Taurus
Moon enters Gemini 2:33 am
Incense: Myrrh

☺ **Friday**
Fiesta of Our Lady of Guadalupe
Waxing Moon
Moon Phase: Full Moon 11:37 am
Color: Pink

Moon Sign: Gemini
Incense: Cypress

---

13 **Saturday**
St. Lucy's Day (Swedish)
Waning Moon
Moon Phase: Third Quarter
Color: Blue

Moon Sign: Gemini
Moon enters Cancer 1:39 am
Incense: Magnolia

---

14 **Sunday**
Warriors' Memorial (Japanese)
Waning Moon
Moon Phase: Third Quarter
Color: Orange

Moon Sign: Cancer
Incense: Almond

15 Monday
Consualia (Roman)
Waning Moon
Moon Phase: Third Quarter
Color: Gray

Moon Sign: Cancer
Moon enters Leo 1:22 am
Incense: Clary sage

16 Tuesday
Posadas (Mexican)
Waning Moon
Moon Phase: Third Quarter
Color: Red

Moon Sign: Leo
Incense: Ylang ylang

17 Wednesday
Saturnalia (Roman)
Waning Moon
Moon Phase: Third Quarter
Color: Topaz

Moon Sign: Leo
Moon enters Virgo 3:35 am
Incense: Marjoram

18 Thursday
Feast of the Virgin of Solitude
Waning Moon
Moon Phase: Third Quarter
Color: Crimson

Moon Sign: Virgo
Incense: Clove

Friday
Opalia (Roman)
Waning Moon
Moon Phase: Fourth Quarter 5:29 am
Color: Purple

Moon Sign: Virgo
Moon enters Libra 9:23 am
Incense: Orchid

20 Saturday
Commerce God Festival (Japanese)
Waning Moon
Moon Phase: Fourth Quarter
Color: Black

Moon Sign: Libra
Incense: Sandalwood

21 Sunday
Yule • Winter Solstice
Waning Moon
Moon Phase: Fourth Quarter
Color: Gold

Moon Sign: Libra
Sun enters Capricorn 7:04 am
Moon enters Scorpio 6:36 pm
Incense: Hyacinth

December

22   Monday
Hanukkah begins   Moon Sign: Scorpio
Waning Moon   Incense: Neroli
Moon Phase: Fourth Quarter
Color: Silver

23   Tuesday
Larentalia (Roman)   Moon Sign: Scorpio
Waning Moon   Incense: Bayberry
Moon Phase: Fourth Quarter
Color: Black

24   Wednesday
Christmas Eve   Moon Sign: Scorpio
Waning Moon   Moon enters Sagittarius 6:13 am
Moon Phase: Fourth Quarter   Incense: Lilac
Color: White

25   Thursday
Christmas Day   Moon Sign: Sagittarius
Waning Moon   Incense: Mulberry
Moon Phase: Fourth Quarter
Color: Purple

26   Friday
Kwanzaa begins   Moon Sign: Sagittarius
Waning Moon   Moon enters Capricorn 6:56 pm
Moon Phase: Fourth Quarter   Incense: Thyme
Color: Coral

☽   Saturday
Boar's Head Supper (English)   Moon Sign: Capricorn
Waning Moon   Incense: Sage
Moon Phase: New Moon 7:22 am
Color: Indigo

28   Sunday
Holy Innocents' Day   Moon Sign: Capricorn
Waxing Moon   Incense: Marigold
Moon Phase: First Quarter
Color: Yellow

29 Monday
Hanukkah ends • Islamic New Year
Waxing Moon
Moon Phase: First Quarter
Color: Ivory

Moon Sign: Capricorn
Moon enters Aquarius 7:42 am
Incense: Narcissus

30 Tuesday
Republic Day (Madagascar)
Waxing Moon
Moon Phase: First Quarter
Color: White

Moon Sign: Aquarius
Incense: Cinnamon

31 Wednesday
New Year's Eve
Waxing Moon
Moon Phase: First Quarter
Color: Topaz

Moon Sign: Aquarius
Moon enters Pisces 7:27 pm
Incense: Lavender

Mideast Fairies

The Mazikeen are winged Jewish Fairies. They were the offspring of Adam and Eve after the Fall. They were supposedly created from a union with spirits. The Mazikeen are expert shape-shifters, are skilled in magical arts and are seers.

The Ekimmu are an ancient Assyrian spirit. This spirit wails before a death, like a Bean Sidhe of Ireland, and can inflict vengeance on those who commit murder.

—Bryony Dwale

Fire Magic

Summer: The Realm of Fire

by Sorita D'Este

Fire, with creative and destructive power contained within every flame, is likely the most challenging element. Fire represents transformation, both in the substances that burn and in the environment around it, as the flames supply both light and heat. It burns with a passion and energy reflected in the human spirit—the purity of fire is akin to our motivation and will, the drive to succeed and shine our own light.

Through the light of fire we receive the illumination we need to follow our paths, giving us the energy to refine our passions and strive for our goals. Fire can leap up and die down again just as suddenly, bringing spontaneity in its flames. It is called the "living element" as its dance is reminiscent of our own dance of life.

In the summer, the heat of the Sun's fire is most present, and the energy of fire fills our bodies and our lives. We spring into activity, motivated by the increased light to do more,

and express the fire of our will in working toward success in achieving our goals.

Creatures associated with fire, such as salamanders and desert beings, are adapted to live in its harsh environment. The salamanders (or Vulcans) of fire appear as dancing flames, or as tall and powerfully built humans. The Ruler of Fire usually appears as a tall and striking red-haired man with flaming eyes and strong musculature. He wears a scarlet robe and is crowned with a wreath of red poppies. He expresses the human form of salamanders.

One of the fieriest creatures, the phoenix (or firebird), was said to burn in its own fire every 500 years. In the ashes, an egg was formed and from it the phoenix would hatch to be reborn again.

Meditation

Make sure you are sitting comfortably and that you won't be disturbed. Light a red candle and gaze into the flame for a while, observing the different colors in the flame. Close your eyes and allow the image of the flame to continue dancing in your mind's eye. In the flame, see a red pentagram, pointing upwards. Then see the pentagon in the center of the pentagram become clear as the flame there shimmers and disappears, opening a doorway to the realm of fire. Feel a blast of dry heat blow through and surround you.

As you look through the doorway, you see the elemental realm of fire. It is a sandy desert with a blistering hot summer Sun in the sky overhead. You can see a river of molten lava running through the sand dunes from a distant volcano, and strange red trees. You send your consciousness through the doorway into the landscape: as you pass through the flames around the pentagram, it transforms you into a body of fire.

Now that your body is suited to the landscape, you start to explore. First you go and look at the trees. You notice they have red bark and that the leaves are all individual flames. Everything here is hot and fiery. You hear a scuttling and see salamanders as small darting flames dancing across the sand,

and see snakes sinuously sliding, creating "s" shapes in the sand they glide across.

You keep looking around and you see a pyre made from the branches of the fire trees burning near the lava river. On a hunch, you gaze up and see a beautiful bird descending, swooping toward the pyre. With gold and crimson and orange plumage, it resembles an eagle. You realize that it is a phoenix as it dives toward the burning pyre, letting out a harsh shriek that seems to call to you.

You jump into the pyre after the phoenix, knowing that the fire will not burn your flame body. As you enter, you realize the pyre is transforming you, the flames of your body becoming whiter with the heat and black flecks falling from it. These black flecks represent old habits that have been holding you back, the "dead wood" that has been slowing you down on your path. It continues to fall from you as the fire consumes it.

You look around for the phoenix, but see it has disappeared, replaced by a golden egg. Sensing the egg needs the whole of the fire, you step out of it, burning with a pure white heat. As you watch, the egg hatches, and from it emerges a baby phoenix, all gold and red. A fully developed, miniature version of the one that it was, it pushes off and flies into the air. As it does so, the flames die down and there is just a pile of ash on the sand in front of you.

Transfixed by the beauty of what you have seen, you look around the landscape with a new appreciation for the beauty of fire. You study the landscape, remembering it for your next visit, and then see the red pentagram standing nearby. Knowing it is time to return to the physical world, you leap through the central doorway, back through the candle flame and into your body. As you return to your body you feel rejuvenated, refreshed, and energized.

Brigid:
Transforming Anger into Creativity

by Denise Dumars

The Celtic goddess Brigid is the patron of both poetry and ironwork. Her symbol is the forge or the cauldron, and her element is fire. Think of her creation this way: just as a blacksmith uses the forge to bend and shape a graceful, useful horseshoe, you too can use the forge to put the fire of your anger to more constructive use. Take the passion that goes into our anger and turn it, shape it, mold it—bending it to your will until it becomes a creative project, a thing of beauty.

Easier said than done, right? Exactly. Many people will tell you to first write down what you are angry about. This sounds like good advice, and it can be. However, there is danger in this method too, especially if you write in the form of a message to whoever has made you angry. Firing off an angry email has caused problems for many people, and etching your anger into written words sometimes solidifies, rather than dispels, that anger.

Remember that fire cleanses. We often think of fire in terms of destruction, but it can also be used creatively. In fact, we speak of "the fire of creation."

When the anger is fresh, do not use this method. Rather, wait until the anger is more of a simmer than a boil. Once you feel you are ready to work with your anger and transmute it into something more positive, get a small cauldron or fireproof pan. You may wish to have a statue or an image of Brigid, although this is not really necessary, as the flame itself is her symbol. You will also need some rubbing alcohol and Epsom salts.

Yes, we are performing a kind of alchemy, but without the dangerous chemicals the alchemists of old used when they tried to transmute lead into gold! We begin our transmutation with a cleansing bath or shower: take rubbing alcohol and Epsom salt into the bathroom with you. If you use the bathtub, take about two cups of the Epsom salts and dissolve them in the bath. If showering, place about the same amount of Epsom salts into a pail and fill with warm water so you can pour it over yourself bit by bit. While bathing or showering think about what you can do to turn anger into creativity. Ask Brigid for guidance. If you like the image, imagine yourself as a dull ol' bar of lead being gracefully forged into a beautiful, golden new you.

Once you're out of the bath, towel dry lightly, then rub your arms and shoulders vigorously with a little of the rubbing alcohol, focusing on them as the blacksmith would focus on strengthening and stretching his arms to prepare for his work. If the rubbing alcohol is too harsh for your skin, you may substitute witch hazel, which contains a little bit of alcohol, but not enough to be irritating. Now that you have chemically transformed yourself, you are ready to do Brigid's cauldron exercise.

We are now going to make Witch fire. Place about a tablespoon of Epsom salts in the bottom of the cauldron, and pour in just enough alcohol to moisten all the salts. Now, on a small piece of paper, write a word that symbolizes your anger—DO NOT write the name of a person! Light the mixture and watch it flame! Drop the paper into the flame. You want to watch the blue and yellow flames consume the paper and the word. Add more salts and alcohol if necessary. Watch the flames to see how they are cleansing away the anger and hurt.

You are now ready to transmute that anger into creativity. Take another sheet of paper from the same tablet or ream and start jotting down ideas. Don't worry about spelling or if the words even make sense. Write what creative ideas come to mind for as long as the words come to you. This is your new raw material that you are going to transform into gold, now that you have released the burden of anger from your body, mind, and soul. You are new, you are clean, you are a thing of beauty before Brigid. Know this and don't forget to thank Brigid for the alchemical wisdom she gives you.

For more ideas on creative projects, talk to Brigid, meditate on her flame, or look to your dreams after you go to sleep following this ritual to experience her creative guidance.

Charmed, I'm Sure

by Ellen Dugan

Almost certainly one of the most popular themes for spellcasting is love. While this is a perennial popular topic, it is also a controversial one. Everybody has an opinion on what is, and what is not, ethical when it comes to love magic. But the bottom line is that yes, working love magic is ethical—as long as you play by the rules. You must make sure that your magic harms none, doesn't target anyone specifically, and is nonmanipulative. You cannot alter the free will of another person by magic. If you try, it will backfire on you, and you will pay the price. Remember, magic is a divine and loving act, performed for the good of all. It works with the powers of nature and all of the elements. Also, you should keep in mind that ethical love magic works on a spiritual level— one that boosts our own personal development.

So how does a Witch go about ethically working love magic? Well, you pull out all the stops and use this amazing part of your personal power—that little thing called charm. The word "charm" is defined in several ways—many of which are very illuminating.

- Charm: something worn about the person to ward off evil or ensure good fortune: Amulet.

- Charm: to affect by or as if by magic: an act or expression believed to have magic power. Compel. b) to please, soothe or delight by compelling attraction.

- Charm: the chanting or reciting of a magic spell. b) a trait that fascinates, allures, or delights. c) to practice magic and enchantment.

When you use your "charm," you are indeed working an act of magic. Tap into this personal power with intention, and the results are pretty spectacular. You don't have to be a beauty queen or Mr.

Universe to use this power either. This power comes from inside of you. It is the magnetic and compelling part of your personality.

The smartest decision for a Witch who wants to attain love to make is to turn the focus internally. By using and working with their own personal power and charisma, basically you cast these spells upon yourself and work to raise the level of your own appeal and magnetism. You can also work to improve your outlook, strengthen your aura, improve your attitude, make yourself more attractive to a potential mate, and boost your own confidence. For when you combine the power of loving change with a desire for personal improvement, you have a winning magical combination.

The loving magic that you wisely perform on yourself will in turn help attract the correct lover for you. With a bit of magical know-how, you can indeed make yourself more fascinating, desirable, and "magnetic."

Magnetism and Magic

When a woman or man is magnetic they posses an extraordinary power to "pull in" and to "attract." To attract what, you wonder? Why, whatever he or she most wants, and is willing to work toward, my dear. This can be a positive change, a new partner in their life,

romance, gaining a new friend, protection for an established relationship, rekindling the flames of a romance that has lost its zing . . . whatever the Witch most desires.

Magnetism is a gift from the goddess. Consider how the divine feminine draws in and attracts her consort to her. Just as the feminine pull of the Moon affects the ocean's tides, it is a force of nature. Witches simply tap into this natural magnetic power, shape it with purpose, and direct it out into their lives. This receptive and enchanting power can be tapped into quite easily. These are natural forces at work here. Magic works with the energies of nature, not against them. And magnetism is a physical phenomenon.

This phenomenon involves a science that deals with fields of force or energy. (As in one that is attracted to another.) Magnetism is also defined as the ability to attract or to "charm." If someone is "charmed" they have been affected by magic. They are gently compelled and delighted, and they are "attracted." This then, leads us neatly to a discussion on receptive power. To be receptive is to be able to receive, to draw in, and to be open and to be responsive. Receptive power is not weak or submissive. Receptive power is magnetic, compelling, and fascinating.

Magnetism happens when there is a polarity of energy. This compelling action is a force of nature that draws in that which it most desires. To be receptive is to be open to all the enchanting possibilities out there—and then to pull them in. A crash course in how to "draw in" energy: Take a deep breath in. When you inhale air you can feel the power of drawing in.

So keeping all this in mind, here is an ethical and practical spell designed to increase your magnetism, and to increase your level of personal power. In other words, here's how to pump up the volume on your charm.

A Charming Sachet
To Increase Your Magnetism

Timing

Try to plan a Friday night in a waxing Moon phase, or the Full Moon. (Friday's are sacred to the love goddesses Venus and Freya. Also be sure to work while the Moon waxes for increase and to pull things to you. Or on a Full Moon night for extra power.)

Supplies

- A handful of fresh red rose petals and red carnation petals. (The rose petals are for romance and love; the carnation petals bring energy and a healthy passion.)
- One pink or red sachet bag. (You may use a square of fabric and tie up the ends with a satin ribbon in a coordinating color, or try a small organza favor bag.)
- One small magnet (a representation of your personal magnetism)
- A small rose quartz tumbled crystal (This crystal brings love, and affection. It is the ultimate "warm fuzzy" stone.)
- One plain white tea light
- A saucer or small plate
- A drop of vanilla extract (for added attraction)
- A photo of yourself
- A safe, flat surface to set up on
- Matches or a lighter

Directions

Set this up in an area where the light of the Moon will fall on your work surface. Place the photo of yourself on the middle of the workspace. Add a drop of vanilla extract to the tea light and set the tea light in the middle of the saucer. Place the saucer holding the tea light directly on top of your photo. (This will protect the photo.) Crumble the petals from the flowers and sprinkle a few in a loose circle around the saucer. Place the rest of the remaining petals, the rose quartz crystal, and the magnet inside of the sachet bag. Tie this closed, knotting it three times and say:

By all the power of three times three,
This charm bag brings luck in love to me.

Set the sachet bag on the work area, making sure it falls under the light of the Moon. Now light the candle and repeat the following charm.

By the light of the waxing/Full Moon,
Let my charm now begin to bloom.
Fragrant petals do add their own powers,
Lady hear my request in this hour.
My personal power is now magnetized,
As I close this spell under the moonlit sky.

Allow the sachet to stay next to the candle until the candle burns out on its own. Once finished, tuck the sachet into your pocket or purse and carry it with you to increase your charm and magnetism. Dispose of the spent candle neatly, and put the saucer and your photo away. The remaining petals that were scattered around the candle you can return to nature and the Lady as an offering.

Now as I am sure you have noticed, not only did the spoken verse work to increase your own personal "charm" . . . but you also created a "charm" or amulet, if you prefer, to carry with you. Pretty clever, eh? Enjoy this spell and be open to the magic that is all around you each and every day. Let your inner magical light shine bright, and allow the essence of love, enchantment, and charm to come into your life.

Magical Laws

by Emely Flak

We did not weave the web of life; we are merely a strand in it. Whatsoever we do to the web, we do to ourselves.

—Chief Seattle, 1855

Following a magical path can sometimes be difficult. Along with the benefits and personal empowerment comes the responsibility. This means accountability for all your actions and magical intent. These key responsibilities are governed by what are known as universal laws. For some, these laws pose a burden, as the expectation is that you stay true to an ethical path and work your intent for the good of all. For most of us, the universal laws provide a framework that helps us understand how magic, spellcraft, and visualization harness the natural energy around us.

Universal Laws

Universal laws represent the collective wisdom of humans, translating into laws that we instinctively already know. They are constant, natural laws that apply to all living things in our universe and relate to forces at work that we invoke through our magical intent. Some writers refer to them as spiritual laws or metaphysical laws.

The universal laws that are most relevant to practicing magic are:

- Law of Cause and Effect
- Law of Accountability
- Law of Attraction
- Law of Abundance

Laws Connect Magical Purposes

The universal laws are related to the fundamental magical purposes of self-protection and manifestation. When you practice responsible magic for your protection, ensure it is safe and ethical and does not intend to harm anyone. Following responsible magic for your self-protection embraces the doctrines of the universal laws of accountability and cause and effect. For example, you cannot justify a spell or revenge in the name of karma—karma works alone. It takes considerable willpower to leave it to cosmic justice to make the adjustment.

When you perform magic to protect yourself, focus on diminishing negative influences around you and rendering others powerless to emotionally harm you. Throughout the ritual, ensure that your thoughts are pure and positive. Do this without anger or hatred, otherwise you could unwittingly wish harm on the person, and return that negative energy onto yourself.

The aspects of magical practice that rely on visualization and manifestation link to the two universal laws of attraction and abundance.

The Law of Cause and Effect

Being responsible for your own actions means being prepared to face the consequences of what you do. This is also known as karmic law, or karma. In the Western world, many people have misunderstood karma to mean fate or destiny. This infers that we cannot influence any outcomes. The real meaning of karma, however, is quite the opposite. Karma is the Sanskrit word for "cause and effect," meaning that for every action there is a consequence. Your choice to act or think in a certain way is the "cause." The outcome of that choice is the "effect."

Everything is shaped by your thoughts or actions, even subconscious or unintentional thoughts. This reinforces the interconnectedness of what we do, what we say, what we think, and what actually happens. For every negative cause or action, expect a negative effect or consequence. The same applies to positive energy. Every positive thought or action you create will result in a positive consequence. Therefore, we create our own karma.

The law of karma is expressed in many ways. No doubt you've heard phrases such as "what goes around comes around," and "you reap what you sow." This law is aligned with the Wiccan law of threefold return, written in the Rede as "Ever mind the rule of three" and, "An it harm no one, do what thou will." Karma has a parallel in conventional religions where it is expressed as the Golden Rule, "Do for others what you want them to do for you." The Golden Rule teaches us that we must accept responsibility for our actions and the consequences of these actions, regardless of our religion.

All world religions have a version of the Golden Rule that endorses this accountability. Belief in the law of karma promotes our accountability, forcing us to think about our actions.

Be patient and watch karmic law at work. Understanding karma helps you deal with apparent injustices and seemingly unpleasant circumstances. It spares you the energy that you might invest in struggles and denial. Karma doesn't mean allowing yourself to be trampled on by tolerating unacceptable circumstances, but it gives you the inner wisdom and calm to manage challenges. Instead of wasting hours devising a way to get even with someone who has hurt you, let go and trust the natural law of karma. Karma reminds us that everything is connected.

The Law of Accountability

The law of accountability is closely linked to the law of cause and effect. Sometimes referred to as the ethic of responsibility, this law simply means that we are responsible for everything we do. Sometimes, we try to blame others for our actions to shift the guilt for an inappropriate behavior. The law of accountability states that as we control all our actions, we must accept responsibility for the outcomes of our behavior. There is no exit route like "the devil made me do it" or "I was under the influence of alcohol."

I recall a situation at work where a married male colleague had a fling with an attractive female co-worker at an out-of-town conference. He was so wracked with guilt and confusion that he blamed her entirely for their brief liaison. He even said to her, "It wasn't my fault, you seduced me. I couldn't say 'no.'" The reality is that no one forced his infidelity. He played a willing role in their intimacy and later he looked for an excuse to ease his guilt. The blame was a weak and misguided attempt to escape his self-responsibility. In each role we play, we are responsible for every action, behavior, word, ritual, or magical practice we invoke or carry out.

The Law of Attraction

The universal law of attraction states "like energy attracts like." Thoughts also have their own energy. If you think negative thoughts, you will surround yourself with a negative vibration that will attract more negativity, resulting in negative choices and attitudes. On the other hand, if you start with positive thoughts, that positive energy from your mind becomes your surrounding force field and you will project and attract positive vibrations. It's a scientific fact that negative particles attract other negative particles. Likewise, positive ions attract positive ions.

Magic is the manipulation of energy. If you are a product of your thoughts, then to manifest change, you need to program the thought processes in your conscious and subconscious mind through creative visualization and positive affirmations. Often, what you need to reprogram is your self-talk—the inner dialogue that has become habit after many years. In your magical practice, visualize what you want to achieve in your mind's eye. Capture the desired image and replay it in your conscious mind. By creating a visual imprint in your subconscious and conscious minds, you mobilize the law of attraction.

The Law of Abundance

The law of abundance teaches us that the universe is abundant in resources for everyone. On a personal level, we must believe in abundance in our lives to allow opportunities to come our way. This belief is essential for the manifestation of your dreams and magic as it paves the way for positive thinking and infinite possibilities. Belief in the law of abundance is closely linked to the law of attraction, because this mindset acknowledges that the universe responds to our thoughts.

Think about this. If your mind is closed to possibilities, then you will never be able to visualize them or manifest your endless options or opportunities. With a closed mind, you may have programmed your mind to believe that you don't deserve positive outcomes. If that mental door to abundance is closed, the breeze of opportunity will not find a way to reach you.

When your magic and spellcraft works in alignment with these universal laws, you are in true harmony with the universe and in the best position to harness the forces of the natural energies around you. Remember your obligation to walk any magical path responsibly. You are accountable for your own actions and your intent. Step away from the power games for authentic inner strength. With your empowerment comes responsibility; a responsibility that lies with you.

The universe is composed of energy and that energy is an abundant resource. With the universal law of attraction, that states that like energy attracts like, you can manifest change through your positive intent. Your thought patterns not only dictate your behavior, but also impact how you create your future, your success, and your magical life.

Altared Spaces:
A Guide to Home Altars

by Lily Gardner

The earliest altars were found in caves in the Swiss Alps dating back to 75,000 BCE. Nearly three feet high, these altars were stone benches on which bear skulls were carefully arranged. Other Stone Age altars were set in homes, close to the hearth fire. Small statues of the Mother Goddess have been found at these ancient altar sites. From the early cave bear constructions in France to the marvelous Buddhist shrines in Thailand, the altar has played a role in every culture. Many Eastern cultures continued their tradition of home altars over the centuries. Sadly, in the West, altars and shrines were mostly used only in churches, but that is changing. In the past twenty years, many of us have adopted the age-old practice of welcoming the sacred into our homes by making altars.

The core belief behind altars and shrines is that everything in our world is composed of energy and consciousness, a mix of mystery and form. Not only are we a part of this energy and consciousness, but by aligning ourselves with the energies of the elements and ancient symbols, we can realize our hopes and

dreams. We can literally change our lives by creating altars in our homes and workspaces.

Using symbols gives form to mystery, a focal point to direct our intention. Using an ancient symbol is more powerful simply because people have used the symbol for the same intention for thousands of years. We are tapping into what noted psychiatrist Carl Jung called the collective unconscious. By arranging ancient symbols—such as a statue of Ganesh, a pentacle, or a cauldron with our sacred souvenirs, such as a photograph, a crow's feather found on a daily walk, or objects saved from childhood—we reach beyond the logical part of us and achieve a direct line to our subconscious. The subconscious is the domain of our inner child, a place where possibilities are endless. Symbols are the language of the subconscious. When we create altars, we build a bridge between the conscious and the subconscious, a language that both realms understand. The communication that results is the essence of magic work.

Altars and shrines can grow out of a kitchen shelf, a window-sill, a stair landing, or a computer stand. Altars can be used for meditation, ritual, honoring ancestors, or performing magic. I would like to offer some suggestions for power altars, altars created for spell work.

How to Begin

Ralph Waldo Emerson said, "Everything in nature contains all the power of nature." Begin every altar with your power grid using the four elements: earth in the north, water in the west, fire in the south, and air in the east.

To represent earth you can use crystals, a dish of salt, a plant, or a vase of flowers. Earth is the plane of manifestation, the realm of growing things, of health, business, and abundance. For water, you may use a small fountain, a fishbowl, a clear bowl of water, or your chalice. Water symbolizes the power of emotion and relationship and rules the subconscious. Fire is typically represented with candles, which come in many shapes, scents, and colors. Consider making your own candles for an even more meaningful altar. Fire represents transformation through passion and will. Fire is the element of change. Hold your intention firmly in your heart when you light your altar candle. Feathers, prayer flags, wind chimes, sticks of incense, and bird figurines all represent air, the place of new beginnings, thoughts, knowledge, dreams, and divination.

In the middle of your altar, place your intention in a small bowl. Think of the bowl as your cupped hands receiving blessings. Your intention can be stated with one word or as an affirmation. Affirmations are positive, present-tense statements. Arrange symbols for your intention on the altar, such as coins for prosperity or a heart for a loving relationship. Add personal objects, your sacred souvenirs, so your altar takes on your individual imprint.

Take the same care choosing these symbols as you would choosing words if you were writing a résumé or a love letter. By care, I don't mean expense. Your altar may very well cost you nothing, but the time you spend choosing symbols, both traditional and personal, will determine how powerful your altar is as a tool for transformation.

Many of us use statues and pictures of gods, goddesses, saints, or angels who serve as patrons for the goals we seek or as symbols of attributes we hope to possess. If the likeness of a god and a statue is unavailable, try downloading an image from the Web or copying a picture from a library book. Handsome picture frames for your god can be found at secondhand stores or drugstores.

Use color in cloth and candles to manifest your goal. Use red for energy, passion, and will; pink for tolerance and love; green for balance, prosperity, and luck; yellow for intellect, communication, and inspiration; indigo for intellect, understanding, and clairvoyance; blue for healing and forgiveness; orange for creativity and stimulation; white for protection, peace, and purity; and black for rebirth, mystery, and power.

Try to engage your five senses when making your altars. Burn incense or scented candles, play music that is sacred to you, and use crystals and cloth to give a varied texture to your space. When your senses are activated, your mind opens to spiritual work.

Remember, altars are a sacred space where we open ourselves to the spiritual energies that help make our dreams come true, so make as many altars as you wish. The spell begins as you keep your intention foremost in your mind while you make your altar.

Prosperity

Ideally, your prosperity altar would be placed on the north wall of your room. North is the realm of earth and abundance. Use the colors green and gold and pine incense or pine-scented candles to invite prosperity. Aventurine, bloodstone, green calcite, chrysoprase, and jade are excellent choices for a prosperity altar.

Find a picture of what you wish to obtain with your newfound prosperity: a house or car or perhaps a picture of someone in a lawn chair without a care in the world. You may want to create a treasure map, a collage of images that spells prosperity for you. To make your treasure map even more powerful, insert photographs of yourself smiling and enjoying life in among the other symbols of prosperity within the collage. This technique is a powerful visualization tool.

Use coins, paper money, a piggy bank, sticks of allspice, basil leaves, dragonfly images, a small container of oats or rice, saffron, and dollar signs. Raid your Monopoly game for all kinds of fun prosperity symbols.

Ganesh, Demeter, Lakshmi, Fortuna, Uriel, Saint Nicholas, and Lu Shing are time-honored patrons of prosperity and abundance.

If you wish to use tarot cards on your altar, the Nine or Ten of Pentacles are good choices, as is the Ten of Cups.

Love

Place your love altar on a west wall. West is the realm of water and relationships. Use the colors pink and red for candles and cloth. Jasmine, rose, violet, ylang-ylang, and lavender are traditional love scents for candles and incense. Alternatively, you may wish to anoint an unscented candle with your own perfume or after-shave. Float rose petals in the element water for your altar. Rose quartz and red jasper are stones that attract love.

Every love altar should have a small vase of flowers. The rose is the most obvious choice, but daisies, violets, tulips, heather, pansies, lilies, and orchids are associated with love as well.

Hearts, apples, and cupids are all ancient love symbols. Combine these symbols with your own sacred souvenirs.

In your asking bowl include a list of attributes you wish to have in a lover. Be as specific as possible.

Aphrodite, Eros, Freya, Parvati, Isis, Hera, the Archangel Gabriel, and Saint Agnes are a few patrons of romantic love.

You may wish to create a collage for your new relationship. Cut out pictures of couples walking on the beach or doing activities you'd like to share with a partner. Paste a photo of your face where appropriate and leave the face of your future lover blank.

The Lovers or the Two of Cups are good choices for a tarot card on your love altar.

Health and Well-Being

Place your healing altar in the north, the realm of earth and good health. If the health you seek is emotional, place your altar in the west. Use the colors white and blue for candles and cloth. Scents appropriate for healing are rosemary, lavender, lime, lemon balm, mugwort, and spearmint.

Guardians of healing are all of the Mother goddesses, Kuan Yin, the Medicine Buddha, Mary, Archangel Michael, Thoth, Mercury, and Bridget. Healing crystals are coral, amber, agate, bloodstone, and jade. If possible, place a piece of coral in your asking bowl along with your healing affirmation.

Use a photograph of yourself having a good time in your life, and place this on your healing altar behind the asking bowl.

If you wish to use a tarot card, Strength or the World are appropriate symbols.

Creativity

Each of us has our own unique voice that longs to create. To nurture your creative self, build your altar in the east and use the colors yellow and orange. Lavender, eucalyptus, peppermint, caraway, and lemongrass are scents associated with creativity. Amber, carnelian, and tiger's eye are good choices for a creativity altar.

Mercury, Saraswati, Brigid, Wodan, Thoth, Athena, Hathor, Minerva, and the Archangel Gabriel are a few of the spiritual mentors that oversee creativity.

Making your altar is a creative act. Carry that spirit of creativity by making a collage of artists, writers, and teachers who inspire you. Hang your creativity collage on the wall by your altar.

Arrange tools you will use as a more creative person on your altar: pencils, paintbrushes, a keyboard, knitting needles, etc.

The tarot cards for your creativity altar would be the Magician, the Star, and the Moon.

Using the Altar

Constructing the altar is of itself a powerful spiritual practice. Make sure the altar is kept dust-free and the flowers fresh. The more time you spend visiting your altar, the sooner the goals you set for yourself will manifest.

Visiting your altar first thing in the morning sets your motivation for the day. Light a candle and a stick of incense and say a short prayer. Try to spend twenty minutes a day visualizing in front of your altar. As your senses flood with symbols you've arranged on your altar, imagine yourself having achieved your goal. Finally, visit your altar briefly just before going to bed so the symbols imprint themselves into your sleeping brain.

Magic is achieved through a combination of imagination and will. The altar serves as an ignition switch for the imagination, a sensual representation of what we wish to achieve. But magic isn't achieved through symbol and visualization alone. Because we live and operate on the physical plane, we need to do everything possible in the mundane world to manifest our desires.

Blessed be.

Message in a Bottle:
The History of the Witches Bottle

by Sally McSweeney

Imagine that you have decided to do some work on the front porch of the eighteenth-century house into which you have just moved. As construction on the foundation proceeds, a worker notices the glint of sunlight on something green, half buried in the earth. Carefully they loosen the soil around it and pull forth a small green bottle that, when opened, reveals small pieces of metal, a nail, and a piece of dark leather. This is exactly what happened in 2005 in Lincolnshire, England. Archeological research showed that it was a Witches Bottle dating to the early 1800s, which is quite late for such a bottle to have been made. A large number have been found dating back to at least the early 1600s in England; the first found in the United States was on Tinicum Island in the Delaware River south of Philadelphia in 1976. This dated back to the mid 1700s and contained six pins, a piece of bird bone, and a pottery shard.

Despite the use of the word "bottle," which we tend to associate with glass, they were more often made of stoneware glazed with salt. These originated in Germany in the sixteenth century and were called "bartmanns" or "bellarmines." The name comes from a man called Cardinal Bellarmine, a Catholic inquisitor, and they carried a picture resembling him that showed a very stern-looking image. Glass was not generally used in England until later centuries. From where we stand today, the early bottles were certainly not made following the recent popular maxim of "harm none." Such a bottle was originally created by a "victim" for counter-sorcery—to banish evil or negative magic directed at them, particularly from a suspected Witch who was thought to have sent a curse. Its contents were used not just to simply repel this energy, but also to actually cause suffering to the Witch. The bottles were filled with objects such as broken pottery or glass, bent rusty nails, pins, thorns, and small pieces of bone. Sometimes the victim added some of their hair or nail clippings—and even urine or blood.

There are a couple of theories behind the use of urine in the bottles. It was believed that the Witch had created a magical and psychic bond between herself and her chosen recipient that could be reversed and/or broken by the making of the bottle. The curse acted most strongly upon the bodily fluids of the victim, so by putting some of her urine in the spell bottle, the curse fell upon this first before it reached the actual person. In this way, the curse was dissolved. Secondly, the urine was thought to hold "part of the vital spirit of the Witch" as a result of the working of her curse through the link. When the Witch next went to pass water, she would supposedly feel all sorts of torment—sharp pain sent by the sympathetic magic of the nails or pins. In this way, the curse was sent back to her. Strong stuff indeed! The bottle was buried in a place where it would not be disturbed, often under the hearth where the heat from the fire was thought to activate the metal objects within the urine, resulting in the breaking of the curse. The hearth was also a logical place for a Witches Bottle because it was believed that Witches entered houses through the chimney. The bottles have also been found in attics and inside walls. The magic of the bottle remained active for as long as the bottle was hidden and unbroken.

Hopefully today, you won't need to be making a Witches Bottle for quite such a grim purpose, but they can be used for a variety of magical reasons and placed in various chosen spots; like all magical tools they are a focal point for your energy and intent. They are most commonly made to capture negative energies without harming the sender. Craft stores and thrift stores are great resources for bottles; there is a plethora available to choose from, but do make sure that it has a tight stopper or lid. You can use glass, earthenware, or stoneware bottles. The items you wish to place in it will determine the size. Most spell bottles are made on the night of the Full Moon, but for those of a banishing nature, the dark Moon phase is appropriate. Be careful when constructing your bottle, as some of the objects will be sharp.

A Witches Bottle can be a powerful means to protect your home or property; bury one at each corner of your land and/or by the front door. If you live in an apartment, bury it in a plant pot by the door. To make such a bottle, you will need some dried rosemary, three pinches of salt, nine pins, three metal nails, and red wine. (You may replace the red wine with urine and/or menstrual blood if you want to stay true to tradition.) Place all the items in the bottle and say:

> *Herb of protection, blood red wine,*
> *Pins and nails, guard me and mine.*

To protect a particular person, place a picture of the person in the jar and surround it with sharp objects such as broken glass, pins or needles, nails, and thorns. The intent is to build a "wall" around the person that will keep any harm at bay. To capture negativity, fill a bottle with similar objects and tangled thread that will ensnare the hostility and prevent it from reaching you. Bury the bottle away from the home

where it is unlikely to be found; an ideal place would be a swamp or a bog.

To protect against psychic attack, you will need to break a small mirror, which, under these circumstances, will not bring bad luck. Put the pieces in your bottle with nine nails. Light a black candle and say:

> *Candle lit, burning low*
> *Stop attacks, here and now.*
> *Broken mirror to reflect*
> *Any harm that comes to wreck.*
> *Nails of steel, nine be true*
> *Allow no evil to get through.*

Variations

To make a **Love Bottle**, try to find a red glass bottle. You will need some dried rose petals, three pinches of dried lavender, three drops of rose oil, a nine-inch piece of red ribbon, a coin, and some red wine. Tie two knots in the ribbon and tie the ends together. This symbolizes the joining of you and a partner. Place the ribbon, rose, lavender, and the coin into the bottle. The coin represents the investment you are going to make in finding the right person for you. Add the rose oil; with each successive drop say "my heart, your heart, our hearts." Fill the bottle with the red wine and imagine your life filling with love as you pour. Put the lid on the bottle and seal with red candle wax. Place the bottle where it will be undisturbed. In the event that the relationship with the person who comes into your life does not work out or you wish to end the relationship, open the bottle, pour out the wine, and cut the ribbon between the knots. Bury all of the contents.

A popular Witches Bottle today is an **Abundance** or **Money Bottle**. For this you will need one made of green glass. You will also need a silver coin, three pinches of cinnamon, three pinches of basil, three corn kernels, and a piece of citrine. If you have a small pentacle add this; if not, draw one on some paper. The pentacle represents wealth in the tarot. Put the items into the bottle and say:

Sparkling silver, shiny and round,
Into my life, may money be bound.
Herbs of abundance, stone and grain,
Work your magic so money I'll gain.

Then, using a green candle, seal the lid.

My personal favorite is a **Psychic Power Bottle**, which can be made in a couple of ways. It should be put together on the night of the New Moon and be left where it can (hopefully) bathe in the waxing moonlight until the Full Moon. I have a wonderful engraved, silver brandy flask that dates from 1810, which is perfect because silver is the metal most associated with the Moon. You can use it for astral travel, divination enhancement, dream work or ritual, and for these purposes you will need to put nine pinches of mugwort in your bottle and then add some virgin olive oil. Anoint yourself with a little of the oil whenever you want to enhance your psychic abilities. As mugwort is considered the most potent herb for divination work, it is also used to cleanse crystals, amulets, crystal balls, and so on. For this purpose, add spring water instead of oil to the mugwort in your bottle and use this to "bathe" your object in. For both bottles, say:

Within the darkness of the night,
By growing light of magical Moon,
And from the herb of second sight,
To me will come this power soon.

As you kneel in the soft earth of the flowerbed beside your front door, the silver light of the Full Moon casts its magical illumination upon the small hole you have dug there. Gently, you place your silver Witches Bottle in the hole; before you cover it with the moist soil, you catch a glimpse of your face reflected in the shiny surface. But was it your face? It looked different somehow. Patting the soil down, you smile as you feel the connection with countless women who have done such magic before you and you wonder if, in years to come, another such woman will find your hidden treasure.

Music in Ritual

by Kari Tauring

Many of the concepts discussed in the movie *What the #$*! Do We (K)now!?* or the *NOVA* episode on string theory on public television and other popular presentations about quantum physics and how we create our own reality are familiar to most ritual practitioners. We understand that there are many more worlds than the three-dimensional one we live in most of the day. Einstein calculated ten dimensions before backing off the whole thing and modern quantum mechanics uses many more in its complex workings. There are some great books on dimensions out there, too, such as *The Dancing Wu Ling Masters* and *The Tao of Physics.*

So what does this have to do with music in ritual? Sound is the key. Sound is the one thing that permeates dimensionally. The sound we make in this moment travels through all the dimensions creating an effect in each reality. Masaru Emoto (on whose work *Messages from Water* the *What the Bleep* movie is based) asserts that the intention behind the sound we make is a powerful force in the universe, affecting everything on the cellular level and inter-dimensionally. His theory postulates that water, exposed to vari-

ous music, chant, and even written thought, will form crystals that are significantly affected in both positive and adverse ways.

Knowing that our sound will travel interdimensionally, it is essential to be accurate and intentionally certain about what we say, sing, or chant. Even more importantly, we must be aware of what key we are in, what note we hold, what rhythm and time signature we desire, and even the duration of the sound we will make. The choice of instruments is also important. There is a different effect achieved with a dumbek than a bodhran, a flute, or a trumpet. As with all ritual practice, awareness of our intention is everything.

As a longtime musician and ritual artist, I have come across many good resources for intentional use of music in ritual and have experimented with it widely. First I would recommend that people get to know which notes affect which chakras. There are some great charts and resources for this. Here is the basic chart:

Chakra	Color	Note
Base	Red	C
2nd	Orange	D
3rd	Yellow	E
4th	Green	F
5th	Blue	G
6th	Indigo	A
7th	Violet to white	B

One way to begin is with toning. This is simply holding a specific note for a specific duration and making observations about physical, emotional, and psychological effects. You could use a keyboard or a guitar to find your note, but with my music students I often have them tone into a tuner. One approach is to record your mood and environment and then pick a tone at random. See where the needle falls . . . does the note you chose correspond to the chakra most depicting your initial feelings, etc.? Another way is to choose a note and tone it for a few minutes. Then record your feelings and thoughts. Did they change as you held the specific notes? Take account of your body. Are the physical effects of the note being held showing up? How is this happening?

Apply this to a ritual. Suppose the intention of the ritual is to increase your capacity for or to attract new love. If you have chosen to tone in F, the love will be of the heart. If you have chosen to tone in C, it is more likely you will attract love of a bodily nature. It's interesting to note that many of the old country and western songs were written in C and F—and most often the content is about the confusion of love and lust, the heart and root chakras! Norwegian women's music, Huldre Stille, is done in A and D, which connects the second chakra (womb space) and sixth chakra (use of brain). This makes sense as Huldre Stille songs are about connecting work (churning, spinning, herding) to the higher mind principle and the feminine divine. This tuning is considered the way into the vibration of the Huldre (the fairy folk of Scandinavia) and is also called Troll Stille, or Troll tuning.

Another fascinating and magic-making aspect of toning is changing the vowel sounds on the tone. Joseph Rael's book *Being in Vibration* is a great resource for the vowel meanings according to his Hopi heritage. The ah, eh, ee, oh, and oo sounds of the Spanish vowels create specific energies and penetrate different levels of our interdimensional bodies. They become keys to open the doors of other, specific dimensions. Much like the chanting of rune tones in Scandinavian shamanic practice, the tones with their specific vowels and consonants can lead from one world to the next and back again. With beginning students, I often have them chant their names. This is a very powerful emotional experience. It is important in these experiments for the practitioner to journal their experiences, emotional and physical conditions. With toning, your body is the instrument. It is unique and built especially for your own tone. We come into this world with our own unique sound and we leave it with that same tone that carries our beings to the next world.

The last aspect to address is the use of the drone tone. From the bagpipe to the didgeridoo, from hardanger fiddles to Gregorian chant, humans use singular drone tones to create a meditative and trance state. Being intentional with your drone tones is important, because the trance state is not always the goal! However, droning on a singular tone for several minutes is a sure way to achieve a meditative or trancelike state.

Music, for me, comes directly from the divine source, penetrates all the bodies on every level and through all the dimensions, and is a steady guide for my spiritual journey. Have fun with music in your ritual and remember to be intentional. As Masaru Emoto points out, sounds change things on the cellular level!

The Illustrated Witch: Creating Magical Body Art

by Mickie Mueller

No tattoos until you're eighteen! That was the family rule and both of my teenagers knew it. Leave it to my girl, the proud daughter of a magical artist, to take my rule and turn it into a rite of passage.

Chelsea had been planning it for years. Here we were, driving our car through the Missouri heat in the middle of the summer, heading toward one of the most reputable tattoo parlors in the area. We had to do it on her actual birthday, not a day later; Chelsea wouldn't have it any other way. As she sat there beaming, holding tight to the hummingbird flash sheet I had drawn her, she had explained to me why she had chosen the hummingbird as her special eighteenth birthday tattoo. She proclaimed that although she was old enough to make a lot of her own choices, as well as "getting ink," she would always keep strong ties to her family. My husband had long ago dubbed her a "hummingbird spirit," a symbol that has ever since reminded her that she is loved, so it made sense that she chose this symbol as her rite of passage.

Body Art, An Ancient Legacy

Ancient people have used both temporary and permanent body art for rites of passage, religious ceremony, folk magic, protection, and many other purposes. For as long as humans have decorated anything, we have decorated ourselves. Red ochre was a mineral used by primitive man to decorate the body for religious funerary rites. It was likely used as an offering as well as purification. Ash was also used to decorate in primitive times, and we still see it used in primitive cultures today around the world.

In India, Africa, and Egypt, henna has been used as far back as 1200 BCE to decorate hair, skin, nails, even horses' manes and hooves. The henna plant paste known as mehndi was (and still is) believed to bring love, good fortune, and protection. Woad, another plant product, produced a blue dye that has existed in Europe since Neolithic times. Julius Caesar describes the Britons as using the blue dye to cover their bodies in battle. Often they would wear nothing into battle except woad paint, which seemed to have a terrifying effect on their enemies. Interestingly, woad also is known to have astringent properties, so it would really offer physical as well as spiritual protection in battle.

The oldest known tattoos that archeologists have found were on a man frozen in ice for over 5,000 years. They were simple dots, and since they were strategically placed over arthritic joints it is believed that these were part of some kind of pain relief or healing application. Some of the oldest known picture tattoos ever found date back as far as the fifth or sixth century BCE. A frozen tomb found near Siberia was excavated and some amazingly well preserved bodies were found. These bodies were covered in highly decorative tattoos portraying beautiful animal figures on the arms and legs. In fact, tattooing was widely practiced in Europe in ancient times, by many cultures including the Celts, Picts, and Vikings. The Polynesians practiced tattooing of the face in intricate designs, and as some of them ended up working on European sailing ships, this is said to be how the popularity of tattoos spread among sailors. The traditional Japanese tattoo is a full body suit. It was used to show status and family affiliations. The beautiful designs and vivid colors perfected by the Japanese are the forerunners of the modern tattoo.

Today's Body Art, More Than Just Decoration

There are many ways the modern Witch can use the many techniques of body art, which range from temporary body painting to permanent tattoos, to boost spellwork, express connections with a deity, and manifest transformation within ourselves.

Because it goes directly on your skin, body art can be a very powerful tool for inner magic. Many of us already use magical symbols and color correspondences for our magic when working with a candle, dressing our altar, or making charm bags. These symbols and colors that you already use can be employed in magical body art. You can do some quick body art magic by drawing Mercury symbols on the soles of your feet for safe travel, or a healing symbol on your solar plexus.

Here is a simple charm to enchant a symbol that you put temporarily on your body. Draw the symbol and then with the intention that it will continually draw power until it is gone, place your right hand (left if you are left-handed) over the symbol and say:

I charge this symbol on my skin
With simple lines that I create.
May it manifest my will within,
And set in motion wheels of fate.
With harm to none, so mote it be.

If you choose to use this method, you may wish to put these symbols in an unobtrusive place that will be covered up. I usually use a ballpoint pen, or fine-line permanent marker to put magical symbols on my body. These pens are formulated to be safe on our skin in small amounts, so I wouldn't recommend scribbling on half of your body, but drawing a small symbol about the size of a half dollar or so, should pose no problem. I have even seen medical staff use them on occasion. If you do Reiki, you can use Reiki symbols in this way. Runes or planetary symbols also work well, and there are also many books full of magical symbols. Here are a few that are pretty easy for anyone to draw (but feel free of course to use any symbols you like):

Pentagram: protection, magic, power
Equal-armed cross: protection, earth, grounding energy
Ankh: life, vitality
Triple Moon: magic, feminine energy
Horned God: strength, masculine energy
Triskelle: protection, magic, power
Caduceus: healing, health

Body Paint

Primitive people often used natural powdered pigments made from plants or minerals mixed with some kind of animal fat to create colorful body paint. Today, there are some wonderful commercial products out there. Of course, if you want to be a purist, you can mix up your own, though I personally have not tried it. If you do, be very careful about what kinds of pigment you use. Some natural pigments are toxic and absorbed by the skin, or at the very least will stain. For these reasons, I prefer to use paints that are created just for body art. There are several good brands of body paint on the market that are nontoxic, nonallergenic, and can be washed off the skin easily. You can pick up a basic set for not too much money. Kryolan Aquacolor is one of the most popular brands used by theater professionals and fine artists alike. You should be able to find it at a local art-supply store or theater/costume shop. If not, try the Internet.

If you simply want to experiment and you don't want to make a big investment, you can try using children's acrylic paint mixed with a tiny amount of face lotion. Now I stress here, use **children's** acrylic paint because it is formulated not to be dangerous if they get it on their skin or even in their mouths.

(Whatever you do, **do not** go to your nearest art supply store and pick up tubes of **professional** acrylic paint. Many of these are toxic. So, that being said, please always be careful about what kind of paint you use. That is why companies make paint specifically for body painting.)

There are many ways that you can use body paint in your magic. Some people use body paint in a manner similar to the way a ritual mask is used. It can be a very transformational experience, drawing upon outer or inner energies and exploring a whole new persona. Imagine casting a circle with participants wearing faces and bodies painted for the elements and the God and Goddess! How about painting everyone to mimic their totem animal? Very dramatic! Even though full body painting requires nudity, if you or your group prefers not to work sky-clad, you can have participants clothed from the waist down, maybe in colorful sarongs, ladies with bikini tops, and paint wherever skin is left showing! Even painted faces would be fabulous. If you do full body paint, don't sit on the high priestess's white couch!

Here is a list of magical color correspondences. If you associate colors other than what is listed here, then feel free to go with that, enjoy, and let your creative Witch show!

Red	fire, passion, south, willpower
Orange	positive influences, justice, career
Yellow	air, inspiration, friendship, Sun, mental focus
Green	earth, abundance, fertility, harmony
Blue	water, truth, healing, higher wisdom
Indigo	life changes, mysticism
Violet	healing, spirituality, psychic ability
Black	banishing negativity, shadow side
White	new beginnings, Moon, protection

Mehndi

Another method for creating temporary magical body art is mehndi (MEN-dee). Popular at many outdoor events and also called henna tattoos, the brownish-orange to mocha shade imprints usually last one to three weeks. Mehndi has been a traditional form of decoration in India for centuries. The ancient Egyptians used it to color nails and hair.

Traditionally, intricate mehndi decorations were put on an Indian bride's hands and feet—the longer the color lasted, the longer and happier the marriage would be! Therefore a darker design was best. In order to achieve this, there were many different formulas for mehndi paste. (Some formulas include lye, called black mehndi, which has been known to cause serious chemical burns; therefore, I do not recommend using any mehndi recipe containing lye.)

Using a premixed mehndi paste is much easier, and there are several varieties from which to choose. Brands of premixed paste that I have used are Shweta or Shelly. Both are excellent, very easy to use, and produce a nice dark stain if used properly. They come in a tube that looks like a toothpaste tube. You can find them in New Age/Metaphysical shops and also in hippie shops. They are fairly easy to find online as well and you can usually get a tube for under ten bucks.

However, it can also be fun to mix your own, and it's really not difficult, just a bit messy. You can also get powdered henna that you mix yourself at the same locations. If you choose this method, here is a good recipe.

Mickie's Magical Mehndi Paste
Ingredients:
Henna powder
Warm water
Lemon juice
Zipper sandwich bag
Mehndi oil, tea tree oil, eucalyptus oil, patchouli oil, or
    lavender oil
Tea light candle

Put the desired amount of henna powder you wish to use in a glass bowl. Add equal parts of warm water and lemon juice until you get a nice paste about the consistency of toothpaste. Really mix it well; you don't want any chunks at all. Now you can add a few drops of the oil you have chosen. You may wish to choose the oil corresponding with your magical purpose. Now comes the hard part; you have to wait. Mehndi has to sit for a while or it won't work, so take the opportunity to magically charge your paste. Put your bowl of mehndi paste or tube of premixed where it will be out of reach of children and pets for a few hours uncovered. Set the tea light next to it, light it and recite this charm several times:

Mehndi, lemon, and oil blend,
Until this magic candle's end,
Containing power deep within,
And leave its mark upon my skin.

Leave your paste undisturbed until the candle burns out (about four hours). While your candle burns, gently exfoliate the area of skin you plan to decorate.

Using a small spoon, fill one corner of the sandwich bag with the paste. Twist the bag to push it into the corner and zip the bag closed. With a pair of scissors, clip just the smallest tip off the corner—remember, you can always make the hole bigger, but you can't make it smaller again! Rub a little eucalyptus oil on your skin where you plan to do your design.

Now, carefully pipe the design onto your skin, much the way you pipe icing on a cake. It will be a raised design. You may use a magical symbol of your choice and add extra decorative symbols around it, make it as simple or intricate as you wish. You may need to keep a toothpick handy to clear the hole out if it gets clogged.

When your design is complete, and it has begun to dry, carefully apply a mixture of equal parts lemon juice and sugar periodically with a cotton ball. Leave the mehndi on for as long as you can, at least six hours or so. The longer you leave it on, the darker it will be.

You can warm it with a blow dryer occasionally, as heat really makes it darken, but be very careful not to burn yourself. When you just can't take it any more, scrape the dried paste off, rinse with clear water, and pat dry. As the mehndi starts to fade over time, visualize that the magic is being absorbed into you. As the design disappears on the physical plane, it will manifest on the spiritual plane.

Tattoos

Tattoos are the most permanent form of illustrating the body. This is an art form that goes back very far and has been seen in many cultures. While they can be removed with lasers, that procedure is usually more expensive than the original tattoo, so be sure about a design before you make it a part of you. Magical people need to be especially aware of this because it is a binding, in a way. Use your wisdom and don't bind yourself to an image that may not serve you in the years to come.

Once you have decided to "get ink," there are a couple of ways that you can turn it into a magical endeavor. The first I will touch on is blessing the skin. The evening before you go to get your tattoo, bless and purify the area to be tattooed. Quite simply, you can use some clean water that you have blessed under the previous Full Moon and wash the areas while repeating a simple chant, something like:

Bless this skin, and make it pure,
The art it wears, shall long endure.

Tattoo artists tend to be pretty open-minded folks, so if you ask nicely they will probably allow you to say a blessing over the ink before they begin. You can call in advance and ask for permission if you like. Hold both hands high over the ink to keep everything safe and clean. You can draw a pentagram or other symbol in the air over the ink, while you can use a blessing of your choice, saying it quietly or to yourself. Write your own, or you can use this one as an all-purpose blessing for tattoo ink:

Lord and Lady, Sun and Moon
Be present here, I ask this boon.
Bless this ink and the art it becomes,
The ink and I, the two made one.

You may wish to memorize this one. You can use it silently in your head while you are getting your tattoo to boost the magic and to give you a focus away from the pain. In this way you can use the experience to reach a transcendental state and therefore build the magic within your new design.

After getting your tattoo, follow the tattooist's instructions explicitly—after all, they do this for a living. When your tattoo is completely healed (all scabbing is gone and it is smooth just like the rest of your skin), you can do something very special to keep adding to the magic of your tattoo. Purchase the very best skin product that you can afford, and use it only for this purpose. If you wish, you can add to the bottle a few drops of oil corresponding to your magical tattoo. Apply it to your tattoo once a week to boost the magical properties of your design.

I created a lotion like this for my daughter's hummingbird tattoo. It took about three weeks for it to heal enough for us to feel comfortable rubbing the magic lotion into it. As it healed, she followed the instructions and washed it and applied the special lotion the tattooist provided and it turned out vibrant and beautiful. She is very proud of the symbol of her coming of age, and wears it with pride. As a mom, I was nervous about it at first, but I am used to it now—and it already seems part of her. In fact it suits her. I continually enjoy finding new ways to incorporate magical art into my everyday life, and body art is a really fun way to do that. Chelsea and I really both like the idea of using body art as a way to mark changes in a person's life, so much that she has informed me that as she becomes a high school senior this fall, she plans to get her bellybutton pierced. Sigh, another form of body art, another potentially transformative experience. I don't know if this mom's heart can take it!

The Magic Diet

by Steven Repko

In our modern society, many of us find ourselves at odds with our lifestyle. We seem to spend more and more time trying to keep up, and less and less time living. For many of us, our spirits suffer as rushing through our day-to-day tasks can leave little time for anything spiritual. As a result, the gods become strangers and our hearts become heavy.

Another symptom of this killing-ourselves-to-live mentality is often the image we see in the mirror each morning. Our eyes become older looking, we lose our immortal zeal for life, the animal spirit and attraction of our youth, and our waistline measurements begin to creep up with our age. This can become a bit frightening as we round forty, fifty—dare we say it—sixty or even seventy inches?

In my own search for health and the balance between the spiritual and physical, I have come to an interesting conclusion: magic, when applied to your lifestyle, promotes healthy modifications that improve your physical condition and overall well-being.

Due to genetic health issues aggravated by a lifestyle of poor physical maintenance in a fast, high-stress environment, I had the good fortune, thanks to the goddess Aradia, to run right into an early and unexpected quadruple bypass. This type of thing does tend to help you get off the merry-go-round, take a deep breath, look around, and contemplate a vision of tomorrow.

The obvious became crystal clear to me: The spirit was great, but the "temple" was falling apart due to neglect. I had come face to face with one of my favorite mantras: "If you don't like it, change it. If you don't change it, deal with it." Something needed to be done, and the only person who was going to do it was me.

I learned a lot in a short time about food and exercise, and the relationship between the two. I knew I needed to make a break from how I lived before, but how?

And then, a light bulb. I needed to take control; I needed a weight-loss spell and a magic diet.

Meditate and Visualize

The first step of any good spell is attained through meditation and visualization, making what you see match up with what you expect to become real. I have found this to be the most important part of both weight-loss and physical conditioning.

It's important to remember that we are all beautiful and meant to be so. We are, after all, the fair-folk—when you look in the mirror what do you see? Do you see the best of what you are or can be, or do you see what you do not like and stop looking?

Each day, take a good look, a magical look. See the you that you are releasing from the self-imposed bondage. See the eyes that sparkle, the turn of the lip, and the line of the shoulder that will remain to support you in every small improvement you make throughout the rest of your life.

Looking our "magical best" is a form of glamour. Any improvement in how we look makes us believe we have power over our appearance. When we believe we have confidence, this confidence convinces others in a magnetic way, and they treat us differently. This treatment once again reinforces our belief in our beauty, the power we have to make change, and the effectiveness of that power. Simply by looking in the mirror to find a more beautiful you, you become more beautiful.

Meditation is something that everyone needs to practice. It keeps us balanced and lets us function with wisdom and patience.

Meditation is the process of separating your mind from your current perceptions of "what's really happening here." The reason many of us do not meditate is because it's boring, but that's because the way many of us try to meditate is boring. If meditation is not fun, don't do it! Meditation is meant to be a pleasant and comfortable release, not a punishment that beats us into submission. Fortunately, there are many ways to meditate.

Find an activity that you enjoy and use it to separate your focus from the here and now—and you have meditated. Make that activity something that includes physical movement and you have just reinvented the home gym. The combination provides a perfect opportunity to make a change in your spiritual and physical condition.

My personal selection was the bicycle. After a news flash from the goddess Hecate, I remembered how I liked to be in motion as a youngster (yes they had bicycles back then). I would spend my days touring the back roads of eastern Long Island exploring the beaches and potato farms. I found it surprising how much I missed those opportunities to clear my head.

This alteration of the here and now allows me a time to separate myself from the current situation and commune with the gods in an altered time and space while getting some sort of exercise. And here's the key—more exercise than I was getting before I started.

This change in our spiritual life allows us to reclaim a benefit that we were lacking, exercise. Of course, physical exercise makes us look better, but, more importantly, it makes us feel better. It changes the chemical processes in our body, helps us sleep better, and improves our mood. Feeling better makes the whole world work in our favor, "magically."

Recent studies have suggested that exercise calms your brain activity, which, coupled with the production of endorphins, can create a very desirable form of meditation. The chemical changes can be helpful in vision-questing exercises, and the exploration of shape-shifting by changing the focus of your consciousness.

Find something that works for you, take a walk with some music, recite some poetry that inspires you, memorize the charge of the god or goddess, get out there and experience the natural/magical world.

Learn your local herbs as you walk, run, or bike, see the changes in your new environment, and feel the changes in yourself. Learn to live the changes of the seasons and the wheel of the year. Jump into a clear pool of water and swim like a fish.

Are there wild berries in your area? Nuts? Are you paying for cinquefoil that grows in a field in your neighborhood?

There are many little bits of exercise that can be added to our lives that improve our physical condition, our spiritual condition, our fun quotient, and our general well-being. Fishing and hunting are great forms of meditation. Fishing in a kayak and walking to the local fishing hole are great forms of exercise that allow us to commune with the gods while exploring and accepting our position in the natural/magical world.

Food

When it comes to food, common sense is the best policy. Doctors consistently offer these three facts of life. We eat too much, we do not get enough exercise, and if you eat 300 calories, you must burn 300 calories or you will gain weight.

You can eat anything you want in a life where you are always in motion, the bad news is most of us don't move much.

The is good news is that exercise is magic. The more we exercise the more muscle we develop, and that muscle requires additional calories to maintain itself. After a while, we eat something that used to make us heavier and, magically, our new exercised level of metabolism burns some of the calories for us, even when we're at rest.

Drink Water

Water has no calories, except for the "little floaty things" but that's another story. Water also helps your body cleanse itself by flushing your systems. Clean systems work better and help us lose weight. Water also takes up space, so if you drink water before a meal, you will feel full faster and consume fewer calories.

Avoid prepared soft drinks. They are loaded with calories and you can get just as much flavor elsewhere. Make lemonade, iced tea, and packet drinks (but use a little less sugar). All drinks should have ice in them. Besides making them wonderfully cool, it dilutes them with water! When in doubt, drink water. If you don't like the taste of water, add a little lemon or sour salt, also known as citric acid (the sourness of fruit). It is refreshing in water and available from spice companies and some supermarkets.

Eat Better

Introduce soups and salads to you lifestyle. As we have become a one-course society, there are many other courses that we are missing out on. Some courses are really good and many have fewer calories than the one course we seem to get stuck on.

Eat Smaller Portions

If you eat a salad, some soup, some meat, and some rice you do not need to eat a lot of any one thing.

Do not live on salad; just eat some. This is a life change, not a punishment. Salad, like water, takes up space and is low in calories. Avoid bottled dressings, and whenever possible, make your own. That way you know what you are eating. A homemade dressing made from a little olive oil, wine, and some shredded cheddar is a very tasty substitute that is cheaper and better for you.

Soups have a lot of taste and fewer calories than most solid foods because they are made of water. These tasty bowls of brew can be whipped up in advance and, when added to your lifestyle, give you added opportunities to reduce calories while you actually still eat.

Indulge

Let's not forget about dessert—if it's fattening and decadent, I want it. And you know what? I still eat it. Not every day and not by the bucket, but I allow myself the freedom to have and enjoy what I want, when I want it. I quickly realized that I could have my cake and ice cream and eat them too, but for the sake of health try not to eat them all on the same night. And remember, one less spoonful of cherry chocolate chip you eat today is a pound saved and another bowlful we can eat in the future. Use a dessert cup, not a soup bowl, and eat some every night if you want. Be creative with your treats. Eat chocolate mousse, but beat the eggs by hand (and perhaps run to the store to get them). Always relate tasty calories to happy exercise.

Snacks

My name is Steve and I'm a chipaholic (Hi Steve). Put your chips in a bowl, preferably a small one. You can eat as many as you want, but a bowl forces you to look at their little faces before they die and realize how many you are actually eating. This is a good rule of thumb for any food you like. Make sure you can see what you are eating, know what you are putting in your body, and take time to enjoy it.

Also remember it is not a crime to eat or skip an exercise session, but every bite of food you forego and every sit-up you do is one more step in a lighter and healthier direction. Don't beat yourself up if you eat three cream-filled cupcakes (or a boxful)—celebrate that. They are tasty and you wanted them. Accept the freedom to eat them and understand the responsibility that goes with it. Then shake off the guilt, walk to the mall, and look at an outfit you will be able to wear as a result of your efforts.

Body and Spirit

My improved spiritual and physical condition makes me happy. Being happy is the most important gift we give ourselves. If eating a jelly doughnut makes you happy, imagine how a homemade blackberry pie that took more calories to gather and make than to eat is going to taste, make you feel, and—after a while—look. Don't forget the vanilla ice cream on top. You've really earned it.

Let us not forget that there are gods, goddesses, and rituals for all these activities. Gods of the forest and field, fruit, and herb. When we nourish our bodies, minds, and spirits together we become the Witches we were meant to be. We learn to celebrate the gods, the world, and our reason for being here, finding joy in the exploration of our magical world. And speaking of celebration, let's not forget to join the god and goddess in the ritual dance of life.

There is nothing more freeing than the ritual dance, and surprisingly enough, more exercise. You may want to go easy at first until you get used to the muscles you will aggravate when you let it all go. Dance is another very effective form of meditation that allows us to transcend time and space. Let the drums pound and the pipes shrill, but do not get caught up in the "what kind of Pagan music can we dance to" trap.

If you like it, it's Pagan music, so dance to it. Light some candles, cast a circle, gather some friends, dance like crazy, raise some energy, and enjoy the worship of the god and goddess from your own personal spot, in the natural/magical world.

Add a little wine, or mead that you have made yourself, perhaps from wild grapes you have collected on a daily walk. Take up a game of ninepins, bocce, or badminton; learn the spiritual grace of archery with Diana or ax throwing with Tyr. The possibilities are endless, and you could soon find yourself a very active Witch.

Does all of this wildcrafting, meditation, and cavorting bring us closer to the god and goddess and the understanding of our own personal spot in the natural/magical world? Sure it does. And it brings us to a new reality, where we are healthy, beautiful, wise, more knowledgeable, spiritual, and happier than we were before.

The Gifts of Pandora
by Gail Wood

Beauty and healing and craft sublime
Creating and merging with divine;
Wild curiosity will reveal
That dark wisdom and bright hope will heal.

Pandora. Her name is evocative as she dances mysteriously into our consciousness as the personification of curiosity run wild, the creatrix of havoc and grief for all humankind. We know her through the stories passed down to us; stories that have survived wars, philosophical conquests, and the deterioration of time. Like so many stories surviving through subjugation, Pandora's tale is cautionary and moralistic, telling us of the dangers of womanly beauty and curiosity.

When we think deeply about these stories we scratch our heads in consternation and ask, "Why should beauty and curiosity lead to betrayal and pain? Who was Pandora really? Who is she now?" Much of the myth comes from the time in Greek civilization that did not particularly honor women, a time when philosophy and stories were aimed at controlling the population and directing them to specific ways of under-standing; thinking that included the polarities of good and evil, woman and man, beauty and corruption. The idea of balancing negatives and finding that every strength was bal-anced by an equally strong evil was born then and these myths about Pandora reflect that.

The Greek myths of the Olympians tell us that Pandora was the first human woman, created at the order of Zeus as a gift to man. The most powerful and magical gods and god-desses attended her birth, watching as she was fashioned from water and earth on the forge of Hephaestus, the god of fire and craftsmen. Each god and goddess gave his or her most treasured talents as gifts. Aphrodite, the goddess of beauty and love, gave her beauty and a gorgeous necklace forged by Hephaestus. Apollo, the god of the Sun, healing arts, and the arts, gave her music and the gift of healing. Hermes, the mes-senger of the gods, gave her the power of persuasion. Athena, goddess of wisdom, craft, political persuasion, and war, gave her manual dexterity and taught her to spin. Demeter taught her to tend a garden, and Hera gave her curiosity. Poseidon, god of the sea, gave her a beautiful pearl and eternal resis-tance to drowning. Pandora was born as a fearless woman of beauty, talent, intelligence, strength, and ability. She was truly blessed with connections to Divinity and all their magic and talents. Her name, Pandora, means "all-gifted."

Conflicting Tales

And then there is a negative turning in her stories as Pandora became the personification of Greek civilization's misogynist theory of "beauty on the outside and evil on the inside." Like that other first woman (Eve), Pandora becomes a baser crea-ture, giving in to instinct and taking the blame for the ills of humankind. While some stories say that Pandora was a genu-ine gift to man, the most well-known ones say that Zeus was lividly angry that fire had been given to men by Prometheus, whose name meant "forethought." In this version, the entire motivation for creating Pandora and endowing her with curiosity and cunning was because Zeus was after revenge on Prometheus and all mankind. So she was given to Prometheus' brother, Epimotheus, whose name means "afterthought" and who was responsible for giving positive traits and strengths to all animals. A woman of beauty, talent, and creative ability would be the perfect partner for such a creative man. It was a joyful occasion with an undercurrent of hidden intention.

Along with Pandora came the infamous box, the mysterious container with the caution that it was never to be opened. Most scholars believe that the box was a mistranslation for what was really an alabaster jar. Cautioned and tantalized about the contents of the jar or box and then left alone with it, Pandora became consumed with curiosity and longed to discover the contents. Finally, she opened it and found that Zeus had placed all the evils—death, disease, sorrow, grief, and more—in the world in there, and they were unleashed into the world of humankind. As she closed the jar, only one thing remained: hope.

A lesser-known tale says that Pandora was created in good faith by the Olympian Gods as a blessing for mankind. Her jar was filled with wedding blessings that flew out into the world when the jar was opened. According to Patricia Monaghan in *The New Book of Goddesses & Heroines* (Llewellyn 1997), Pandora was probably one of the original chthonic earth goddesses and the bestower of gifts. Her name meant "rich in gifts" and her nature was generous, fruitful, and beautiful. So rather than a passive recipient of gifts, she becomes the active, powerful, and wondrous giver of all.

The story and symbolism that comes down to us through the Greek myths give us a philosophy that is no longer relevant in Pagan thought. Her story is skewed because, as is often the case with human nature, we remember the negative rather than the magically positive. The Greeks saw this beautiful and talented woman as suspicious, a gift too good to be true. Even details such as whether the container is a box or a jar is interesting, and perhaps the mistranslation was an unconscious revulsion toward women's sensual and sexual power. Box is slang for vagina, and her box might be a passageway to the deeper mysteries of women and their wild sexuality. This wild and unpredictable women's power was something that needed to be controlled by equating the passageway to women's ecstasy with all the evils found on earth. Her control of disease, heartache, sorrow, and grief is the role of the Dark Goddess—she who guides us into the lands of fear and dread. Her beauty is a terrible one and her love is reserved for those who will journey the passageways of destruction and creation. It is a wild journey that brings us hope and reunion with our divine selves.

Beyond the Box

When I think about the contents of the box that contained all the evils that beset mankind, I wonder if that is only half the story. It does seem to be human nature to de-emphasize the positive and focus on the negative. What if there were more? An herbalist friend tells me that whenever a poisonous plant grows wild, the herb that provides the antidote is always growing nearby. What if, when the evils of the world were released, the remedy was also released? Because we only train ourselves to see the negative, we often miss the beauty that lingers near. What if we shift our focus and soften our vision to see the good?

What if we returned to those older stories of the earth, chthonic goddess, the giver of death and life? I think the true story of Pandora as the chthonic giver of gifts, the loving and beautiful goddess generously sharing is something that we can retrieve and revitalize. Doing so would not only make her relevant to us today, but also allow us to work with her on a magical and spiritual level. We can begin with new stories, seeing Pandora as the giver of all gifts, death and life, dark and light, giving and receiving. It is not necessary for us to maintain the misogynistic picture of Pandora. We can reclaim her as a wild beautiful goddess of light and dark.

In meditation, we can journey to become who she is now. To set the stage for this meditation, create a meditation space that is full of grace and beauty. Place items on you altar that symbolize opposites, the dark and the light, beauty and ugliness . . . don't favor the positive over the negative, but achieve a balance between that which you fear and that which you love.

If you have a drum, begin by drumming the rhythm of the heartbeat. If not, sing a single tone. Connect yourself with the firm solidity of the earth. Close your eyes and take a deep breath. As you breathe deeply, find yourself in your favorite outdoor place. Drink in the beauty of that space. Breathe deeply the calm and the safety you feel there. With another breath, you see a pathway extending outward from you. You walk on that pathway, noticing the landscape as you walk. Finally, you come to a valley and in the center is a circle surrounding a fire pit. You know it is a dancing floor. You hear drumming and laughter—and suddenly the dancing floor is filled with dancing women, swirling and circling in flashes of color. Their laughter fills your ears. All but one woman recedes from your vision. Her beauty and power fill you as you watch her wild dance. You realize that she is the first Woman, Pandora, and she chants to you:

> *I conjure the powers of dark and light*
> *I dance the pathways of Sun and Moon*
> *I call to you to see my truth*
> *Open your heart and enrich your soul.*

You feel your heart open as her chant fills your being; she reaches out and pulls you into the dance. Finally, when the dancing stops she takes you by the hand to a piece of ground and tells you to lie down on the earth. You lie down and merge with the earth. You become the earth.

Suddenly, you feel a powerful hand scoop you up and place you on the forge, beating you into shape. It feels glorious, the time of becoming. Water washes over you and you find yourself taking on a wonderful shape. You are beautiful, perfect. These hands take you and place you in the middle of a circle, and you realize you are surrounded by the divine creatures, beings of talent, beauty, and strength. As you watch and listen, they come forward and identify themselves. Each one gives you a gift, something you need now in your life. (Take a long pause to listen as the meditation unfolds.)

When the creation is finished, these divine beings encircle you with their arms and chant your name over and over again, raising energy upward and upward, bursting into the sky, empowering you and the world to new magic and new understanding. At the end, Pandora comes and takes you by the hand.

She leads you back to the dancing floor where you are surrounded by dancing women, the dancers of divine energy. You dance together as time disappears. Finally, it is time to leave and she leads you back to your favorite outdoor place. She smiles at you and hands you a beautiful box. She gives you final words, special to you, and then leaves you with a final message, "all gifts are yours to receive, and all gifts are yours to give. Take these and use them for you and yours." And with a hug and a kiss, she is gone.

And you take a deep breath and return to this space and time. Breathe again and remember your connection to Mother Earth. Take some time to write down the wisdom of your meditation. Also take some time to work with this new, fuller, older, and beautiful image of Pandora. You will find that she will help you discover more gifts and you will discover her to be not only larger than life, but larger than her stories—more expansive and full of wonder as she brings fresh joy to you. Call on her to reveal the darkness and the light and find that she gives you the gifts of healing, survival, pleasure, intelligence, beauty, power, and, most of all, curiosity.

The Magic of Evolution

by Paniteowl

Evolution is such a magical process that many spend their lives studying the patterns of change that have occurred throughout the ages. Magic is an evolutionary process of recognizing patterns and flowing with, or adjusting to, the patterns to suit ourselves. I know that sounds a bit simplistic, but magic happens when we understand how things work, and how certain elements work with each other. The most fascinating magical evolution is life itself!

Science has shown that every species on this planet is a carbon-based life form. This raw material is so adaptive that we have hundreds of thousands of species sharing our world. It's truly amazing the variety of life forms our ecosystem can sustain. Exploring the patterns of adaptability is fascinating, but discovering how it all happens is a wonderful experience of great significance to the magical practitioner! When the first diagrams of the double helix DNA strand were shown to the world, many Witches smiled and clapped their hands in glee. The spiral dance of life was actually being shown in a scientific manner! Buried deep in all those lumps of carbon, in all their various configurations, the DNA was programming the patterns of life . . . spiraling around in wanton abandonment, creating wondrous beings such as you and me!

Yes, the magical practitioner, the cunning man, the Witch doctors, the seers, and the Witches had an understanding of the basic workings that create and preserve life. The carbon-based material is the clay, and the DNA is the sculptor. Depending on the arrangement of the molecules, we may be a bug, or a plant, or a human, but we all have that spiral dictating who and what we are. We may not have all described this awareness in the same way, but each culture had, in the teachings of the Wise Ones, a firm understanding of the balance of life.

Scientists have figured out the coding for approximately 97 percent of the DNA structure. They know which molecules affect our general make-up, but the other 3 percent—which is really a lot of molecules—is still a mystery. So let's look at a possibility. What if that 3 percent of DNA is the "input" component of our programming? Like the keyboard of a computer, that 3 percent takes in the experience of the individual and translates that to adjust the basic programming within the 97 percent that controls our physical reality.

Perhaps we should look at the DNA as a huge computer program. The basic program is configured to run in a specific pattern, and each species (plant, mineral, animal) has its own unique lines of code. The variables of input then create a new database from which we can extract information or examine the patterns of data to create other programs as needed. So we may have 20, or 2,000 variants of bluebirds. We may have a thousand variants of goldfish! The basic program dictates one is a bird or one is a fish . . . but the experiences of the individuals begins to create a new database, and future generations use the basic program along with the input data, to adapt to specific conditions that affected their ancestors. That database now becomes an integral part of the basic program.

A Collective, Intergenerational Experience

How would that work for humans? Well, when we develop a program, we input certain lines of code to tell it what to do. We also build in "What if?" codes so that the program itself adapts to information and makes modifications as it receives input from the keyboard. Let's say that the genetic information we get from our parents is the basic program. In that 97 percent of our DNA, the genetic factors govern our height, our hair color, our eye color, and our bone structure. It can even carry some factors that make us allergic to things, or others that make us prone to certain diseases. It can also carry the talents for artistry, or math, or any number of disciplines. That other 3 percent—the "keyboard"—is just waiting for us to input additional information that makes each of us unique.

So genetics are more than the original programming code; they are also the experiential factors that have impact on current practice and future generations. Each of us is the product of our genetic coding along with all of the input that went before us. If we look at it this way, isn't that a good explanation for evolution?

As we look at the evolution of different species, we can understand how the hummingbird developed a long and slender beak to sip nectar from flowers, while the pelican developed a huge beak with a deep pouch in order to scoop fish from the waters. Their particular evolution came from necessity and living in a specific environment.

A fascinating program about African elephants explained the phenomenon of a herd that was struggling for survival during a drought, the likes of which hadn't been seen in over a hundred years. This was much longer than the oldest elephant of the herd had been alive. At a certain point, when it was evident the herd was in mortal danger, the matriarch began to lead the herd out of its territory along a path that was unfamiliar to them. She led them to a watering hole far from their home turf. How did she know where to find water in times of drought, even though they had never been to that particular watering place? Somewhere, in their collective memory, they recalled the pathway, and the existence of that which they needed for survival. Were they recalling a past life? Or were they tapping into a special awareness? Either way, they were "remembering" what was learned before, even though it was not their own personal experience.

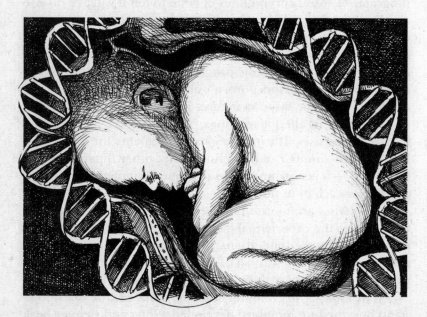

In studying the various species, we often neglect to consider the human evolution. Yes, we know that today we are taller, stronger, and living longer than our ancestors of a few centuries ago. But it's not only the physical part of our being that is subject to evolution. Our awareness of our environment, our culture, our society is constantly undergoing an evolution. The more we know, the more we change. New knowledge encourages an evolution on all levels, not just the physical.

We know that DNA is used in police investigations to identify victims and criminals alike. However, DNA is also being used to trace ancestry of various groups. A prime example is the Lost Tribes of Israel. DNA testing shows that groups of people in such places as Ethiopia, China, and the West Indies can indeed be traced to common parentage in Israel centuries ago. This tracing is done through the specific patterns of DNA, which is simply the ability to recognize the matriarchal lineage.

Studies done in European communities by Bryan Sykes, professor of human genetics at Oxford University, claim to have traced origins back to seven original mothers. Calling them "The Seven Daughters of Eve," professor Sykes has individually named them Ursula, Xenia, Tara, Helena, Katrine, Valda, and Jasmine. Professor Sykes arrived at his conclusion by studying mitochondrial DNA, which is passed down from mothers to children. From 6,000 random samples, and allowing for naturally occurring mutations, he established seven different clusters of DNA. Professor Sykes says that the ancestry of 99 percent of Europeans can now be traced back to the seven women who founded the clans.

Since the number seven is significant in many cultures, it doesn't come as a surprise to those of us who study old lore. Celtic belief says the people came from beyond the seven waves. Could this be a reference to the original seven birth waters of the first mothers? The Seven Sisters of the Pleiades are well known through astrology, and other cultures also have similar references to the Seven, who created life as we know it. Are we recalling a specific memory of importance in our ancestry?

Taking this premise one step further, let's look at what happens when a person achieves something spectacular in human history. Years ago, running the four-minute mile was thought to be impossible, until Roger Bannister actually did it on May 6, 1954. According to physiologists of the time, it was dangerous to the health of any athlete who attempted to reach that goal. Within months of his accomplishment, a number of runners achieved that milestone, and today, it's a common occurrence at meets all over the country. All the subsequent generations of runners who have broken that record are not the progeny of the original record breaker. It is not just the physical ability that is passed on to others, but the awareness of the possibility changed the future generations. Awareness of another person's achievement caused an evolution in the sport of running. Once our species realized we could do something, future generations took it in stride and adapted.

Magical Applications of DNA

How does this relate to magical practices? Well, one of the most interesting topics of conversation in the magical community is reincarnation. How would it work if we applied this theory of "DNA as a computer program" with the ability to have "input" to the program's development? For most of us, it's difficult to take our egos out of the equation. We do a past-life regression and are surprised when we recall a memory that makes us realize we were a different gender, or that we were not all kings, queens, or exciting personages of recorded history. Most of us were average, working people who lived lives of commonplace experience. But in each lifetime, our experiences, and life lessons, have an impact on who we are today. What about those who claim to have been Cleopatra or Attila the Hun? Are they actually recalling a prior existence as that person? Or are they recalling a memory of someone being affected by these personages during their own lifetime, or perhaps recalling the memory of an ancestor reading about the infamous personalities?

Are we actually reborn again and again, or are we a "live recording" of a genetic memory experience? Might it be that we have the ability to tap into the cosmic awareness that Jung proposed? Or could all of the experiences of our ancestors be stored somewhere in that 97 percent of our DNA? In order for evolution to occur, we must be aware of our past on a very basic level. How much more basic can it be that the record of our history is passed on within the very fiber of our being? Well, what if we can access the memory of those changes in our DNA? What if our past life regression techniques are bringing up our code changes? What if the ancients understood this better than we do, and named the phenomenon, "Akashic Records?" What if the gods and goddesses have built-in the capability to retrieve the old files, just as we do today when we make backups of our programs? What if our meditations and regression therapies are the means of accessing the history of that 3 percent input function?

Have I given you something to think about?

Harness the Power of the Sun with Sunstone!

by Muse

There is nothing quite like the power of the Sun. It infuses the world with life and energy. Sunrise wakes us in the morning, and sunset leads the way into the night. Sunlight energizes us, staves off depression, gives us light to see by, and can heal minor skin irritations. But it can also burn the skin, scorch the Earth, prevent rest, and be harnessed into destructive flames. The Sun's power is unmistakable and relentless.

Much focus has been brought to Moon power since the days of women's rights have begun. And justly so, as women are linked to the Moon intrinsically. However, as in all things, there must be balance. Women and men alike pull power from the Sun as well as the Moon—psychic, physical, and spiritual power. Without the Sun, the Moon cannot shine her light upon us.

The Sun's energy is inherently male. It is positive, energizing, forceful, physical, and dynamic. But that does not mean it affects only men. Indeed, women can benefit from its power just as greatly. Men and women can use the Sun's energy for protection, sexual energy, and health. It can also be used to give strength in times of weakness.

One way to harness the Sun's energy is to use a sunstone in your magical practices. True sunstone, a form of feldspar, has the same opalescence as a moonstone, only with the fiery orange and gold of the Sun. It is linked to the Greek Sun god Helios, son of Hyperion and Theia. The Greeks believed that each morning at dawn, Helios rises from the east in his chariot, pulled by four horses.

Sunstone is beautiful set in a necklace or ring, and protects the wearer while also increasing self-esteem and self-confidence. Wearing sunstone in any form, though, whether in a piece of jewelry or in a mojo bag or magical pouch, increases your positive energy, improves your attitude, and battles depression. It promotes cheerfulness and good temper. But the most powerful influence this stone has is strengthening. It increases stamina and lends extra energy to the body during times of illness. Sunstone truly embodies the physical energy of the Sun.

Physically, sunstone is effective for increasing blood circulation, and has an invigorating effect overall. It is a wonderful tool to help heal the heart, eyes, and kidneys. Placed near the sexual region, it acts as an aphrodisiac, increasing blood flow to the sexual organs and stimulating arousal. Sexual energy and stamina are increased as well.

If you do not wish to physically carry the stone on you, sunstone water is a great way to draw on the energy of this stone. Place a sunstone in a glass of water and put in a place where the Sun will shine on it for a few hours during the day. At the end of the day, remove the sunstone from the water and drink up! When you drink the water, imagine you are soaking in the power of the Sun—great waves of orange and gold energy enter your body and infuse you with life.

While the Moon is often seen as the mistress of creativity, the Sun can also help keep the creative juices flowing. Any artist knows how frustrating it can be when you are "on a roll" and your physical energy starts lapsing, or when your creative energy is fluctuating too much to complete a piece. Place a sunstone at the base of a white candle, and light the candle. Imagine the candle is pulling the sunstone's fiery energy up into it and the energy is being released into the air through the flame. Soak in that energy and you will find your stamina increases and creativity can continue on. This is, of course, best done at your place of work. But if you cannot perform this ritual in the location where you create, perform it at home before you leave for the office or creative setting.

Another use of sunstone is in a healing pouch. Take a green or white drawstring bag and place in it healing herbs such as sage, rosemary, juniper, chamomile, goldenseal, garlic, feverfew, ginger, or licorice. Then place a sunstone in the bag and chant over it:

> *I call upon the Sun,*
> *Great giver of life*
> *Infuse this bag with your energy,*
> *Bless it with your strength,*
> *Fill it with your power.*

The sunstone will increase the power of the healing herbs. If you keep the bag on you, it will increase your own physical energy as well.

I have found that sunstone is the gemstone version of caffeine. Besides increasing physical energy and stamina, it also boosts the power of your spells. With this powerful energy, however, I would recommend not having sunstone on your person when trying to meditate!

Sunstone is not an easy stone to find. Unfortunately, it does not share the hype of its cousin, the moonstone, thus many shops where you can find stones for magical use will simply not have them. However, I have had some luck finding them online with certain larger metaphysical supply distributors, and also at metaphysical fairs. If you do not live near these fairs, online will be your best bet. Treasure what you find. The sparkling energy of these stones is potent and you will find many uses for them.

The Bully Buster

For Wiccan and Pagan Children, Teens, and Young Adults–And Their Parents

by A. C. Fisher Aldag

Bullying is an unpleasant topic, but a very necessary one for the parents of Wiccan and Pagan children to consider. In-school bullying has had terrible consequences over the past few years. In Oklahoma, a young woman of Native American descent, Brandi Blackbear, was ostracized by her peers and suspended from school for studying Wicca—but not actually practicing the religion. Near Detroit, Michigan, a twelve-year-old Wiccan girl named Tempest Smith was teased by her classmates so badly that she took her own life. And we are all painfully aware of what happened when two boys at Columbine High School in Littleton, Colorado, were bullied by their peers. Because Wicca, Paganism, and other nature religions are sometimes misunderstood, because the Goth subculture and a gay lifestyle are often feared, kids who may look or act differently from other students could be singled out—sometimes with disastrous results.

As a mother and as a Pagan clergyperson, I've had to confront the topic of bullying in school. My daughter Rhiannon is a Goth and an openly practicing Pagan. She is also a cheerleader, 4-H teen leader, and good student who has many friends. She also had some serious enemies. My son Brandyn has very long hair, as do many of the men in our Celtic Pagan culture. People sometimes made rude comments about my children's beliefs—including teachers, a scout leader, and a cheerleading coach. We developed several coping strategies, both mundane and magical, to diffuse this type of bad behavior. As an advocate for other young victims, my goal is to help educate their peers, and often to inform the teachers, administrators, community leaders, and other adults who should be providing leadership and guidance. I don't have all the answers, yet I believe that everything happens for a reason, that every event is part of a pattern, and that the gods direct us in situations that help our growth and spiritual development. So I will try to share with readers some ideas and techniques we developed to help children deal with difficult peers.

First, a parent must identify that a problem exists. Is your child reluctant to go to school? Is she afraid to get on the bus, to attend extracurricular activities? Does she have a lot of "tummy-aches" in the morning? Are his grades dropping? Does he complain of having no friends? Does your child seem fearful of one individual, dislike one specific class, or express mistrust of one particular teacher? Talk to your child. Find out if there is a bully problem, or if your son just hates math, or if Miss Jones is mean to everyone equally. Your problem may be solved by a tutor, a classroom reassignment, or by walking your child to the bus stop. He may feel clumsy in Little League, and need glasses. He might just need to learn to ignore spiteful remarks.

Some kids will make hurtful comments to everyone just to get a reaction. "You're fat, you're ugly, you worship the devil." Your child might need to learn to choose his battles, and to consider when it's appropriate to ignore a taunt, necessary to answer back, or time to report dangerous behavior to an authority. When my son was teased for his long hair, he retorted, "Yeah, I might look like a girl, but you look like a sheared sheep. So, you wanna play catch, or just stand there making dumb comments?" The other boys soon became his friends, and the teasing is now good-natured. When another child insisted on poking my daughter on the bus, she replied with a low, powerful voice, and bellowed:

"Stop that right now, that hurts me!" This response attracted the kind of attention the bully didn't want.

You might also consider helping your child to find a new peer group where he is more accepted. Not everyone is going to get along with everyone else. Your kid may be the belle of the band, the king of the chess club, but a nerd on the ball field. She may have to learn to acknowledge her shortcomings. Try to involve your children in various clubs, organizations, or different peer situations where they can excel. Your kids may have to go outside the mainstream to find friends who accept them. There are many covens and religious groups for Pagan teens, online and in person. Spiral Scouts, a program oriented toward nature spirituality, or an Internet chat group for teen Witches might be the answer. Llewellyn Publishing has information and books just for young people. Silver Ravenwolf's *Teen Witch* is a great resource for both covens and solitaries. If there isn't a Pagan organization for kids near you, you and your child may consider forming your own religious society. Our Pagan church started its own youth group with service projects, field trips, and campouts. My children made lifelong friends at the Pagan festival we attend annually. When things got rough at school, my daughter could call other young Witches for support.

A word of caution: As parents, you must ensure that your children are safe. Get to know their friends. Unfortunately, there are predators within the Pagan, Goth, and vampire subcultures who may take advantage of young people (just as there are predators in Christian churches, mainstream scouting, youth camps, or anywhere else). Be aware of who your kids are associating with, who is in charge, and what is going on there. Any decent coven, study group, or teen club will allow parents to sit in. If your presence is unwelcome, this is a red flag.

Your child's newfound acceptance in a different peer group may be enough to bolster self-image, raise confidence, and stop them from being the target of any bullying. However, the school situation or team dynamic might still have a negative impact. If peer behavior is physically harmful, or contains repeated hateful slurs or racial comments, and continues even though you and your child have made an effort to diffuse it, you might have a serious bully issue. "Joan ripped up my music and hid my trumpet." "All the boys are calling me a slut." "They put a smoke bomb in my locker again." Or it might be something even more dangerous, like the football team threatening a gay boy with locker-room beatings. Then it's time for parents to intervene.

Role of Agency Support

Psychologists say that bullies suffer from low self-esteem and that their attitude may come from feeling threatened themselves. They may feel powerless and weak in their own home environment. In this case, a constructive confrontation can be beneficial. Talk to the parents of a disgruntled student. Talk to the teacher and/or the principal, and if you don't get a response, talk to the school board. If this does not work, you may have to speak to the police and the juvenile authorities. If a child is bullying because he is being harmed or threatened at home, it may be appropriate to discuss the matter with a social service agency.

Sometimes, the officials themselves are the problem. If a bus driver is making unacceptable comments to your child, talk to the bus garage manager or transportation director. If a teacher is singling your child out for punishment, first meet with the teacher, then with the authorities, including the principal or school board. You may have to speak to the teacher's union. If a coach is behaving in an inappropriate way, you may have to discuss the matter with other parents or even the businesses that help sponsor the team. Occasionally, a teacher will behave in a very unprofessional manner. "Mr. Smith said my pentacle is the sign of the devil, and made me take it off." If it is a clear case of ongoing religious discrimination, which continues long after discussion, education, and counseling, it might be time to contact an attorney.

Your child has the same right to practice his religion as any other child. As long as he is obeying reasonable school rules—and the rules are equally enforced on all children—a student can wear his religious symbol, pray to his deities before meals, refuse to salute the flag or take an oath, or draw a picture of the Goddess in art class. You may have to insist that your daughter be allowed to miss school on Imbolc or not eat meat at the sports banquet. If comments from teachers or authorities involve racism, sexism, unreasonable demands, inappropriate remarks, or hate speech about your child's religion, then this creates a hostile environment for education. This is unlawful.

When addressing school authorities or community leaders, remain calm. State the problem in clear, specific terms, without calling names or making unfounded accusations. "On six occasions, my daughter Suzie was confronted in the locker room before gym class. The girls said that she was a Witch and that they were going to burn her. I want this intolerable behavior to stop." Magically speaking, you might wish to carry a talisman for protection, strength, courage, or justice in your pocket, arrange to have the meeting on an auspicious day, wear empowering colors in your clothing, and perform a ritual beforehand (more on this topic appears below).

It always helps if you have some backup. After Tempest Smith's tragic suicide, her mother dedicated her life to educating young people and teachers about religious tolerance. The Tempest Smith Foundation has a wonderful brochure entitled "No Hate" available online. Other groups, including the Pagan Educational Network and the Pagan Pride Project, have pamphlets, fliers, and informational brochures designed to inform non-Pagans about the beliefs and practices of nature spirituality. Most of this literature is available at minimal cost. Pagan and Wiccan organizations such as Circle Sanctuary's Lady Liberty League, Covenant of the Goddess, AREN, and non-sectarian groups such as ReligiousTolerance.org, can help you with coaching, educational information, and referrals for legal assistance.

If it is a separation of church and state issue, governmental interference with the practice of religion, or tax dollars being used to favor one religion over another, you may get assistance from the American Civil Liberties Union or a similar constitutional foundation. If authorities are unresponsive, you may wish to hire an attorney specializing in civil rights issues. This solution is often effective, but it's rather extreme. Dealing with the court system can consume a great deal of time and energy, it's expensive, it's mentally and spiritually exhausting for a family, and therefore should only be considered as a last resort. Before making any decision to consult an attorney or yank your kid out of class in favor of homeschooling, talk with trusted friends or clergypersons, consult your oracles, perform divination, and pray. Your guides may have a better solution for your family.

Sometimes, a bully is just a very mean person who enjoys threatening and intimidating someone perceived to be weaker. In this case, you might have to take more drastic measures. As you would in your magical workings, carefully consider the consequences of your actions. While I can't endorse using threats, violence, or pepper spray (or any activity that could result in getting suspended from school for a week), aggressive behavior is something that bullies often understand—and it might be worth it if the bullying will cease and desist. My daughter Rhiannon had to take similar action. When a group of thugs at her small rural high school surrounded a gay lad and threatened to put him in the hospital, she shouted, "Don't make me ruin my cheerleading uniform!" and began rolling up her sleeves and wading into the fray. Yes, she attracted the attention of the hall monitors. Yes, she got in trouble. But it stopped the attack, and made the bullies feel ashamed of themselves for threatening a physically smaller person. And I was very proud of her for defending a young man who may have otherwise been badly hurt.

Magical Alternatives

A better idea may be performing magical rituals with the idea of stopping the negative behavior. Even though a bully might be a danger to others, he still has free will, and to interfere can have magical repercussions. Remember that you want to change the situation, but it is up to the gods to change an individual person. Your magical workings should be aimed toward modifying your circumstances, making your child's environment more tolerable, raising her self-image, creating new friendships, and granting her the strength to cope with a difficult problem. If your child is being harmed by a teacher's unacceptable comments, it may be appropriate to ask the deities for justice and to invoke proper authority. If your son is being physically threatened, then it is OK to perform a binding spell on a person who is capable of actually causing serious harm. Remember the law of return (any energy you send out shall return to you three-fold) still applies. "Joan's behavior cannot and will not harm me or my property" or

"Mr. Smith has no effect on our religious beliefs or practices" are examples of spell wording that does no harm, yet brings about effective change.

Magically speaking, remember that new projects should begin at the New Moon, that banishing rituals should occur during the waning Moon, and that ceremonies to invoke a better situation should be performed during the waxing Moon. A request for power and authority should happen during the Full Moon. The day of the week may be used to correspond with a particular outcome, for instance, requesting justice on a Thursday, calling for loving friendships on a Friday, summoning the entities related to education on a Wednesday. Look in tables of correspondences

for the proper color of candle to burn, magical sigils, suggestions for spellwork, and appropriate herbs and gemstones used to create a particular condition. (Scott Cunningham has some really good ones.)

An example of a bully-busting spell: Inscribe runes and symbols of protection on a royal blue candle, anoint it with frankincense oil, and burn it on Tuesday. As it burns, chant, "I call protection unto me, safety and security, as my will so mote it be." (Kids are creative, I'm sure you can come up with a better rhyme!) Keep a piece of sodalite or malachite in your pocket. Visualize a shining, royal blue light shimmering around you, creating an impenetrable shield, especially when in the presence of the bully.

Call for strength, courage, and dignity for yourself and your loved ones. Your child may feel safer after summoning Nike or Athena for protection, Lugh for bravery, or Danu for motherly comfort away from home. The very act of performing magic can help a child to feel empowered. And don't forget to apply doses of humor. One young Goth gentleman wore a T-shirt proclaiming "I only wear black because all my pink clothes are in the laundry!" This statement made people laugh with him, not at him.

However, such self-ridicule might not have been as effective in the past. Pagans and other practitioners of nature spirituality have made great strides over the past twenty years. Children have won the right to wear their pentacle necklace or Triple Moon symbol to class. In most places, parents do not have to hide their religious beliefs from the authorities, fearing loss of custody or visits from social services. Books about Wicca can be found in many public libraries. Yet we still have a long way to go.

Good luck and blessings to children of Pagan, Wiccan, heathen, and other nature spirituality paths.

Mail Magic

by Elizabeth Hazel

Good old snail mail benefits from magical improvement, especially when a specific concern or need is involved. As an inveterate card sender (and happy recipient), the following procedures have been tested and proven to yield good results.

Merry Mailbox

To attract good news, friendly cards, and invitations—pick a small bouquet of golden yarrow, wormwood, and lavender under a nearly Full Moon. Tie together with a red ribbon and dry upside down, and then tie it to the mailbox. If a bouquet won't work, put herbs in a small cloth pouch. Place this inside of the mailbox for the same effect.

Put crystals in a mailbox for specific types of mail. If you're waiting for a check, put a piece of malachite or bloodstone in the mailbox. For getting news from a loved one, use a rose quartz. For good news on test results, use either citrine or clear crystal quartz. To repel negativity (and junk mail), use carnelian.

Mail Supplies

To add a touch of magic to everything you send, find a nice box to transform into your Magical Stationery Box. Smudge the box with sage or incense. Sprinkle with consecrated sand, herbs, and spices. Add a cotton ball saturated with oil or perfume, crystals or stones, and a picture of a favorite god or goddess. Fill the box with everything you might need to send mail. This might include a consecrated pen, stamps, return address stickers, envelopes, personal stationery, and cards.

Sending Magic Through the Mail

Yule cards: Add a whiff of good cheer to Yule cards by saturating a cotton ball with essential pine, orange, and cinnamon oils. Put the cotton ball with the cards in a plastic container.

Seal it tightly, and leave undisturbed for a couple of weeks. The cards will have a lovely, seasonal fragrance.

To bind Yule blessings to a card, get a hole-puncher and cut pieces of yellow, green, and red ribbon (string works too if no thin ribbon is available). Punch a hole near the top of the card, thread the ribbon through the hole, and fold both ends of the ribbons together. Tie three knots from the top to the bottom of the strand and proclaim a wish for health, wealth, and happiness with each knot. **Variations:** Braid the strands, or attach a small Witches ladder to the card. Cut a piece of red ribbon and tie a feather into each knot, making wishes for the recipient as each knot is tied. Any kind of binding charm works well in the mail.

Magical herbs make a nice addition: pick fragrant herbs and long, fragrant pine needles. Tie into tiny bouquets with gold and red ribbon or string. Dry in a press or between two heavy books. Enclose in Yule cards in protective tissue paper.

Valentine's cards and love letters: Add dried petals of a red rose to a letter that expresses deep feelings and tenderness. Sprinkle dried lavender into a card for a good friend.

St. Patrick's Day or Ostara: Send a lasting good-luck token. Pick fresh cloverleaves and cut a piece of 1 × 6 inch parchment or card stock. Stack a paper towel, a piece of wax paper, and the piece of parchment and arrange the fresh cloverleaves. Stack another piece of wax paper and paper towel, then iron until the wax paper seals the strip. Trim the edges, punch a hole in the top, and tie a knot to bind in the good luck with gold and green ribbon. If clover-shaped and/or egg-shaped glitter is available, add this to the card, too.

Get well cards: Sprinkle dried lavender and thyme inside of a get well card. Another thoughtful addition is a piece of rice paper saturated with Florida water or orange water. Let the recipient know that they should place this in their pillow for healing dreams.

Blessing cards: Purchase or create a card with a blessing image: fairies, angels, butterflies, dragonflies, ladybugs, koi (big goldfish), elephants, doves, or bluebirds. Write a note about the blessing you're sending, and sprinkle glitter or herbs in the card. Blessing cards are sweet for new babies, weddings, or other significant and life-changing events. This is also a clever way to spice up a thank-you card.

Special events: If you're planning a performance, gallery opening, or premiere and are sending announcement post-cards, consider charming these invitations en masse. Place the stamped, addressed stack(s) on a pentagram, or put them within a circle made of consecrated sand. Smudge the cards with sage and surround with bay leaves (for success). Compose a spell that indicates what you want to accomplish by sending these cards: to increase attendance, to attract attention and positive publicity, etc. For best results, mail the cards when the Moon is in a Mercury-ruled sign (Gemini or Virgo) and when Mercury is not retrograde.

Mailing Prosperity

If you're sending prosperity wishes to a friend, sprinkle cinnamon (a powerful money attractor) or cedar powder in the card, along with a dollar bill saturated in money oil or cinnamon extract. Tell the recipient to place the card in the location where they normally store their checkbook or wallet, or to simply put the dollar bill in their wallet while imagining it filled with money. It's amazing how well this works for a quick money fix.

To attract prosperity to your household through the mail (or to increase payments, or to get somebody who owes you to pay), try this variation on the "Law of Abundance" spell. Check an astrological calendar and find out when the waxing Moon is trine Jupiter (or ask an astrologer for the exact date and time). When the Moon-Jupiter trine aspect is exact, write a check to "Law of Abundance." Leave the amount blank. Date and sign the check, and say:

> *Law of Abundance, hear my plea*
> *Shower money down on me!*

Wrap the check in a piece of paper, and seal it in an envelope addressed to yourself, with "Law of Abundance" as the return address. For swift results, sprinkle a little yarrow and cinnamon in the envelope. Mail it from the largest post office in your area. When it arrives in your mailbox, put the sealed envelope in your checkbook or wallet.

Helping Others

If there is a person you're worried about, take any letter or card that individual has sent you and place it on a pentagram. Invoke a circle of protection around the pentagram, and imagine a silvery orb of light surrounding the letter that extends to your friend. Ask the deities to protect that individual. Burn a white candle with his/her name inscribed on it.

For someone who works too hard, or has many burdens, mail a surprise gift in a box. It could be a good book, a doll or stuffed toy, a red Chinese money envelope, or any other little treat. The arrival of your gift will give the recipient a magically uplifting "warm fuzzy."

Clearing Negativity

To clear the path to your mailbox and banish negative energies (to eliminate debt, misfortunes, bad luck, hexes, a persistent former lover, etc.), create a banishing pentagram. Working within a circle of protection, draw the star within a circle on a small piece of parchment. Smudge it with sage, and sprinkle with Four Thieves Vinegar. Put the pentagram in an envelope, and add crushed rosemary, cayenne, and basil, and consecrated sand. Mail this to yourself from a post office that is far away from your home. For large-scale banishing, place stamped, addressed, sealed letters into larger envelopes, and mail them to friends across the country along with a note requesting that they mail them to you from their location.

To halt the actions of an adversary (particularly in legal matters), take a letter from that person and put it in the freezer. This doesn't harm the other person, but it will make attacks less effective.

Consecrated Sand

This is an excellent substance to make for mail spells, and can be used for other spells, too. Gather sand three days after a New Moon. Open a circle of protection, and place the bowl of sand on top of a pentagram surrounded by four directional votives. As you light each candle, sprinkle these ingredients over the sand:

Fire: powdered sulphur (crushed match tip is OK)
Water: saved from rainfall or gathered from a river, lake, or ocean
Air: wave feather over the bowl, and stick in the sand
Earth: a pinch of mustard seed

Place a charged quartz crystal or a crystal ball on top of the sand and say:

> *By the power of spirit,*
> *I charge you —*
> *May the blessings you bring*
> *Be as abundant as grains of sand on an endless beach.*
> *So mote it be.*

Let the candles burn down, and leave undisturbed on the altar until the Full Moon. On the night of the Full Moon, place the bowl outside in the Moon's light to complete the charging. The next day, put it in a jar for use. (Thanks to Lord Abriothur for this spell.)

Halloween Hocus~Pocus

by Ellen Dugan

By pumpkins fat and Witches lean . . .
By coal black cats, with eyes of green
By all the magic ever seen . . .
I wish you luck this Halloween!
—Victorian Halloween Postcard

Ah, it's that wonderful time of the year when Witches are suddenly in vogue. A vast array of bewitching themed items can be found in every store across the land. Houses and shops are decorated with orange lights, fall leaves, blooming mums, colorful gourds, pumpkins, and scarecrows. Oh, and of course, ghosts, Witches, and screeching black cats. In all the excitement of decorating and preparing for the sabbat, it is easy to forget that often the most practical and magical of items are to be found very affordably, courtesy of good old Mother Nature. This Halloween why not keep things simple? For your celebrations, consider the seasonal trimmings that are to be found within nature's bounty.

Why the focus on natural items? Because this popular holiday is one of the major sabbats of our earth religion. So as we celebrate the earth and her cycles and seasons, it makes much more sense to work with earthy and natural accessories. Plus, it helps to keep us connected to nature. Much of our Samhain/Halloween folklore comes from fruits, flowers, and such. So why not fly with this idea and see what we can conjure up for your Halloween festivities?

Jack~O'~Lantern

Halloween just wouldn't be the same without the supernatural flicker of jack-o'-lanterns. There is something about those carved and glowing pumpkin faces that put us in a festive mood. The jack-o'-lantern was a Celtic custom, though the ancient people originally used a hollowed out turnip or a cabbage to make their lanterns. These lanterns were a handy way to light their path home after the community bonfires on Samhain night. An ember was dropped inside the hollowed-out cabbage or turnip, so the vegetable was thick enough to illuminate, but not burn.

This night marked a time when the veil between our world and the world of the spirit was thin. So faces were carved in the turnip lanterns to frighten away angry ghosts or spirits that were thought to be wandering about looking for trouble. Years later when Irish, Scots, and English immigrants arrived in the New World, the pumpkin became an ideal choice to replace the turnip. It was in season, readily available, and a gorgeous harvest color. Plus this fruit was large, inexpensive, and very easy to carve.

This Halloween why not use the jack-o'-lantern as it was originally intended? To scare away evil and to frighten off negativity. Those flickering faces can do more than just serve as a beacon for the neighborhood trick-or-treaters. The jack-o'-lantern can also be put to good practical magic use in your Samhain/Halloween festivities.

Here is a fun jack-o'-lantern spell to ward your property. First prep your pumpkins. Scoop and clean out the pumpkins. Then carve your jack-o'-lantern into any expression or bewitching pattern that you desire. Afterwards, arrange the pumpkins in a place of prominence. Perhaps they can flank your front door, or line your walkway. Have the jack-o'-lanterns march up your front steps, tuck them inside of planters or arrange them across an old bench or hay bale. Once you have the pumpkins in place, add a few tea lights in the bottoms of the pumpkins. When dusk falls, light all the candles in your pumpkins. Repeat this Halloween jack-o'-lantern charm as you go along.

> *See this pumpkin all glowing gold?*
> *Protection for my home it holds.*
> *Frighten off evil and turn back, negativity,*
> *This spell is cast, by the magic of All Hallow's Eve.*

When the last of your jack-o'-lanterns is lit, close the spell with these lines.

> *By all the powers of three times three,*
> *As I will it, then so must it be.*

A Fall Flower Fascination

A Chrysanthemum Spell to Ward Off Ghosts

These big, bold, spicy blossoms add glorious color and fragrance to many a yard or container at this time of year. Chrysanthemums are probably one of the most unsung flowers when it comes to magic, because they are so common. The chrysanthemum (*Dendranthema* hybrids)—are affectionately known today as "mums." The name of this flower comes from the Greek words "chrysos," meaning gold, and "anthos," meaning flower. In ancient times, Greeks would wear garlands of chrysanthemums to keep away those dreaded "evil spirits."

For the modern, practical Witch, the mum is a fabulous, protective fall flower that wards the home and keeps away wandering ghosts. Since these flowers are available in a wide range of jewel-toned colors, you can also match the color of the mum to specialize your Halloween spellwork. Red mums mean, "I love you." White signifies "truth," yellow means "happiness," and the gold tones are employed for protection (just like the Romans once did). For the other available jewel tones, I would go with "energy and bounty" for the orange mum, and a "happy hearth and home" for the bronze colors. The amethyst-colored mum could be added to spells worked to promote "power and protection."

These flowers do pack quite a protective punch, and since they are readily available in the fall months, why not work with the seasonal magic already inherent within these flowers? Here is a Chrysanthemum charm for you to perform on Halloween. Choose whichever color you think would match your intention and add a few blossoms to a vase. Or just bless the mums that are already growing in the yard. Happy spellcasting.

A flower fascination I spin on this Halloween night.
Keep spooks and specters far away, repel bad luck from my sight.
Hear my words, and let the magic flow, both hither and yon
This spell will last, and ward my home, until the break of dawn.

Close the flower fascination with:

By the magic of Halloween, as I will it, so must it be.

An Apple Spell for Love Divination

The apple is sacred to the Roman goddess Pomona. Pomona was the keeper of the apple orchards and she traveled the land with her pruning knife tending to and caring for all the apple trees. Pomona was an independent soul, but she too eventually found love with a very determined young man named Vertumnus. Working with apples in your Halloween spells and charms makes good magical sense. Apples are both a fruit of love and a fruit of wisdom. Inside the apple is the star of knowledge, and of course slicing an apple horizontally, will reveal the Witches' star hidden within.

Considering the folkloric significance of this fruit, it's not surprising that in the old days, young women believed that on Halloween night they could divine the name of their future husband by reading apple parings. To perform the old apple peel trick, you must pare an apple in an unbroken chain and then flip the apple peel over your shoulder into a previously placed pot or cauldron of water. The peel will unfurl in the water, taking the shape of the first letter, of the first name, of your true love. Try this Halloween night spell to go along with your love apple divination.

Apple peel, apple peel, let's you and I play a game,
Take the shape, of the first letter, of my true love's name.
By the mystery of love, and the magic of Halloween,
With the help of Pomona, now make your symbol clear to me.

Happy Halloween!

May your Halloween be an enchanted one. Filled with the colors and scents of this most bewitching season. Arrange multicolored leaves around your home. Plant some colorful mums in your garden and allow their natural energies to ward your property. Display your jack-o'-lanterns with Pagan pride, and set a bowl full of bright gold and red apples in the kitchen to inspire love and wisdom. Let the bounty that nature has to offer us inspire your natural and practical magic. My best wishes for a soulful Samhain and of course, a Happy Halloween!

Water Magic

Autumn: The Realm of Water

by Sorita D'Este

Water is essential for life. Life began in water, and it is all around us, covering much of our planet, and making up the bulk of our bodies. Our emotions ebb and flow like the tides of the sea, and can be as serene as a calm lake or as wild and overwhelming as a tsunami. Water also symbolizes our dreams, which rise from the depths of our unconscious minds like a whale surfacing from the deeps.

Water can be nurturing, the "waters of life," or it can represent death, the journey beyond the physical into the unknown, which has always been represented as a journey over water. Because of this, water can also represent rebirth and the compassion that comes from accepting inevitable change.

Water is unique in that it can be solid (ice), liquid, or gaseous (water vapor and steam). Its ability to change state reflects its quality of transformation and adaptability to the appropriate condition, hence the saying, "water always finds its level." In autumn, we encounter the elemental tide of water in the rains that fall and the sense of change that fills the air around us as the tide of the year begins to ebb.

The beings of water are those that live in and around water. The undines or nymphs of water appear as water creatures like dolphins, fish, mermaids, and water-horses. The Ruler of Water usually appears as a voluptuous, beautiful woman with gray-green hair like seaweed and sea-blue eyes. She wears flowing blue robes and is crowned with a wreath of blue lotuses.

Meditation

If possible, this meditation should be done next to a lake, a pond, or by the sea. If not, sit with a small bowl of water (from a natural source) in front of you as you undergo this journey into the watery realms.

Close your eyes and focus on the water in the air around you. Feel the damp on your skin and the moisture as you breathe in deeply. In your mind's eye, visualize a huge blue pentagram, pointing upward, on a sea green background. See the pentagon in the center of the pentagram shimmer and disappear, opening a doorway to the elemental realm of water. Through the doorway you see waves breaking on the seashore. See a cliff on the right and a Full Moon in the night sky above.

The pentagram grows larger as it moves closer to you, with its lower points sinking into the ground beneath. You see yourself walking through the central pentagon and as you do so, you hear the crashing of waves on the shore and the sound of falling water. You look more closely at the cliff, seeing a river tumbling over its edge, forming a mighty waterfall down into the sea. You continue to look around, you observe the waves breaking on the beach, the fresh and saltwater mingling, and notice the beach curving away on the horizon.

Feeling the call of the water drawing you toward the sea, you step into the water. Continue walking into the water and feel the water covering your legs, your chest—then dive into the water and swim around. As you do so, focus on the limitations of your body in the water and how that differs from the sea creatures, which often have tails. Hold your legs together,

focus and feel your legs merging together, becoming a large tail, as you transform into a mer-person. In this form you are free to explore the ocean, dive under the surface of the water and swim easily.

Swimming around, you see coral reefs with shoals of multicolored fish swimming through and between them. Dolphins playfully chase each other, and you see other creatures like octopi, whales, and even a sea-goat all swimming through the waters. You realize that as a mer-person you can breathe underwater and are not restricted in your movements in the ocean, so you swim around and explore your surroundings with joy and wonder.

As you swim and explore, you appreciate the freedom the sea offers, and your senses respond to a different set of stimuli. You hear the songs of whales and the chattering of dolphins carried in the water. You feel the currents within the water, the different temperatures, a cooling sensation as you descend to greater depths. The sheer magnitude and diversity of the watery realm and the life inhabiting it leave you amazed, and you understand why the oceans are known as "inner space" and you come to a greater appreciation of them.

After a while, you decide it is time to return to land and swim back toward the shore, the powerful strokes of your tail quickly propelling you through the water. As the water gets shallower, you know you will need to return to your human form, so you concentrate on your tail and feel it turn back into your legs and feet as you make a final kick up to the surface and your head breaks through into the air. You walk back to the shore and see the open pentagon doorway in the pentagram waiting. You continue through the doorway to your original position, take a few deep breaths and open your eyes.

Hapi: God of the River Nile

by Denise Dumars

The river Nile is the lifeline, bloodline, and origin of all fertility and abundance in Egypt. The Egyptians are grateful for, and indebted to, the Nile. The river Nile gave abundance not only in the form of fish to eat, but of water to drink; beautiful and useful water plants such as lotuses and lilies of the Nile; birds; and the rich black silt that spilled over onto the land of Egypt every year. Without the yearly inundation of the rich black silt from the Nile, there could be no agriculture in Egypt.

Even before Osiris and Isis and the other deities of Egypt, there was a god of the river Nile. His name has come down to us as Hapi. Pharaohs prayed to him and one of the four sons of Horus is named for him.

Hapi was seen as a boatman. His boat metaphorically brings abundance to the Nile; the Egyptians worried that without Hapi, the Nile might have been a barren stretch of stagnant water. Hapi imbued the river with life.

Depicted as a somewhat androgynous figure, Hapi is drawn as a mature man wearing the artificial beard of a pharaoh. He has a potbelly and the pendulous breasts of a nursing mother! What is the purpose of his strange appearance? Some say he is an androgynous figure, sort of like Shiva/Shakti in the Hindu beliefs: male and female in one. Others say that his large belly could either be seen as symbolic of wealth—to some extent being plump is still a hallmark of prosperity in the Middle East. Or it could have been a symbol of fertility and meant to be interpreted as a pregnant woman's belly. Hapi is sometimes a twin god; there are friezes of two Hapis facing each other, and each had a consort. One was Nehkebet, the vulture goddess, and the other was Wadjet, the cobra goddess. Hapi as a singular god had a composite goddess for a consort: Nehebka, the winged cobra and goddess of magic who has aspects of both Nehkebet and Wadjet.

In any case, followers of the Isian religion—and those who just wish to revere the ancient Egyptians and their belief in a god of abundance—would do well to honor Hapi. This is easy to do; for example, on the West Coast the flowers called "lily of the Nile" are abundant; they grow in tall stalks topped with either periwinkle or white blossoms. To bring abundance into your life or even give thanks for the abundance that exists today, here is a brief offering to Hapi: place a few lilies of the Nile in a tall vase, or if these are not available, place a water lily or a lotus in a bowl of water. Place an image of Hapi on the altar with the flowers. In your own words, thank him for the abundance in your life. Meditate on the idea of abundance to keep impoverished thinking from your mind.

To explore the abundance in our own lives, all you have to do is go to a large supermarket or farmers' market. Survey the different types of fruits and vegetables available. If you are in a large supermarket, count the different types of fruits that you find in the produce section. You will be amazed at how we take so much for granted! Browse around and see if there is one item that strikes your fancy. It is doubtful you would find a single piece of fruit or a vegetable that you cannot afford to buy. (Whether or not you feel the item is overpriced is beside the point!) Buy the piece of fruit or vegetable that appeals to you, and place it and a green candle on Hapi's altar; Hapi is sometimes shown with green skin in his aspect as a vegetation god.

Think of Hapi as a happy god, a party god! Have a good time and enjoy the abundance that we have by honoring him.

Red Alert Witchcraft

by Elizabeth Barrette

Sometimes the universe grants you the luxury of dedicated magical space, appropriate tools and supplies, planning time, and everything else you need for elaborate ritual magic. Other times a problem pops up that must be dealt with immediately, right where you are, with little or nothing in the way of tools and ceremony. Magic is wonderfully versatile—and the power lies within the practitioner more than in any tool or ceremony.

You can use magic to solve metaphysical problems, or in conjunction with mundane efforts to address mundane problems; it is especially good for preventing small issues from snowballing into a major crisis. Advance preparation helps to make you ready for whatever challenges may come your way. Here are some ideas to get you started.

First Steps

Step #1: Stay calm. In order to respond appropriately to a challenge, you need a clear head. By remaining calm, you can use your magical and mundane skills to best advantage. Likewise, keep everyone else calm. Few situations are so bad that panic can't make things a whole lot worse.

Step #2: Ground, center, and shield. Grounding connects you to an outside power source so you don't exhaust your personal energy. Centering lets you keep your mental feet under you, protecting you from internal stress and making it harder for people to confuse you or push you around. Shielding raises a barrier between you and others, protecting you from external stress due to other people or hostile energies. Together these magical techniques give you a firm foundation from which to work—and after some practice, they can be done instantly with a flick of your will, with no outward sign at all.

Step #3: Identify the problem. Take time to figure out exactly what is wrong, as best you can tell. Is the matter small or large? Magical or mundane? In progress, imminent, or merely approaching? Who does it affect? How did it get started? Ask other people for information if possible, but also use all of your physical and metaphysical powers of observation. The more you know about the situation, the better your chance of resolving it in a positive manner.

Step #4: Make a plan. Take time to use your cool head and your observations to decide on a course of action. Don't just do the first thing you think of. Whether you have seconds, minutes, or hours to respond—make the best of that time. Then act on your plan to improve the situation.

Emergency Supplies

One excellent way to prepare for the unexpected is to carry a few simple items that are useful in a variety of situations. These fit neatly in a purse, pocket, backpack, suitcase, the glove compartment of a car, and so forth. Most are inconspicuous, thus unlikely to attract attention from curious onlookers.

Essences and oils: If you have a favorite flower essence or essential oil for use in a crisis, carry some with you in a perfume bottle or pendant. Bach's Rescue Remedy is a popular choice, a blend of flower essences designed to soothe and balance. For essential oil, consider a "protection" blend, such as Spellbound offered by Kamala Perfumes, ideal for shielding. Magical liquids can be used to draw runes, protective symbols, etc. Fragrant oils and flower essences both represent elemental air, which brings clarity of mind.

Lighter: Even if you don't smoke, a cigarette lighter makes a discreet source of flame. It serves as a representation of elemental fire, which purifies and protects. Of course, if you've got candles, you can also light them; but in a pinch, the lighter alone will work.

Mirror: A compact mirror, signal mirror for campers, or other tiny portable mirror will suffice; a large one is not necessary. Pointed away from you, mirrors reflect negativity. Just carrying one repels some malicious entities. A mirror also makes a good focus for scrying. In dim light, gaze into the reflective surface and let your mind wander until images form.

Pencil: A wooden pencil makes an excellent magic wand. (A mechanical pencil or a pen can work, but usually not as well as natural wood.) Holding it as you would your regular wand, use it to direct and focus energy. It's also ideal for writing runes, protective symbols, and so forth to affect other objects.

Pentacle: Wear a pentacle for protection, preferably under your clothes next to your skin. It is also a place to store magical energy. Fill it up during a quiet time, and you'll have that energy available when things get tense. Magical tools can be charged in many ways including energy manipulation, repeated ritual use, and leaving them out in sunlight or moonlight. A pentacle represents all the magical elements combined.

Salt: This representation of elemental earth purifies, protects, and blesses. Salt repels or banishes many hostile entities. Sprinkle it dry or mix it with water. In either form, salt can be used to trace wards or protective symbols. Draw a circle with salt or salt water to keep out unwanted influences. Dabbing it on a lock discourages anyone else from messing with the lock, and protects the locked item or space. The easiest and most discreet way to carry salt is to save those little paper packets used in fast-food restaurants.

Stones: Many semiprecious stones have magical qualities. Wear them as jewelry, carry them on a keychain, stash them in the glove compartment of your car, etc. At a minimum, carry a quartz crystal, which adapts to serve any magical purpose. Other good choices include: amethyst (increases psychic powers), garnet (gives courage), aventurine (calms), jade (brings luck), obsidian (protects), jasper (aids with grounding). Any ordinary rock can represent earth or assist grounding, too. Hold the stone and concentrate on your goal to activate a stone's magical qualities—although some qualities tend to be active continually, like protection or luck.

Thread: Lighter and easier to conceal than rope, thread (or string) works just as well for knot magic. With it you can work a quick charm to bind an enemy, tangle the path of a pursuer, slow blood loss, bind or loosen the wind—anything traditionally done with knot magic. To bind, slow, stop, or prevent something, tie one or more knots in a thread. To release, set loose, or open something, untie one or more knots. To obscure a trail, tie a tangle of thread and drop it where a pursuer will step on it. A traveler's sewing kit contains several different colors of thread, and the smallest kits fit in the palm of a hand. A stray thread pulled from your clothing also works.

Water: In all forms, water purifies. Running water forms a protective boundary, and ice binds. To banish something, draw it or write its name on a piece of toilet paper, and flush it down a toilet. To cleanse yourself of unwanted energies, go to the nearest restroom and wash your hands. Water is usually easy to find even if you don't carry it. Still, bottled water or a perfume bottle full of water is easy and unobtrusive to keep with you. Of course, it also represents elemental water.

Inconspicuous Magic

Some types of magic are flashy. Others are discreet, giving little or no outward sign of their presence. Inconspicuous magic is often faster because it relies more on the caster and less on outside tools. Also, magic works best when given a framework to support it, so it's easier to layer a shield over an existing wall than to create one in midair. It's easier to shift probabilities to match your mundane actions than to make something happen by magic alone. This also helps hide magic by providing an alternative explanation—instead of "witchcraft" you're benefiting from "favorable coincidences." (One definition of magic is "coincidence control.")

Energy manipulation is the most basic type of magic. You simply grab the power and shape it into the form you need. Mold it into a wall or bubble to shield yourself or others. (Do not try to stop onrushing energy and objects directly, just deflect them harmlessly to one side.) To clear negative energy from an area, imagine a wind or broom sweeping it all away. If you need to pass quickly through a crowd, shape your aura into a wedge and extend it ahead of you to move people apart. Energy manipulation comes entirely from inside you, so there's nothing for nonmagical people to notice.

Folk charms include a wide range of simple actions and objects, each creating a specific effect. A penny in your shoe for wealth, an obsidian bead on your cell phone to protect it from loss or theft, a four-leaf clover for luck—these are all passive folk charms that require no action from you to do their thing. Making a fig hand (thumb between first two fingers) to avert evil, tying a knot to calm a storm, scuffing your shoe on a threshold to shed hostility—these are active charms that are easily concealed, perhaps behind your back or under a table. Another option is to layer such charms over a similar action required for mundane reasons; for instance, if you're wrapping gauze over a cut, concentrate on stopping the bleeding when you knot the bandage in place. Most of the items mentioned previously in "Emergency Supplies" can be used in folk charms.

Meditation works well in any situation where you need to wait for something to happen, stay alert, or remain calm for an extended period of time. You can meditate by focusing your attention on a sound, like a ticking clock or a soothing phrase; by staring at a pattern, such as a scrollwork carpet or the dance of shadows under a tree; and so forth. The "alert" version works by spreading your awareness evenly throughout your environment, noticing everything but not focusing on anything—until something requires a response, when you will be ready to act immediately. Meditation keeps you from exhausting yourself with worry, and recharges your energy after working magic or other exertion. Being completely internal, it tends to be undetectable.

Prayer serves a similar function to meditation. It soothes, heals, and restores energy. But unlike the other forms of magic discussed here, prayer asks a higher power for assistance rather than creating the desired effect through the practitioner's own will. It requires the least amount of effort, making it useful when you lack the energy for anything more exertive; and it needs no outward sign, although you can add some (such as a hand gesture or a holy symbol) if you wish.

Symbols represent a certain energy or goal in a visual pattern. Good symbols for emergencies include algiz (shield), Eye of Horus (protects against the evil eye), lightning bolt (power, success), nauthiz (need, petition for aid), om (meditation), peace symbol (neutralizes hostility), pentagram (protection, containment), raido (safe travel), and Thor's hammer or tau cross (averts misfortune). Symbols may be traced in the air, drawn with a pencil, or traced on objects using magical liquids such as essential oil. The above symbols and uses will fit on an index card, which can be folded and kept in a wallet or glove compartment for reference.

Visualization is a technique used to facilitate many magical effects. It involves forming an intense sensory image—visual, auditory, tactile, etc.—of what you wish to happen. For instance, when manipulating energy to make someone leave you alone, you might imagine yourself concealed by fog and the bothersome person walking away. For safe travel on icy roads, you could throw down a pinch of salt while imagining the ice melting and your car tires gripping the road securely. The harder you concentrate, and the more detailed your visualization, the more effective it will be.

Wherever you go, you will find challenges—and a little magical preparation will help you to meet them gracefully. Practice with different techniques and tools so you'll learn which ones work best for you. Then when life sends you a "red alert," you'll be ready!

Apples and Magic

by K. D. Spitzer

Apples have a long association with the gods, their magical powers called upon in deceit, distraction, and generally in divination—an association that continues today. The Romans introduced apple orchards to Britain; their goddess Pomona gave it powers of fertility and love.

The most famous place in legendary Britain is the Isle of Apples. Surrounded by water, it can be only glimpsed through the mists. It is Avalon, where Excalibur was forged and King Arthur awaits with his sister Morgana for his call to England's gravest peril.

The magic of apples is forever linked to the Celtic other-world; it is an endless source of sustenance, satisfying hunger, yet always entire. Reminding us of its spiritual roots, it holds a special place at Samhain, the Celtic festival honoring the dead. We drink apple cider, make candy apples, and bob for apples. Some even bury apples so the souls waiting to be reborn will have food for the journey.

The apples are placed in a large pan of water, which symbolizes the journey of the soul across the water to the far shore of Avalon and immortality. Trying to grab an apple with only the teeth reveals the difficulty of the trip. And as is the custom, the first person at the party to do so will have the kiss of the goddess and thus be the first to marry in the coming year.

Apple magic can be enhanced by dropping apples in water to see how they float on the surface; they don't always ride with the stem side up. Carefully carve a small indent in the top of the apple, and then insert a pink tea light. Place a bowl of these lights on your altar and burn them to honor Venus and Pomona to attract love or enhance fertility. Use yellow tea lights if you want to increase your fertile imagination.

There are many ways of using an apple to find one's own true love. Country girls in the United States, following the customs of their European grandmothers, would light a candle in the dark. Then, looking in a mirror, they would pare an apple. This spell guaranteed that the face of their future husband would be revealed in the mirror before they finished peeling. Possibly a slug of hard cider or applejack helped in this vision.

If the mirror did not display the identity of their own true love, another spell likely would. Again, it required peeling an apple. Back in the olden days, peeling an apple in one continuous unbroken piece was considered a housewifely virtue. So an unmarried woman would take her best paring knife and get to work. Once she had the peel, she would throw it over her left shoulder. When it landed on the floor, the peel's shape would form a letter of the alphabet—the first letter of the name of her future husband.

It is not a secret that if you cut an apple through the middle you reveal a pentacle, which is one of the reasons this fruit is so dear to the goddess. However, it was once quite common on New Year's Day to cut the apple through from top to bottom. If you could do this without slicing any of the seeds you would have a healthy and prosperous year.

And, of course, the best of apple magic requires eating an apple every day, thanking the goddess for her blessings. It keeps the doctor away.

Reconnect with Your Magical DNA

by Karen Glasgow-Follett

You don't have be involved with magical thought and practice for too long before you hear the same old lament from a new (or not so new) practitioner. This generally commences with the expressed experiences of spells that have "gone wrong" or have proven ineffective. The conclusion of this lament is typically the double-barreled self-blame of "what's wrong with me," which is quickly followed by the finger-pointing blame of "why can't anyone write a good spell."

In the thirty-five years that I have been practicing magic, I will be honest—I have had my share of "oopsies." Either my intent was askew, I was distracted, I was holding my tongue wrong, or I encountered any of the other myriad excuses that can lead to spells running amok. But in spite of the fact that most practitioners experience the occasional spell that produces an untoward result—or none at all—I can unequivocally declare that all spells have a good productive potential. All spells work.

As magical practitioners, we are conduits for the magical energy. The magic is that flame of the divine energy that is within. Spells act to fan our magical flame. Spells provide the ignition of intent and statement of desire. But in the final analysis, the practitioner is responsible for the results.

Any untoward or lackluster result is not the fault of the spell. Even though the spell's result begins and ends with the spellcaster, the problem of ineffective magic is not generally even harbored within the practitioner's techniques. The main problem that renders magic ineffective or untoward lies in evolution and in our disassociation to the magical DNA of our origin.

Nothing in life, or in the creation of life, is static. Evolution embodies this theory in the cycle of cellular adaptation. The change that elicits the adaptation of cellular structure and function can occur in either the perceived external or internal environment.

Adaptation to external change is widely chronicled from the historical adaptive changes seen from the primal to the modern species. Even recent evidence of evolution exists as lifestyles change with effects that are seen in the structure and function of our adaptive responses, which are required to survive and thrive in a nonstatic existence.

The external environment does not operate independently from the internal environment when interacting with the stimulus of change. In fact, the internal environment can initiate evolutionary change. Environment, external or internal, is based on perception.

When any change, external or internal is perceived, the neural pathways distribute the "oh this is different, we must adapt" signal throughout our bodies, down to the cellular level. Our bodies then respond whether the change is real or imagined.

Internal perception includes recognizing the thought response to a stimulus. While this stimulus—the catalyst of change—can be a part of communal tangibility, the evolution that has undermined the activation of our magical DNA began with the thought response to intangible belief and bigotry.

Since the external and internal environments are synchronous, the thoughts have unfortunately evolved to produce this physical outcome of disassociation and disconnection.

The magical DNA material still exists, as evidenced by the energy that we can raise and by the results that are found in matter created by the catalyst of the mind. But unfortunately, either by total disuse or by the continued impression of very limited and limiting thoughts onto magical ability, the signals from these strands of coding may not be operating to their fullest capacity. The results of the limited thoughts and beliefs may be a thin veneer of "positive magical thinking" that covers overwhelming layers of negative thought and expectation.

Reconnect, Reactivate

The reactivating of and reconnection to these strands can increase the capacity that can alter cell structure and function to the peak of magical energy flow.

The tools for reconnection and reactivation presented in this article will begin with the magic of guided-imagery meditation. The magic of guided-imagery meditation is the magic of stated intent in the imagery coupled with the physiological energy generated in meditation.

Incorporating guided imagery and the induction of meditation can occur in any fashion that speaks to you. One of the most useful ways that I have found to magically imagine and meditate involves three stages. Theses stages begin with the reading of the script. The reading is then replayed in imagery that takes on the attributes of daydreams. (This shifts the brainwaves into an alpha state, which opens the gates of subconscious and conscious perception. The energy generated in the alpha state is synchronous with the energy of the earth.) The stages culminate with the mind's travels being independent of conscious guidance. (This elicits the theta state of brain wave function; opening the mind and body to the realms of the divine universal consciousness.)

Capture the Thoughts

Regardless of the techniques employed in guided imagery meditation, there is one tool that will prove of immense value. This tool is a journal.

Useful information to include in your journal would be the documentation of emotional, physical, and mental perceptions during and after the meditation. This can be quite valuable as messages are often revealed during and even after the openness of the meditative state. Even the act of writing works to "ground" some of the "lofty, not quite tangible" concepts that may float into your mind. So with journal nearby, let's begin your process of reconnection.

In a comfortable position, focus on your breathing. Each inhalation possesses the cleansing, calming essence that is the vital breath of the earth. Each exhalation harmlessly releases the blockages and the toxins that have been harbored in your body. Each breath relaxes you in mind and in body. Each breath awakens your union with your Divine Spirit.

Shift your senses from your physical body to the subtle landscape of your inner senses and of your etheric body. Focus on the flow of energy movement feeling each wave pulsating in rhythm with the beating of your heart. You feel the denseness of your physical body yield to the energy field of your etheric self. Your inner senses feel the ebb and flow of energy in cadence with the flow of your breath. Your breath directs the current to the vortices of your chakras. Each breath that you take encircles the wheels with cleansing light. Light energy encircling the root—extending to the belly, the solar plexus, the heart, the throat, and to the brow. Your senses are open to any perceptions that arise at these vortices.

The energy encompasses the crown chakra. You feel a ribbony flow extend, uniting you with your Divine Self. Along the ribbon, rivulets of golden warmth enter your crown. Flowing gold cascades through the vortices . . . balancing . . . extending . . . opening the energy to the power of reconnection and reactivation. Waves of warmth fill every cell with the limitless energy of divinity.

The Magic Habit

The preparatory stage is complete. The next stage of your journey begins with your most recent magical rite. Your mindscape builds the physical events. You inner senses discern the response of your energy body. You feel the energy's strength and origin as it flows within you. You become aware of the layers of your intent. You allow the inner senses to speak their perceptions to your conscious mind. When you feel comfortable with what you have learned, you allow the image to fade.

Transcending all manmade limits of time and space, your etheric body introduces you to the magical person of your soul and to the magical place of practice. You may perceive this person as a past life or as a magical aspect of yourself. Allow your mind to unfold the surroundings and events. This aspect of you is alive in this time when magic wasn't merely "something that you do;" magic was "who you are." Allow the rite to unfold on your mindscape. Again feel the energy flow. Feel the flow reach beyond your etheric field to blend with the magic of the vision. Again focus on any perceptions shared by your inner senses. As you feel comfortable, allow the image to fade.

The limiting vision of passive participator is discarded. Your vision is the sight of your true being. Your being as the creator. Your creator's vision sees the emergence of images in brilliant light. As these images become clear, you sense that you have transcended to the realms of the ancients. Your etheric body is glowing with the transclucent brilliance that emanates from the crystals surrounding this temple of the Old Ones.

Rainbows of color reach to you and through you. These strands of color intertwine to form the double helix of DNA. These interconnecting strands of mind-manifesting matter weave their energy through your energy vortices. Every cell is alive with the DNA of pure divinity as your defined etheric body merges with the universal flow of light and reactivation.

As your etheric body begins to redefine and reclaim its energy field, you feel the grounding heaviness of "near matter." Each breath that you take attunes the magical double helix with the cells of your etheric body. Then your etheric energy acclimates to the flow of DNA and merges with the density of your physical self. Each breath blends and adjusts the magical flow to the physical self. You release any energy excess with each exhalation.

As your energy balances and you feel comfortable, you shift your inner senses to the sensing of your physical world. You allow your energy to ground as you journal the perceptions gained in this reconnection experience. Magic is a living essence that interacts with each person on a personally distinctive level. All perceptions are valid for you.

Keep your journal close at hand for the final stage of magical DNA reactivation. This final stage is the repetition of the magical stimulus that sends the DNA coded messages to the cells. This repetition honors the reactivation and reconnection that will alter cellular structure and function.

It is said that it takes approximately one month for the body to learn or unlearn a stimulus. This theory is often referred to in the creation of, or the breaking of, habits. So, in the next month, our bodies will learn the habit of magic.

Every day perform a simple act of magic. The spells can be as simple as a direct statement of intent or as complex as a full rite. The results should be clearly measurable and realistically achievable in a short period of time. Keep the "as above, so below" principle of magic at the forefront of your mind. It is the mundane effort that is enacted in the "so below" that connects with and actualizes the magic released in the "as above." Refer to your journal as needed to compare the sensations and perceptions of magical energy. Record your perceptions and the results as you progress through your month.

Regardless of the outcome, each act of magic is positive self-learning. Each act of magic attunes your physical body to your magical DNA. Each magical experience opens you to the spirit of the true creator that is within you; a creator that is released with your reconnection of divine magical DNA.

Caffeine & Nicotine:
Their Magic, Their Danger

by Raven Digitalis

In our fast-paced, heavily demanding society, little emphasis is placed on our spiritual selves. Today's society is greatly motivated by the instinct of self-preservation, psychologically forcing citizens to fight for financial success and stability in the physical world. Things like sleep, relaxation, daydreaming, and general "chilling out" are so often pushed aside because of social demands. As a result of the world's heavy demands, many people turn to stimulating substances to stay alert, living up to this world's stipulations, be this by necessity or perceived expectation. Unfortunately, some go a bit overboard and engulf themselves in harmful drugs that push the body to—and even well beyond—its limits. However, the majority of stimulant-taking individuals tend to have a soft spot for coffee and/or tobacco; the two most widely used stimulants in this society.

Both caffeine and nicotine act as stimulants and relaxants. Not only can they get the "blood flowing and the mind working," they can also give relaxing breaks when a person is amidst the day's chaos. Whether used throughout the day or only at the top of the morning to help wake up, caffeine and nicotine help users deal with daily life.

Caffeine

Caffeine is highly addictive, but luckily, relatively harmless. Caffeine, a plant alkaloid, triggers the release of glucose in the blood, giving the effect of a buzz. Coffee contains a high amount of caffeine compared to tea—generally twice the amount. Soda also contains less caffeine than coffee (the caffeine in soda is added rather than naturally occurring), and many forms of chocolate contain next to no caffeine. Coffee is said to have come from Kaffa, Ethiopia, where the plant originates. Local legend says that when a goatherd named Kaldi discovered his animals eating the berries (beans) of the coffee bush and becoming increasingly energetic, he tried it himself and discovered similar effects.

In a ritual context, drinking a cup of coffee at the beginning of a ceremony is said to bring the practitioner insight into the working at hand. In particular, it is used to give the caster greater clarity of the magical purpose within the ritual, helping to specify and understand the motivations and mechanisms of ritual. Since the physical effects of caffeine can provide alertness to a person, the same traits are echoed on the metaphysical plane by providing spiritual awareness. These magical effects can be imbued in a practitioner by consuming magically charged caffeine (physical) or by using its metaphysical properties alone, such as including a bit of coffee in a medicine bag.

Individual Consumers, Global Impact

The effects and perks of coffee for individual consumers are easy to identify, but its spiritual effects are far reaching. Like many products, global economics come into play because coffee is produced worldwide.

The economic state of the world is not cross-culturally beneficial. Many people, particularly Westerners, belong to a culture in which those in positions of power often have little concern for the welfare of others. However, consumers can voice their concerns to those in power when considering choices in purchasing coffee. It's best to buy coffee listed as fair trade rather than not; the majority unlabeled as such is often referred to as "blood coffee." In the case of the latter, Third World or developing countries are exploited by "rich" countries in a modern form of slave labor. While the poverty-producing effects on the coffee harvesters are grave—even life threatening—the benefits the exploiting country receives through such tactics are monetarily immense and ethically slim. To counter these cruel and unfair conditions designed at making the rich richer and the poor poorer, the fair-trade movement was begun to ensure ethical social standards for exported goods, of which coffee is one of the main crops. In order to continue a moral and humanitarian cycle, we must give absolute awareness to the products we buy, especially those produced in remote countries. Choosing coffee wisely indeed promotes social justice across the board.

As a further word of warning, coffee is known to cause ulcers and gastrointestinal discomfort with extended use. An alternative

many people are beginning to use is the South American herb yerba maté, an antioxidant-rich substitute for coffee, which contains caffeine in the form of matine. Its "buzz" keeps one going steadily throughout the day and is ideal for people who get overly jolted or ill-affected from caffeine. It also tends to have a more pleasant effect on the stomach than does coffee.

Nicotine

Nicotine is most easily consumed in a "stick" form as a cigarette, especially for those who either don't have the patience to smoke a pipe or don't have the urge to use chewing tobacco. Numerous Native American tribes have long made use of tobacco in a spiritual/ritual context. The Yokut tribe's creation myth associates the plant with wisdom and creation. Many Native mythological systems include the belief that the gods and deities themselves smoke sacred tobacco. Some tribes see the plant as being protected by astral beings similar to the gnomes recognized in many Pagan and Wiccan systems.

Smoking a tobacco peace pipe is a method of communion in Native American spiritual systems, and many tribes smoke a communal pipe following a sweat lodge, drumming circle, and other religious ceremonies. Tobacco is also believed to be the best herb for making offerings to the spirits; an idea with which no Pagan I know would disagree!

Tobacco smoke is said to part the veil between this world and that, which is one method the herb can be used magically. Because tobacco smoke is believed to penetrate the overlapping planes of existence, wishes and prayers can be sent with each puff. Personally, I find it good practice to send well-wishes and illuminating energy to a different person with each puff of tobacco. When practiced, the ease of projecting this energy long-distance becomes recognizable. Some spiritualists, Native and otherwise, incorporate tobacco smoke into hands-on healing rituals to aid in metaphysical sight when working on a patient. The smoke itself is also healing and can be blown on an "ill area" to assist the healing process by helping to banish harmful energies.

Native American cultures honor the tobacco spirit and promote respecting it rather than developing an addiction to it. Its sacred properties are immense, but the fact remains: tobacco is related to belladonna and other deadly poisonous herbs, and is far from safe. Little to no negative effects occur if tobacco is used sparingly, especially for ritualistic communion alone. But looking at modern statistics, we see just how dangerous it really is. In the year 2000, 18 percent of all deaths in the United States were tobacco-related, earning it the No. 1 cause of death for that year, according to the March 10, 2004, *Journal of the American Medical Association.*

Nearly all manufactured tobacco contains thousands upon thousands of chemical additives. Luckily, chemical additive-free tobacco does exist and is available for purchase. For a spiritual person who cares both about their physical health and tobacco's metaphysical uses, this is undoubtedly the best option if tobacco is chosen to be consumed. If prayers are sent via tobacco containing thousands of chemical additives, the magic projected immediately becomes diffused and diluted with toxicity—not to mention the distress it puts on the lungs! If using tobacco for spiritual use (as well as physical consumption, ideally), the chemical- and additive-free varieties are the way to go.

Conquer Addictive Habits Spiritually

Most people who use caffeine and nicotine do so habitually. Once the substances prove themselves effective or pleasurable, an addiction can result that may not have the best of consequences. A number of individuals are instead able to restrict their usage of caffeine and nicotine to special circumstances. While some may have a cup a' joe every morning, others use it sparingly when the need is more intense. While some may smoke a pack-a-day, others limit their tobacco use to social situations. Indeed one's use is a personal choice and any variant of usage is individually decided.

As magical folk, it's both our duty and motivation to develop self-awareness. If a spiritual person uses caffeine, nicotine or any other substance, they must strive to bring as much self-awareness as possible to the situation. Addiction is prevalent all over the world, especially dependence on these legal drugs, and it is most definitely a spiritual procedure to conquer addictive behavior. If the energy of a substance has more control over a person than they themselves do, both spiritual focus and magical intention can easily become convoluted.

An ideal method of spiritual progression for a person addicted to caffeine or nicotine is to undertake abstinence. Abstaining from one's substance of choice is a form of fasting that forces the person to objectively witness their body's physical reaction to withdrawal. Denying the body a familiar, external substance pushes the body away from its learned patterning. As the body withdraws from a substance, it aches to be satiated. Filling the body with energy through acts of magic and meditation has a profound effect when ritualized at this time. Fasting from a substance for a period of three days initially can be a dedicatory act of self-realization. Once accomplished, the next attempt can be seven days, and so on, perhaps until dependence is eliminated entirely.

Fasting from caffeine and/or nicotine can prove a very difficult task for one attached to the drugs' effects. It's best to set a period of days aside for the fasting (such as a weekend) and assign yourself various tasks and duties to accomplish throughout the day to prevent becoming overly distracted by the body's outcries for the drug. Of course, it's ideal to not surround yourself with people using the substance, as well as to remove the substance from the household entirely if possible. If caffeine is the addiction, try caffeine-free herbal tea or another antioxidant-filled beverage. If nicotine is the addiction, an herbal smoking blend may be a good substitute. Many blends are available, the most effective of which contain dried mullein, sage, coltsfoot, and rose petals. Chewing gum and gnawing on dried licorice sticks (the roots of the herb *Glycyrrhiza glabra*—not the candy) also help ease the oral fixation.

At the end of the day, we magicians, Witches, and spiritualists must account for our actions, our desires and our dependencies. It's up to us alone to live our lives in a progressive and mind-ful manner, which necessarily includes giving awareness to our own behavior and its effect on our holistic health. Furthermore, our effects on other people mustn't be overlooked. Our choices (in this case, what we consume) must also be those that cause the least amount of cyclical burdening and suffering worldwide. Everything we do influences the greater whole.

DNA Dowsing

by AarTiana

To define DNA dowsing, one must first know what dowsing is: a method of tapping into the universal energy using a tool (in this case a pendulum) for measurement. Dowsing has been likened to a "spiritual telephone" in which one communicates with the source, or higher self. The pendulum can either be purchased, created, or in a pinch you can use a key on a piece of string or a pendant on a neck chain. Whatever you use, make sure it is weighted and swings freely in all directions. You may wish to smudge it with sage or herbal smoke to cleanse it before use. You also need some charts so you can read the pendulum's swing. You can purchase them, make your own, or get them free from the Internet. If you do not have charts available, you can visualize the chart in your mind underneath where you swing the pendulum.

Begin by centering and grounding yourself. The pendulum's accuracy is diluted (to the point of rendering it unusable) if the person swinging the pendulum is distracted or distraught. Clear your mind of desires so that you may accurately read the true energy. Hold the pendulum in front of you so it can swing and, without moving it intentionally, ask it to show you a "yes" answer. You can also program your "yes" answer by seeing it swing away from you, then toward you (forward and backward, or a "nodding"). It may not swing much at first, but practice allows you to see the swing better, so don't give up. Then, ask it to show you a "no" answer, or you can program your "no" answer by seeing it swing left to right (likened to shaking your head "no"). Some people show "yes" as a circle clockwise, and "no" counterclockwise, vice versa, or another way that makes sense to them. This is also OK, but the trick here is to be consistent. You can also read your response for "maybe," "rephrase the question," and "not enough information available."

Once you establish your system, ask the pendulum if you are in the highest good and ready to pose your question. It might say no for a number of reasons, but the most common are that you are not centered and focused, or that your emotional desires will make any answer inaccurate. If you find it too hard to separate from external activity or your emotions, you may wish for another person to pendulum dowse for you to get a more accurate read.

Charting Energy Flow

When you get really comfortable with yes/no type questions, you can use charts (or imagined charts) to measure the energy present in a situation. Remember, any future forecast is similar to a weather forecast—if energy flows in the current direction, the outcome will happen, but unexpected energies can change this outcome. The good news is you can usually predict a situation better than most meteorologists predict the weather!

One application I like to use is a watch-face, which would be numbered 1 to 12 or 1 to 60, whatever you intend. If you don't have a chart available to read the pendulum swing, you can just use your watch, or imagine a watch-face under the pendulum. This system is very good for predicting time. Once your pendulum is programmed to read time in hours, days, weeks, months, or years (determine which interval is best via yes/no queries or a chart with these specifications); then you can use the watch-face, numbered either way you intend before swinging, to arrive at the time involved in the situation, provided there is no interruption of energy.

Now that you know how to read the energy available, you can also by intention change the outcome as long as the change harms none and is balanced. For instance, if you are expecting a check in the mail and the pendulum tells you it will take two weeks to arrive—but you actually need the money sooner than that so you can go to an event—you can then ask the pendulum to change this energy, harming none, to bring it faster. If it gives permission, you can then ask how soon it can arrive without harm. Then read again (let's say it says eight days, and that will work for you), and then with strong intention, ask the pendulum to make it so. You can then read this energy on a half-circle percentage table (with 0 percent on the left and 100 percent on the right). See the pendulum swing to 0 percent at the beginning of the energy change, then watch it move through the percentages to 100 percent when the energy change is "set" or completed. Then your chances are very high that you receive your item within eight days (unless energy is interrupted). This shift of energy happens because clearly focused intention changes the energy field, which includes your own DNA patterning.

Cellular Dowsing

DNA dowsing is my interpretation of a technique taught by master dowser Walt Woods, but the term itself was coined in 2003 by Reiki master and shaman, Standing Bear Thunder Heart. DNA dowsing is the ability to change energy manifestation as shown above by changing the programming of your DNA using a pendulum. The example of bringing mail more quickly is one application, but as you can imagine, applications of this technique are endless. When you set intention as described, you are actually sending a message to your DNA via all the cells in your body. Then they align with the new message and create magnetic attraction of energy so these new events manifest. One of two things will happen: one, the changes are integrated in the body without much conscious effort, or two, you are led to experiences so these changes can take place.

As an example that Mr. Woods would use, ask your pendulum if you need vitamin C, something known by science that the human body needs, but, unlike most animals, cannot manufacture and must get from external sources. Unless you take high amounts of vitamin C or just ate an orange, the pendulum will likely say yes. You can then have a balance chart in which to measure how much vitamin C you have—the middle being balanced, the left side showing shortage, and the right side showing an overage. You can then read your energetic level of vitamin C (and it will usually show deficiency). Then take some vitamin C or eat an orange and read your level again. Because it is very difficult to have too much vitamin C, the chart will now likely show a balance.

However, some nutrients can accumulate excessively rather easily, and the idea is to strive for balance.

You can then program your DNA by asking at this time that your vitamin C levels at all times remain balanced, and with no harm, to make it so. You can then see this change happening on the percentage table like before. Either your body will adapt by conserving usage, learn how to manufacture the vitamin for itself, or lead you to a way you can always have balanced vitamin C levels. It is known that our DNA and that of animals are nearly identical, so if animals can program their DNA for their bodies to manufacture vitamin C, it is possible that we can do the same. We need to open our mind to infinite possibility—and to use it responsibly.

Expanding on this, let's say you wish to grow a thicker head of hair. Be very clear on how you wish for this to happen (for instance, you may not want thicker hair if it means you have more body hair too). Be very clear about the hair texture (i.e. straight, shiny, curly, porous, etc.), thickness of the individual hairs, the amount of hairs on your head, and location if that is important. Also set intention about body hair remaining the same or decreasing. Once your intentions are very clear, ask if it is the highest good with no harm for you to have your hair change in this way. If it says no, you can find out which things will upset the balance and then work accordingly. When it says yes, tell the pendulum to make it so. Again, you can see the energy changing on the percentage chart, from 0 to 100 percent as before. Then you can read the pendulum for how long it will be before you notice the changes in place. For instance, it may say nine months. You can also ask when your ideal is fully implemented (which could be a number of years). Either your body will make these changes on its own, or bring you to nutrition, products, or even a whole new way of life, in order to manifest these changes.

Whether you wish to smooth wrinkles, seek a cure for cancer, create a new source of continual income, or just be in the right place at the right time to embrace opportunities—these same techniques apply. As long as your requests are allowed by the universe, and are in balance, they will manifest. However, if the pendulum does not give permission, do not try to force the requested change, no matter how badly you wish to do so. There are likely larger problems unforeseen for you or others. The price to pay energetically for such change may not be worth it at all. You have heard this before: Be careful what you wish for!

Also you can keep track of your goals by measuring how much percentage of the energy is in place periodically, and also to read percentage of the finished physical, tangible results. For instance, say it would take nine months to begin to see tangible results with your hair wishes. If you wish to see if you are on track for this, you can ask in three months what percentage of the work is done (and hopefully it says you are approximately one-third of the way). Again, you may speed up the process, but only if no harm is done.

If things are going too slowly to see change and the pendulum says harm would be done if things were to speed up, try another form of divination to reveal what might be happening. Maybe there is a reason for the delay that will work in your favor later. For instance, using the mail example, let's say the pendulum did not give you permission to speed up your letter and you missed your event. But then you find out the event was not all it was cracked up to be. Or maybe the event was great, but you subsequently find a sweet deal on something else you have wanted for a long time—a deal you could not take advantage of had you gone to the event. Or maybe your car breaks down and you need the money to fix your car instead. After much experience with the pendulum, you will learn to trust the information it brings to you, as it is in fact a wonderful method for communicating directly with the source, your higher self.

You may have seen that this is a wonderful way to do spellwork. In fact, these techniques can be interchangeable in almost every situation. Happy DNA dowsing, and remember, practice makes perfect (or at least very accurate)!

Regaining Our Balance in Spring: The Difficulty with Easter

by Kari Tauring

In *Mastering Herbalism,* Paul Huson describes accounts of mid-wives giving tansy cakes to the maidens at Easter time. The priests and monks frowned at this practice partly because of ties with pre-Christian spring rituals and partly because everyone knows that tansy is a powerful emmenagogue and can cause abortion. The old wives justified it by saying that the bitter herb reminds young girls of the bitterness of Christ's suffering.

This tension over tansy is but a small reminder that Easter is an oddity, not only among various religions, but within Christianity itself. Most holidays were fixed on or within a few days of the astronomical events they represented. Jesus was born as the Son/Sun god at Winter Solstice, Mary ascended in a crown of flowers as Queen of Heaven and Queen of the May at Beltane—everything had correlations that made sense and gave us easy transitions from the old ways to the new ways imposed on our cultures. Everything but Easter. What is the significance of creating a movable feast at the Spring Equinox?

Astronomy and Tradition

Historically, astronomical cycles have served humankind well. Our Earth-based spiritual traditions ask us to observe and do ritual as the Moon waxes and wanes. We are to chronicle the changes in ourselves and the Earth through the Sun and Moon cycles as we gather in community at the solstices and equinoxes and the points in between. Both men and women report an increased intimacy with their biorhythmic cycles physically, emotionally, and spiritually when they do this. As the Earth changes, we change. It is part of the "as above, so below" concept of Earth-based spiritual practice. Doing ritual in conjunction with nature's seasonal cycles increases intimacy and awareness of humanity's unity with the whole of the natural world.

Women who track the Moon cycles report that their own menstrual cycles tend to sync up with the Moon. Their periods become more predictable and through ritual practice are able to ease the cramping and bloating that accompanies these "Moon times." Starhawk's "making friends with your womb" ritual from her book, *Spiral Dance*, was just what I needed as a teen with no one to guide me in the blessings of my cycles. Through this and other rituals, women can observe bodily fluids, temperature shifts, and emotional and dreamtime changes. Medically speaking, this intimate relationship with our bodies is called the "rhythm method," used to help a woman avoid becoming pregnant. She knows the weeks she is fertile and can choose whether to conceive or not.

By maintaining intimacy with my body relative to the Moon, Sun, and other cycles over the years, I developed the confidence and freedom to use my powerful biorhythmic cycle toward my own life goals. I believe it is the right and responsibility of all women to develop this awareness so that we can practice conscious conception literally and metaphorically. It is the cornerstone to our goddess-hood, sexual freedom, and autonomy of being.

Through careful tracking, I discovered that my cycle shifts at Spring and Fall Equinox. During the light half of the year I ovulate on the dark Moon and during the dark half of the year on the Full Moon. Though uncertain of the exact meaning, this shift clearly held significance. Then, a few years later, I began raising three heirloom chickens, Old English Bantams. We didn't heat or light their roosting house artificially and, as chickens naturally ovulate on the Sun cycle, they began laying at Spring Equinox and Fall Equinox. (The amount of light received stimulates a chicken's body to ovulate. Many egg producers control the heat and light of chicken coops to promote egg-laying year-round. Some hybrid chickens can also lay eggs all year.) This added to my curiosity about these two astronomical events.

In researching global traditions for theatrical performances related to the solstices and equinoxes, my performance group unearthed the origins of modern customs. Interestingly, the most recent religious layer placed on these astronomical times was Christianity, the kind developed by Rome after Constantine—to be used as a political power base for converting and controlling conquered populations.

Origins of the Moveable Feast

Easter is a derivative of the goddess Eostar, a spring goddess who would appear as the March Hare. She would come up from the world of the dead and shake life into the trees so the sap would start running in the sugar bush. Eostar would infuse the chickens with light and they would start to ovulate. She would infuse the women too. Egg rituals at Easter abound, and the bunny imagery persists. Herb lore surrounding this time of year has to do with cleansing, fasting, and purging the blood. In particular, nettles, dandelion greens, and roots and sometimes tansy, (all considered powerful emmenagogues, were recommended as the springtime herbs for women. It was a time for women to revisit their fertility and balance menstrual cycles. And one had better get it together because the may pole will be rising on the Full Moon of May (anywhere from six to eight weeks).

But, oops, Easter was declared a "moveable feast" by the church fathers at Nicea after the triumph of Constantine ended the persecution of Christians in 323 AD. The resurrection of Jesus was set to occur on the first Sunday after the first Full Moon after Equinox and was to be called Easter. The rituals of Eostar's women from this time forward would never again occur directly on Equinox. In fact, there are times when these rituals would have to wait until we are perilously close to the May Day celebrations with its sexual freedom, fertility ritual, and debauchery, which was extremely difficult to expunge through the rural areas as many a monk and priest would note. Sometimes Easter and

May Day (in its fixed location of April 30/May 1) are a mere ten days apart! This would give many a maiden need for the midwives' tansy cakes.

Disconnect and Control

The placement of Easter has created cross-cultural obstacles for egg and bunny rituals on the Equinox for me personally, with my family, and in writing for Equinox shows. Even the secular world follows the moveable feast. Was this decision a conscious effort by the patriarchy to subvert women's power? There is a mountain of evidence that supports the patriarchal necessity of men to control women completely. Creating laws to control women's fertility cycles is, in my opinion, more insidious than the laws created to control their land, inheritances, and ability to earn income. And let us not forget that at the same council of Nicea where the date of Easter celebrations was chosen, the official Gospels were canonized (Matthew, Mark, Luke, and John were chosen; the rest of the Gospels were declared heretical), and the official creed was created. These 300 bishops on the council also debated whether or not women had souls.

Everything about women and nature had to be controlled for the patriarchy to work. When there are strong, independent women, hierarchies don't work so well. Women will make decisions based on what is good for the whole culture, the elders, the children, the crops, and the animals. Women's work has ever been intimately connected to the cycles of the culture—perpetuating the culture and educating the next generation. In hierarchies, decisions are made that benefit the elites and must therefore find ways to control those underneath them to maintain their fragile foothold as the few on top. As a patriarchy, then, the idea was to put children and the elderly at the bottom, then women, then worker men, then the men who rule all of this, and on top was God, created in an image that best expresses oppression.

Something modern culture has done to dislodge us from our understanding of our seasonal cycles is to call Spring Equinox the beginning of spring rather than mid-spring. On the old agricultural calendars, the beginning of the seasons occurred at the lunar-marked midpoints between the solar events. The beginning of spring is Imbolc, February 2, as the ice starts to melt.

The beginning of summer is May Day. Summer Solstice is still celebrated in Scandinavia as midsommersdag (midsummer's day). Calculating my year this old-fashioned way has led to a new world of understanding and connection to the seasons.

Ultimately it doesn't matter if the effects of disrupting Equinox/Eostar ritual were conscious and intentional. The effects are as they are and the lesson is simple. We as a culture need to create awareness of all the cycles we are so intimately connected to. We must educate our young to celebrate these transitional astronomical events by doing the proper rituals in their proper time. We are continually fighting for the basic human rights and empowerment of women around the globe. One sure way of creating a sea change for all oppressed people is to reconnect our cycles with those of the Earth, Sun, Moon, and stars.

Henna Magic

by Sybil Fogg

Henna smells like dirt and is cold when applied to skin. The eucalyptus oil used to prepare the skin smells like life and is pleasantly warm. When combined with incantations, a Full Moon, and expectant parents, henna can create some potent magic.

Early in my fourth pregnancy, the life of my unborn child became threatened. My midwives were at odds: one thought that my pregnancy would not declare itself and another felt that bed rest and reduced stress could allow the pregnancy to continue.

When those measures didn't work, I decided to use henna magic. I felt handing over the fate of my unborn child to the Goddess and God was a necessary step to remove stress from myself. I had already followed all of the recommendations of my midwives to no avail. I needed something that would help me focus my energy away from what was happening to me and direct it toward making something happen for me. That is what magic is all about.

It also helped that my partner is a skilled henna artist.

Henna art is called mehndi and draws its traditions from the Middle East and India. The action consists of applying a thin coat of a paste made from ground henna plant mixed with black tea and eucalyptus oil. There are many variations in the recipe with people trying a little of this and a little of that to find the desired consistency. Personally, I find that mixing equal amounts of henna powder and brewed black tea with a quarter amount of eucalyptus oil creates the best paste. For example, mix a half tablespoon of eucalyptus oil with two tablespoons each of henna powder and black tea. Henna paste should have the consistency of toothpaste.

Henna works by staining the skin. This happens almost immediately, but to assure a darker, longer-lasting design, it is best to coat the henna with sugared lemon water and to leave it on for at least eight hours. Once dry, henna can be brushed off. A cotton ball dipped in olive oil can be used to loosen any stubborn residue. The image that is left will be light to dark reddish-brown depending on the color of your skin.

Henna magic is powerful. You are using earth to draw your intention from your own body. It incorporates all aspects of spell

casting, from mixing the powder to creating the design to applying the paste to your skin. Henna magic should be approached
with extreme care and respect, for you will be wearing your design
for about one month, the time it takes the Moon to go from
round to dark to round again. As with anything being applied to
your skin, you should test a small area first to be certain that you
won't have any reactions to the henna paste.

To begin any magic, you should first determine the nature of
your intention. In the case of my possible miscarriage, mine was
specific. I didn't want to lose my baby. Henna magic can be used
for any type of spell: prosperity, love, self-confidence, happiness.

Once the nature of your spell has been decided, it is important to choose the correct correspondences to go with your magic.
The day, time of month, and astrological influence should be
researched and observed. In my case, I chose to do my spell during a Full Moon to represent the pregnant goddess and picked
a day that the Moon was in its governing sign, Cancer, because I
wanted all influences to be as strong as possible for my request.

When choosing your time, keep in mind that mixing henna
paste is time consuming. You will need about two days to make
the henna, one twenty-four-hour cycle to brew the black tea (two
tablespoons in one cup of hot water) and then another twenty-
four-hour cycle once the paste is mixed. Once ready, the prepared
henna will only last three to four days, so timing is critical.

It is useful to add a pinch of certain herbs to your henna
mixture. Be sure to check your lore and to grind the herb into
powder so that it is absorbed into the mixture and doesn't clog
up your applicator (the easiest vessels for applying henna are
the plastic tubes used for silk screening found in most art supply stores). A coffee grinder works well to grind the henna with
the herbs, but make sure you clean the grinder thoroughly or
purchase one solely for spell casting. There are many books on
herbal use in magic if you are having trouble choosing. To keep
the henna paste smooth, use a minute amount of only one or two
herbs. For example, I used lavender for protection of children
and rose petals for love in my spell.

Once you have determined all correspondences, direct your
attention to the design. Are you going to simply write out the words
of your spell? Perhaps this is not what you want to wear for the next

four to six weeks. Maybe you will settle on symbols to represent words. Or one image. For my spell, I let my partner create a more traditional Indian motif in which he inscribed symbols representing our intentions.

Once you have your henna paste and your design picked out, you will need to choose what part of your body to decorate. If you are working solo, you are pretty much limited to your feet, legs, or the hand/arm opposite your writing hand. If you are fortunate enough to be working with an artist, then the options are limited only by your body and the nature of your spell. Because of the circumstances, I chose my navel.

Now that you have everything you need and all is planned out, it's time to do some magic. Start by casting a circle in the way you normally would. Feel free to call the quarters, though this is by no means necessary. When I do magic, I like to burn incense and candles appropriately scented and decorated to my intent. Then I call the quarters and cast my circle, at which point, I draw down the Moon by reciting my version of "The Charge of the Goddess." It is in the center that I chant for what I want while my partner applies the henna. When finished, we both say, "From full to dark to full again, please grant for us (me) our (my) wish by then" over and over raising the cone of power, inhaling deeply with the words. Once we are filled to the brim, we release the cone by exhaling loudly. At this point, blow out the candles, close the circle and thank the guardians of the four quarters. The henna will last for the Moon's cycle if care is taken to not scrub vigorously while washing, wearing gloves for dishes (if the design is on the hands) and keeping the area dry. As the henna fades, your wish will come to fruition. In my case, I am now the proud mother of a son born at the Winter Solstice of 2005.

Brightest Blessings

by Sybil Fogg

Pregnancy and birth are undoubtedly the most empowering feats in a mother's life. In an act that brings us down a road traveled by our ancestors dating back to the dawn of humankind, we must put our faith into the hands of the great mystery. Because birth is as equally painful and blissful for the newborn, this life we have brought forth from our own flesh deserves recognition. And acknowledgement of the spiritual side of our children is best done via some sort of blessing, whether it is a Wiccaning, Christening, Baptism, Naming, or a combination of ceremonies.

A ceremony honoring the birth of your child about to embark on a spiritual journey is a time not only for introducing your belief system to your offspring, but also to embrace your own spirituality in a joyous and relaxing manner. Focus on creating minimal stress for the new mother and father in all aspects of planning the event, so careful thought should be put into choosing the time, place, and scope of the ritual.

When choosing a time to bless your child, consider the child's sex, birth date, and temperament. An infant who strictly adheres to a schedule and always lies down at eight o'clock will not appreciate being kept awake for a Full Moon blessing.

The baby's age is also important. A newborn will most likely sleep through any ceremony, but an older child may want to play or explore. Some babies take well to consistent schedules and get fussy with any slight change in daily routine. In this case, picking a time when the baby is alert and happy is integral to having the kind of experience that all involved remember fondly. Other infants do well with a more carefree lifestyle, thriving while nursing on demand and napping wherever they fall asleep. Picking a time is simple for parents of these types of these babies.

As well, awareness of one's own heritage should come into play to make the child's spiritual adventure poignant and deeply rooted in the parents' belief system. I chose to bless my son on a solstice holiday, not only because he was born on the Winter Solstice, but also to celebrate his gender by choosing a sabbat dedicated to the God. In my tradition, the Summer Solstice is sacred to father archetypes and a time to honor the men in our lives.

After determining the date, think about what type of dedication ceremony would be most appropriate. The parents need to discuss this issue thoroughly to be certain they are on the same page. Major factors include the length of the ceremony, how many people will be involved, and who will preside.

Sometimes a simple recitation and passing charmed objects over the child are all that is necessary. Other families are large and want every member to be involved. Some families want to incorporate the traditions they were raised with and spend time speaking with clergy from their family's church. Some of the most beautiful and lingering blessings are the ones that combine traditions.

Once the type and length of ritual has been determined, it is time to figure out the guest list. Every family has different needs in this regard. Some will want all their family and friends to attend. Some will want to keep it small. Others prefer a blessing privately with a larger celebration afterward. This decision is probably the most important, especially if the blessing takes place close to the birth. Every consideration regarding the mother's comfort and stress level must come into play.

Finally, location must be planned out. Will the ritual be indoors or outdoors? Is it feasible to be near a body of water? How about the forest? Or desert? Correspondences to call upon for this decision could be astrological influences of the child and siblings, parents, and grandparents. Perhaps you live near a sacred place or have an outdoor shrine in which you do all of your magic and rituals. As with any event, the practical aspects to consider are the length of ritual, the size of your group, the laws governing parks and recreational areas in your community, the weather, and the logistics of transporting people and supplies.

In the case of my son's blessing, I knew I wanted the ritual to incorporate all of Sam's extended family, his half-sisters on either side, as well as his paternal and maternal grandmothers along with his father and myself. Equally significant was that this ritual be done outdoors without an audience. We chose the ocean because all four elements are present there—water, air, earth, and fire (which we brought in the form of candles). However you go about it, the blessing of a new family member is a sacred act full of love and will only strengthen the bonds between mother, father, goddess, god, and child(ren).

A Family Blessing

Tools needed: White candle, working knife, small cauldron or incense diffuser, charcoal blocks, lavender, patchouli and sage leaves (for love, protection, growth, and wisdom). Blessed water, blessed earth or salt, rose quartz, and a small table (or use one of the picnic tables that are readily available at most state parks. If you do this, you may want to bring an altar cloth).

Place: The ocean. This can be either a beach or state park or cliff side.

Time: The Summer Solstice. Sunrise or early morning.

Preparation

Sometime before the day of the ritual, wash the candle and charge it under a Full Moon. If possible, charge it when the Moon is in the astrological sign of your child. Bless the candle with water and sea salt. Using a working knife, carve symbols corresponding to the child's astrological sign, a goddess sign, a god sign, a pentacle for protection, and whatever blessing symbol you recognize. I like to use the three droplets of water.

On the day of the ritual, mix your herbs together and roll the candle through them reciting what each herb was chosen for: "Lavender for love and protection, patchouli for growth, and sage for wisdom." Chant over and over again until you feel that the candle is sufficiently charged.

1. Using the table as the center of your circle, set out your tools. Put the charcoal block inside the cauldron and lay the herbs on the table.

2. Call the quarters and cast the circle.

3. Light the candle.

4. Light the charcoal and add the herbs, saying:

   Lavender for love and protection (add the lavender)
   Patchouli for growth (add the patchouli)
   Sage for wisdom (add the sage)

5. Pass your baby through the smoke (with extreme care) and say: *With air, the lady and lord give you intellect and creativity.*

6. Pass the candle over the baby. Say: *With fire, the lady and lord give you spirit and heart.*

7. Sprinkle some water over your baby and say: *With water, the lady and lord give you fluidity and freedom.*

8. Rub some dirt onto your child's forehead (where his or her third eye is) and say: *And with earth, the lady and lord give you strength and determination.*

9. Press the rose quartz into his or her palm and state: *Bless this child by the earth that is her flesh and the air that is her breath and the fire that is her will and the water that is her life-giving mystery. May she (he) go forth in this mortal journey and live richly and generously with love for all that inhabit this world. So she (he) wills it, so it must be.*

10. Pass the rose quartz around the circle and have each person make a wish for the child's future. They need not say anything out loud.

11. Press the stone back into the baby's hand. At this point, the baby's age may dictate that the stone be removed and placed on the table.

12. Pass the baby around the circle, allowing time for each wish bearer to feel and commune with the child.

13. When the baby returns to the mother and father, close the circle and celebrate with food and drink, dance and be merry. Later, place the rose quartz somewhere safe in the child's room.

Artemis: Protectress of Girls & Goddess of Childbirth

by Sorita D'Este

Throughout the ancient Greek world, Artemis was celebrated as a goddess of childbirth and of initiation rites for young girls. Her mysteries were celebrated by women and children throughout the ancient world in the temples, shrines, and sanctuaries that were erected in her honor. The most famous of these, the Temple of Artemis at Ephesus, is recognized as one of the Seven Wonders of the Ancient World. Artemis is the only goddess who can claim such an achievement and it reflects the importance that she held in the hearts and minds of those who worshipped her.

Many of the earlier depictions of Artemis show her as a winged goddess surrounded by wild animals, hinting at her earlier role as Lady of the Wild Beasts. During the Hellenistic period, she was shown as a young woman dressed in a short tunic with her hunting bow and arrows, sometimes with a stag

or with large feline creatures. However, the depiction of Artemis at Ephesus is one of the most unusual, showing the goddess with numerous breasts, hinting at her associations with childbirth and her origins in the cult of the Great Mother.

The Birth of Artemis

The story of the birth of Artemis and her twin brother Apollo sets the scene for many later adventures and also gives a clear explanation for the associations Artemis has with the trials and tribulations of pregnancy and childbirth. The twins were conceived of a union between the Titan goddess Leto and the Olympian king of the gods, Zeus, who was known for his many amorous conquests. Zeus was married to the goddess of marriage, Hera, who was both angry and extremely jealous of Zeus's affair with Leto.

As a result, Hera forced the pregnant Leto into the wilds to give birth to her children. She also sent the Python of Delphi, a giant serpent, to chase Leto across the land, forcing the rulers of all the kingdoms to refuse Leto sanctuary, cursing her so that she would be unable to give birth on solid land. Leto fled across the lands, escaping the wrath of Hera, tired and exhausted and unable to find a place to rest in safety.

Eventually, at the very last hour, Zeus came to Leto's rescue by commanding the North Wind, Boreas, to bear her safely away from the Python to the floating island of Delos. Here Leto was finally able to give birth to the divine twins under an old palm tree. The myth tells us that Artemis's birth was quick, easy, and painless for Leto, but that Apollo's was difficult. Some myths tell us that this was because Eileithyia, the goddess of childbirth, was being kept busy on Olympus by Hera, preventing her from attending the birth. It wasn't until some other goddesses intervened and sent Iris the messenger goddess to fetch Eileithyia to the birth, that Apollo was finally born. It is here, helping in the delivery of her own twin brother, whilst still just a baby herself, that Artemis first takes the role of divine midwife.

Goddess of Childbirth

Many of the Greek goddesses had associations with childbirth, but Artemis was particularly associated with the role of divine midwife and protector of young children. As such, votive offerings were made to her for help with the birth itself and to protect the newborn child. It was believed that she was able to ensure a painless and successful birth for both mortal and divine women. Furthermore, mistreating children with Artemis present was also considered unwise, even if you were a goddess. This is illustrated in the story recounting how Artemis became wrathful following the birth of the babies of the Titan goddess Aura. The goddess ate one of her own babies following the birth in which Artemis assisted.

Protectress of Children

Artemis was the protectress of young children, a role she shared with her twin brother Apollo. Artemis was assisted by the Oceanides (clouds) to look after the girls, and Apollo by the Potamoi (rivers) in protecting young boys. Both twins were known to be fiercely protective and would go to great lengths to exact revenge on those who caused damage to the children in their care. Artemis was, however, alone in her role as Kourotrophos (child's nurse), protecting babies from birth to the end of their weaning period. Interestingly, this is a role she held not only for human babies, but also for infant animals.

Girls would be under the protection of Artemis until such time that they received their consecration into adulthood. At this point they would be rededicated to either Aphrodite, the goddess of love, or to Hera, the goddess of marriage. At coming-of-age ceremonies, girls would cut a lock of hair and dedicate it to Artemis as a symbolic gesture to thank her for her protection and to indicate that they were ready to leave their maidenhood behind. Girls who were about to lose their virginity would dedicate their virginal clothes to Artemis in a similar gesture. The clothes of women who died in childbirth were left to Iphigeneia, the companion of Artemis.

Artemis of Brauron

This temple sanctuary of Artemis was also known as the "Parthenon of the Bear Maidens," a reference to one of the most famous rites performed there in ancient times in honor of Artemis. At this site, votive offerings dating to the ninth and eighth century BCE have been found, and many believed that the early worship at this site focused on the sacred spring and cave, both of which were incorporated into the later temple complex.

The famous stone temple that stood on the site was first built in the sixth century BCE, and was flooded in the third century BCE—never to be rebuilt. But centuries later, a Christian basilica to St. George was built near the sacred well, just outside the temple boundaries.

At Brauron, Artemis' followers worshipped her primarily as a goddess of protection during childbirth and of young girls until they reached puberty. Women would travel from afar to make offerings to Artemis at Brauron, presenting Artemis with their most prized possessions and asking for her protection and help during childbirth. Countless gems, mirrors, and rings have been recovered from the stream and the sacred well, emphasizing the importance that was placed on Artemis in help with such matters.

The Brauronia festival itself was a spectacular event held largely for women that took place every four years at the temple. In the festivities, young girls participated by "dancing the she-bear," taking the role of a bear in the ceremonies. This custom is said to have its origins in a story that recounts the killing of a tame she-bear who lived at, or frequented, the temple and also participated in some of the celebrations there. On one such visit to the temple, the bear was agitated by a young girl who was teasing her. It attacked the girl, ripping out her eye. The girl's brother subsequently took revenge on the bear by killing it. Artemis, upon hearing of the murder of her sacred bear, sent a plague to the sanctuary, which caused a great illness to befall many there. In desperation, the people turned to the oracle and were told that the only way they would be able to appease Artemis was through ceremonies that required the girls to take the role of the she-bear who was killed.

Many depictions from that period show young girls, often naked, dancing and running near an altar. These girls were sometimes shown bearing torches, carrying twigs, and wearing crowns of leaves. Sometimes they were also depicted as wearing garlands made from leaves. The girls who went to Brauron were sometimes as young as five, but most were in their pre-puberty years (about ten to thirteen years old).

Brauron was primarily a sanctuary for women, but statues and depictions of young boys have also been found on the site alongside those of girls. Many people believe that it is possible that male-female twins, reflecting the divine twins Apollo and Artemis, would also be dedicated at Brauron.

Modern Bear Song

This song is for young girls "playing the bear." The girls can be encouraged to dress as bears, and mimic bear movements whilst they dance and sing, and could be done at birthday parties or whenever they feel inspired. Of course, adults can also join in and sing and dance too!

I dance and lumber like a bear
The trees and caves are in my care
My growl the animals does scare
I dance for Artemis so fair

Artemis Blessing Ceremony (For Girls)

Entering puberty brings with it not only hormonal and physical changes in the life of a young woman, but also a change in outlook toward the world in general. This is why many ancient cultures had ceremonies to mark this transition.

The ceremony that follows is for a girl who has reached puberty, and should be performed by the women in her life. Accordingly, the girl's mother or guardian should lead the rite if possible. Remember, you can personalize it to suit your own relationships with each other and with the goddess.

Preparation: Set up an altar to Artemis. In addition to your usual ritual items, you will need an image of Artemis, white flowers, a small bowl of olive oil, a glass vial, and a pair of scissors. Also make (or buy) a necklace to present to the girl as a gift to mark the occasion.

The Ceremony

Create a sacred space or circle in your usual way with all the participants present. Once this has been done, the girl should be taken to stand in the center of the circle. Everyone else should dance around her and sing:

> *Holy Maiden Huntress, Artemis, Artemis, Maiden come to us*

Invoke Artemis (if possible, this should be done by the girl's mother):

> *Artemis, thou beautiful and chaste maiden huntress, come to us*
> *Strong-voiced lady of the lake,*
> *Leader of the dance, protector of children*
> *Be with us and bless [Name] on this night*
> *Guide her footsteps that they may be as true as your golden arrows*
> *Bless her with your protection, ferocious defender of the innocent*
> *Lady of the wilds, come from the woods and walk among us*
> *That we may honor you as of old*
> *Mistress of bears, helper of children, persuasive soother*
> *We dance in your honor and we bid you hail and welcome.*

The mother (or guardian) should now lead the girl to the altar and cut off a small lock of her hair. This should be placed in the vial in honor of Artemis, and left by the image of Artemis. The girl should now be anointed with the olive oil and with personal words of blessing from her mother, stressing the relationship of love and caring. Any other women present may do the same. They can each present a promise to help the girl with particular aspects of her life in the coming years (example: to teach her a skill or be an agony aunt).

Next, the necklace should be taken and placed around the girl's neck, and she should join the other women dancing in a circle whilst chanting:

Earth my body, water my blood, air my breath, and fire my spirit.

End the ceremony by thanking Artemis for her blessings and protection, opening the circle, and feasting.

Artemis Charm for a Painless Birth

This invocation, inspired by the Orphic Hymn, should be used to create a charm calling on Artemis for an easy and painless birth. It should be spoken three times whilst holding a piece of silver moonstone jewelry over a censer burning storax. The jewelry should then be worn throughout the pregnancy and birth:

O venerable goddess hear my prayer
For labor pains are in thy care
Guardian of children, imbued with gentle mind
To helpless babes thou art gentle and kind
Give to me relief from labor pain
An easy birth that is not in vain
Grief and heartache do me spare
And make my child your constant care
Artemis thou holy maid
By my true intent be thou swayed.

Gods of Sleep

by Janina Renée

Normal sleep consists of several stages, all of which are important for our health and ability to function. Two phases of light sleep have been identified, followed by two states of deep sleep, and then REM (rapid eye movement) sleep during which dreaming occurs. Disruptions of any stage, whether for internal or external reasons, results in problems. In the more extreme examples, some people with bipolar disorder have a problem with their sleep stages cycling too fast, sufferers of fibromyalgia are unable to get enough REM sleep, and certain autistic persons may get too much REM and not enough deep delta sleep.

Whether you have sleep problems that are mild and occasional, or more chronic, the following ritual is designed to help your inner archetypes of sleep produce a balance that is right for you. It calls upon a family of figures from classical mythology as a way of personifying and communicating with whatever body-mind functions regulate the different aspects of sleep. Many other cultures have named gods, angels, fairies, and spirits as guardians of sleep and dreams, but to my knowledge, the Greco-Roman pantheon is the most elaborate. However, this ritual avoids being too specific about what you need, relying on your body-mind's natural wisdom, because needs vary among individuals and also during different stages of life.

You can perform this ritual simply by saying the invocations aloud or in your mind. However, for more of a ritual experience, get a bowl of dry potpourri (you might want to pick out a special bowl for this), a spoon, and a bottle of essential oil such as chamomile, marjoram, hops, lavender, Melissa, ylang ylang, rose geranium, vetiver, sandalwood, juniper, cypress, or any fragrance that you find soothing, and proceed as follows:

When you are ready for bed, inhale the scent of the oil, and then stir a drop into the potpourri as you prepare to call upon Nyx (Roman Nox), the Night herself. In addition to the fact that the goddess Night was believed to influence sleep and dreams, we are concerned with circadian rhythms here, so we can view night (and day) as both external and internal states. You may picture this goddess as a winged, full-bosomed woman, wearing a blue-black headband or a garland of poppies on her brow. As she wraps the heavens in her black cloak, she dispenses sleep by sprinkling the world with an infusion of herbs and poppies. Invoke her by saying:

I greet you kindly Lady Night,
*   most ancient goddess, refresher of the mind,*
*   mother of Sleep and Dreams.*
Please enfold me in your starry mantle,
*   and lull me to sweet repose*
*   in this good hour of evening.*
Please grant me swift, deep, restorative sleep,
*   that I may arise in a good hour of morning,*
even as your daughter, the goddess Dawn,
*   brings in the brightening day,*
*   and infuses my body and mind with light.*

Again, inhale the fragrance of the oil and add another drop to the potpourri, stirring it as you call upon Hypnos, god of sleep. You may picture him as either a young or old man with heavy eyelids and the wings of a hawk or night bird on his shoulders or temples. Sometimes he is depicted with a lizard standing beside him, and he has been portrayed lulling a lion to sleep. He possesses a wand that rations sleep, and a horn from which he pours liquid sleep. He wields his power over gods as well as mortals. Invoke:

I greet you shadowy, all-powerful Hypnos,
*   also called Sopor and Somnus,*
*   and Epidotes the Bountiful One.*
As you gather the silent world to your embrace,
*   please also bring me your balm and peace*
*   in this good hour of evening.*
Please grant me swift, deep, restorative sleep,
*   that I may rise in a good hour of morning.*

Next, inhale the fragrance and stir another drop in to the potpourri as you call upon Morpheus and Oneiros, and the other dream spirits. Oneiros is sometimes seen as one entity, the

personification of dreams, though there are also a thousand Oneiroi, of which Morpheus is the best known. Morpheus is also an overseer of dreams. The Oneiroi do the bidding of Hypnos, and follow in the train of Nyx.

> *I greet you Morpheus and Oneiros,*
> *   you black-winged gods of dreaming.*
> *Sons of Sleep, please guard and measure my dreams,*
> *   that I may receive the right proportion*
> *   of deep rest and pleasant dreaming.*
> *Likewise I greet you Ikelos, Phobetos, and Phantasos,*
> *   who bring us dreams that are lifelike,*
> *   frightening, or fantastic,*
> *   and you, the entire tribe of Oneiroi,*
> *   also called the Somnia,*
> *   children of Night and Darkness,*
> *   swift-winged and of countless shapes.*
> *Please allow me a wholesome measure*
> *   of deep rest and pleasant dreaming.*

You can wrap up the ritual by once more inhaling the fragrance of the oil or potpourri, and then setting it aside, saying, "and now, I bid good night to one and all."

If you don't relate to classical mythology, or if you want a shorter ritual, you can say a simple prayer: "Dear God (or Gods of Sleep), please enfold me in your protective care, and grant me quick, deep, restorative sleep, that I may awaken refreshed and ready to greet my day. Thank you for being with me—as ever, amen."

It is not necessary to repeat this ritual every night for the rest of your life, but you might want to try it every night for a week, as it may take your sleeping mind some time to adjust its cycles, especially if you have a sleep deficit to pay off (making up for previous inadequate sleep). After a while, you can condense your bedtime ritual, signaling your deep mind by stirring a little oil into the potpourri, or just by sniffing your herbs or oil before lying down.

By the way, I had difficulty composing this ritual because I kept drowsing off. Invoke the gods of sleep only when you are ready to get into bed.

Preparing to Live:
A Meditation on Death

by Christine Jette

Dying is a wild night and a new road.
—Emily Dickinson

We are not truly prepared to live until we are prepared to die. Life assumes a greater meaning and purpose when we fully appreciate the fact that we are going to die. Our death is real and will be marked by a specific day on the calendar. All the days leading up to that one assume a special significance. Time passes so quickly.

Comprehending the end of our existence is hard, if not impossible. But to the extent that we can, doing so helps us appreciate life and living all the more. A life review can help us make peace with our lives as we have lived them. Once we make peace with our lives—yes, I've made mistakes, but I've done as well as I can—we can make changes in our lives. Also helpful is understanding how our attitudes toward death and loss shape our significant relationships.

This meditation is designed to enhance awareness of your own mortality and the mortality of those you love. Loss is part of the human story, after all, and sooner or later we will all face it. When you are able to accept your own death, and the deaths of your loved ones, as inevitable, you gain a broader perspective of your life direction and the choices you are now making. Priorities become clearer and change is easier to make.

The death meditation will not ease the pain of loss. Grief is an expression of your love for the one who has died. The meditation will, however, help you acknowledge death as a part of life. As you do this, you prepare to make the most of the time you have left. You prepare to live.

The Death card of tarot, No. 13, traditionally means transformation, rebirth, letting go, and permanent change. Rarely does it signify physical death, but for the purposes of this meditation, that is exactly what it means: coming to terms with your own mortality.

Find a quiet space. Play gentle music if this comforts you. Use the Death card as a focal point. Sit comfortably and prop the card up in front of you. Allow the edges of the card to soften. You may want to look at a picture of yourself, or your loved one, as you meditate. Concentrate on slow, deep breathing as you relax and let go.

Continue to breathe deeply as you contemplate the questions. Allow thoughts to come and go. Images may appear in your mind's eye. Record your responses in a journal or on tape for later review. Think about your own death as you gaze at the Death card or meditate.

To get you started, answer the following questions: What does dying mean to you? Are you afraid to die? How long do you expect to live? What do you most want to accomplish with your life? What is the one thing you wish you could do before you die that you have not yet done? If you believe in life after death, what do you want the keeper of the gate to say to you when you get to the other side?

Pretend you are writing your own obituary. Let your whole life pass before you. How do you want to be remembered? What are your accomplishments? What gives your life real meaning and purpose? Do you have regrets? What are they? Who are the most important people in your life? What will your loved ones say about you at your funeral? What do you want them to say?

What has been the most significant death in your own life? Describe your life before and after the death of your loved one. How has the death of your loved one changed you? If you have not yet experienced the death of a close friend or loved one, anticipate how you would feel if a significant person in your life dies tomorrow. What do you dread or fear most about this death? How would you behave differently today if you knew the person you most loved were to die tomorrow? What would you say to him or her? Imagine what he or she might say back to you.

The questions in the above paragraph will also help heal unresolved hurts and misunderstandings if you are mourning the loss of a loved one. As you look at a picture of your deceased loved one, imagine a conversation between you and the one for whom you grieve: What would you say? What would he or she say in return?

Would you want that person to be without flaws? Such a person would bear little resemblance to the one you love. (No more than that person would want perfection from you. You wouldn't be recognizable, either.) Love makes all kinds of allowances—and keeps on loving.

When we prepare to live with the full knowledge that we will die, we stop taking life and the people we love for granted. Our own lives and our significant relationships, become authentic. Review your responses to the death meditation at a later date. Has anything changed?

Magical Anchors

by Diana Rajchel

You've heard of anchors before. Anchors keep boats from floating away when you moor them. In magic, anchors also keep you from floating away. In simple visualization practice, you may see an apple, or your bedroom, or a street you walk every day. As your skill grows, these visualizations become more vivid. After a certain point, visualizations become so complex that it's possible to get lost in them. While imaginative universes have their place, nasty side effects can emerge that strongly resemble schizophrenia. This can be prevented by the use of a magical anchor, whether physical or an alternate visualization.

Magical anchors range from physically present objects to geographic concepts. Any geographic body must remain still the majority of the time. Rivers, lakes, oceans, or active volcanoes make poor anchors. As a rule, the speed of an anchor should never outpace a glacier. Small anchors, usually talismans like a rabbit's foot or mojo bag, may be located away from you or on your person depending on what you wish to achieve. The talisman's composition rarely matters: what matters is that after extensive prayer and meditation, it bears a psychic link to you.

As an example of a good geographic anchor, Minnesota State University–Mankato has a clock tower standing alone in the center of an arboretum. Almost everyone visiting Mankato has seen its simple, distinctive shape, and can recall it easily in the mind's eye. Its distinctiveness has made it the butt of jokes at the university campus—some students refer to it as "the Penis on the Prairie"—and its distinctiveness has created a lasting psychic imprint that can be drawn on from anywhere.

One of the main blocks to astral projection is a fear that there will be trouble, or even damage, upon returning. While generally the body itself is an anchor, and a visualized silver

cord for the con-
sciousness is the stan-
dard for travel, intro-
ducing a secondary
anchor acts as addi-
tional insurance that
you won't float off and
get lost in your trav-
els. Thus, the large
anchors are for larger
magical processes,
particularly those that
may leave you con-
fused as to where and
when you are. No matter how bizarrely your familiar world
changes in the astral, some objects persist. A tall building or
sculpture that is iconic to the area, a stationary geographic
feature like a mountain, and even a long-standing biological
presence such as a large historical tree, over time create their
own imprint. Each of these items appears consistently on an
astral plane, has a place in the collective unconscious making
it easy to visualize, and will be around for a long time. Sometimes, even after a building or tree falls, it leaves a psychic
imprint like a phantom limb, disconnected yet present, to its
body of surrounding land. These are the qualities needed for
a magical anchor.

Portable Anchors?

Smaller anchors can be used, but are not necessarily for
smaller workings. There are situations where these anchors
simply fit better into the ritual scheme, such as when you go
on long hikes or other occasions in which you venture into
areas where you might get lost. Something small, even trivial,
that would be completely incongruous to what you are doing
is exactly what you'd need as a way to focus, should you get
physically lost along your way. A small anchor should be utterly
mundane. Its incongruity in a magical environment is its most

important aspect. Work or building passes are especially useful. They symbolize safety because security offices make them, and it triggers the "every day" part of your mind—nothing is more mundane than work, and everything from demeanor to dress to thought pattern changes as part of going into "work mode." This moves you out of magical consciousness into the ideal space for grounding and centering.

Some items work better as talismanic anchors than others. I would advise against anything on a household altar, such as your athame or any other item used to guide you toward magical consciousness. Anchors should weigh you down and pull you back. It's possible that you'll just float off again if you try to use a designated magical object for your anchor. If you can think of nothing else as an anchor, think of a toilet that you use often. Toilets stay ordinary.

There are circumstances where having a talismanic anchor on your person comes in handy. In this case, anchors serve as a super-efficient method of grounding rather than as gates or keys between perceptual realities. These anchors may be worn as pendants or carried in your pocket as charms. In circumstances where you are meditating in a public space where interruption is inevitable, you can grasp your anchor and return to normal awareness. You may not ground completely, but you will become conscious enough to get to "normal ground."

To use a geographic anchor while astral projecting, do a dual visualization. Focus one part of your mind on the anchor itself; view it directly, look at a picture, or envision it. While holding the image of the anchor, perform your second visualization or meditation. If you want to astral project, focus on your anchor. While holding that image in your mind, make your routine mental preparations for projection. Breathe yourself down, see the white glow of light around your body, and off to the side remember your anchor. While thinking of your anchor, sense yourself lifting out of your body. This works because your anchor visualization occupies your unconscious mind, thus keeping your conscious mind from wandering while you direct most of your attention to your primary activity.

The distraction-reduction effect of the anchor can apply to far more than just astral projection. College students who practice magic know plenty about executing a working in a distracting environment. The constant noise in student housing can even distract a person with earplugs and a blindfold. Using an anchor can distance your mind from the extraneous noises, smells, and sights. And strengthening your attachment to the anchor can lead to deep meditation in the most difficult-to-concentrate situations.

In terms of limiting disruptions, anchors extend a step beyond shielding, which helps filter out a good portion of what disrupts a working, but can only muffle distractions (or cause you to perceive the distractions as muffled). Use of an anchor makes the distraction inconsequential. It's like hearing sirens after you move near a fire station—if you use earplugs to shield your ears, the noise is lessened, but it still gets through and can wake you; if you have something else to think about when the sirens go by, such as an anchor, you may not even realize you heard sirens.

Knowing what anchors are tells you how to use them, whether they are used as a filter or as a back-up plan. Anchors assist in sharp returns to ordinary consciousness, they filter distractions while in altered states, and they add an additional safety feature to magical and meditative exploration. If stuck at a point in magical development, add an anchor—it may actually provide the counterweight needed to propel you forward with the work, especially in astral projection. Linking your mind to a steady point of reference gives you one more way to return safely home.

When the Rains Came:
First Nations Stories of the Flood

by Nancy Bennett

According to the Bible, the floods came down upon mankind and destroyed all but Noah and his family. Could such a flood happen and, if so, was it only in the land of Moses?

The Welsh, Hindi, African, and Australian aborigines and many other cultures have their own version of a flood during early times. Perhaps some of the most colorful tales come from the First Nations tribes of North America. Here are a few stories of "When the Rains Came."

A Fishing Dispute

According to Yokut lore, at first there was only water. The world that we know today did not exist. There had been a flood a long time ago that had covered almost everything. Each night rain fell upon the world. From the sky came two birds, the Crow and the Eagle, looking for somewhere to land. They finally found a tree stump. Here for many days they fished and had contests to see who could catch the most. They shared what they caught, and occasionally took flights to see if they could find any land. But there was none to be found.

Duck came along one day and was very hungry. But when he dived down to catch the small fish he brought up mud instead. This gave Eagle and Crow an idea. "If we cannot find land, we can make it with Duck's help." They began to leave fish out for Duck, one fish for one mouthful of mud.

Soon each bird had a pile beginning to grow on either side of the stump. Though they had promised to share the land, one day when Eagle was away searching, Crow put out two fish and got twice as much mud. Eagle was angry with Crow and the next day left more fish out for Duck. Eagle's land rose high and tall, while Crow's remained flat.

One day a strange ribbon of many colors appeared in the sky. It was a rainbow, and from then on the Sun beat down upon the earth. The birds continued to work hard and gradually the land was revealed. Later humans came and the population grew.

It is said that the tall land of Eagle is today known as the Sierra Nevada Mountains. Crow's land is the Coast mountain range.

On the Back of a Tortoise

The Iroquois tell of a time when no men existed. The Earth was covered with water, and in these waters great monsters lived. Birds flew and sometimes landed on the waters. One day as they flew they saw something fall from the sky. It was a beautiful woman. The birds held a quick council and it was agreed that they should try and save her. So the ducks flew up to where she was falling and spread their wings, making a soft place for her to land.

But they could not carry her forever, and as they flew, the monsters under the water (who had also seen her fall) held a council of their own. They had decided to save the celestial woman, but they would need someone strong to carry her. It was then that Giant Tortoise (or Turtle in some myths) was sent to the surface of the water and here, the ducks placed her.

From this woman all manners of people came. In one legend it is said she first gave birth to a daughter, who was mother to twin boys. In another, she gives birth to twin boys: one the Good Spirit (who gives such things as corn and tobacco), and the other the Evil Spirit (who is in charge of things like worms, weeds, and

harmful things.) Later, more people were born and that is how the world of men began.

The true hero is the Tortoise, on whose back we still live. He has stretched and stretched himself to make land. Other animals are heroes too, like Beaver and Duck, who placed earth upon him so food may grow. Sometimes when Tortoise is tired or annoyed, he shakes himself. That is where earthquakes come from.

A Vision and a Cedar Raft

The Cowichan people tell of a time before the white men. In the village there were many people. Food became scarce and soon the people began to argue amongst themselves. Some of the elders began to have dreams and visions about a great flood coming. They told the others of the village, but many laughed and did not believe the prophetic warnings.

Those who believed began working on a great raft and gathering food. They used the mighty cedar trees and lashed them together. With a great rope they tied the raft to the top of Mount Cowichan. When the rains began to fall, those who had built the raft gathered their families. As the waters rose they were safe. The earth was soon covered with water. The people lived on the raft for many days, until the rain stopped and the waters began to recede. One day, land was revealed and the people were pleased. They rebuilt their homes and started life again, in harmony.

However it was not long before fights began to break out again and the tribe split into several groups. This is how the people first spread across the world.

How We Came to Speak Different Languages

The Haida People tell of a strange-looking woman who came into camp one day. The children of the tribe began to taunt her as she had funny clothes and a crooked spine. The parents warned them not to act in such a disrespectful way, but they continued with their teasing.

The strange woman went and sat by the shore. As she sat, the tide lapped at her toes. As she moved back the tide followed farther and farther up the land. The people realized she must be a magical being and they were in very grave danger.

They gathered together on rafts and fastened them together with twisted ropes of cedar bark. The waters grew bigger and soon the land was flooded. Some of the ropes held fast, but some of the rafts broke loose and the people on those were separated from the tribe. Eventually the waters subsided and the people began to rebuild. Those who were on other rafts landed in different places, and this is how the people began to speak different languages.

The Fight of Thunderbird and Whale

In a paper cited from the seismological research letters March/April 2005, a scientific community tried to find a relationship between the flood stories of the coastal First Nations and an earthquake and consequential tsunami in the 1700s. The myths for this event came down in story for the past seven generations.

The Quileute and Hoh tribes of the Pacific Northwest describe an epic battle between Whale (on whose back we live) and Thunderbird. Thunderbird dug deep into the whale's back, causing the land to quake. Whale tried to drag Thunderbird underneath the waves to drown him. Unfortunately, the humans on his back were shaken off and many died. The land was torn apart and the water rumbled and rose. Whole villages were washed away. This

was what the elders say happened. Thunderbird and Whale continue to play a major part in tribal tradition to this day. Both are to be respected for they hold power over us all.

The story is uncannily descriptive. If we were to look at floods of today and hand them down in an oral tradition instead of the media, how would we tell the story?

The biblical story is one of a vengeful God who drowns all but a select group, causing fear and insinuating that only the perfect shall be spared. Personally, I think I would rather be on the back of a giant turtle, or on a strong cedar raft, waiting for the rain to stop falling.